Creating Flannery O'Connor

Creating Flannery O'Connor

Her Critics, Her Publishers, Her Readers

DANIEL MORAN

THE UNIVERSITY OF GEORGIA PRESS *Athens*

Paperback edition, 2017
© 2016 by the University of Georgia Press
Athens, Georgia 30602
www.ugapress.org
All rights reserved
Set in Adobe Caslon Pro by Graphic Composition, Inc., Bogart, GA

Most University of Georgia Press titles are available from popular e-book vendors.

Printed digitally

Library of Congress has cataloged the hardcover edition of this book as follows:

Names: Moran, Daniel, 1968– author.
Title: Creating Flannery O'Connor : her critics, her publishers, her
readers / Daniel Moran.
Description: Athens : The University of Georgia Press, 2016. | Includes
bibliographical references and index.
Identifiers: LCCN 2015043074| ISBN 9780820349541 (hardcover : alk. paper)
| ISBN 9780820349558 (ebook)
Subjects: LCSH: O'Connor, Flannery—Criticism and interpretation—
History. |O'Connor, Flannery—Religion. | O'Connor, Flannery—
Relations with publishers. | Literature publishing—United
States—History—20th century. | Authors and publishers—United
States—History—20th century. | Authors and readers—
United States—History—20th century.
Classification: LCC PS3565.C57 Z789 2016 | DDC 813/ .54—dc23 LC record
available at http://lccn.loc.gov/2015043074

Paperback ISBN 978-0-8203-5293-0

Contents

Acknowledgments

It has become a cliché to state in such pages, "This work could not have been possible without the support of many people," but this may be one cliché a reader may forgive, since it's true. James L. W. West III, John Francis X. Judge, Roxanna Bikadoroff, Georgia Newman, Peter B. Hirtle, and Janice T. Pilch shared their insights and offered advice on subjects both aesthetic and legal. Karin Coonrod, Alfred Corn, Wally Lamb, Mary Jo Bang, Julia Whitworth, and Marilyn Nelson all kindly spoke to me about O'Connor's induction into the American Poets Corner. Gordon Thomas and Marshall Bruce Gentry, both of Georgia College, answered all my queries with the enthusiasm one would expect from fellow admirers of O'Connor.

The staff of the Manuscripts and Archives Division of the New York Public Library made the imposing task of sifting through hundreds of documents manageable and enjoyable, as did their colleagues at the New York Public Library for the Performing Arts. Victoria Fox at Farrar, Straus and Giroux was patient and invaluable in helping me obtain the necessary permissions.

At the University of Georgia Press, Walter Biggins believed in the project from the beginning and responded to my many emails throughout the writing and preparation of the book; Beth Snead and John Joerschke helped get the manuscript in its present form. Daniel Simon provided expert copyediting. Kevin Mulchahey at the Rutgers University Library provided invaluable help with locating sources and tracking down stray reviews of O'Connor's work as I delved more deeply into the topic. Elizabeth Teets of the Weinberg Memorial Library at the University of Scranton helped me locate an original copy of *Esprit* that celebrated O'Connor soon after her death. Barry Qualls of Rutgers University provided helpful comments about the book after its first draft was completed; his good humor and kindness will not be forgotten. And Father Robert Lynam of St. Augustine of Canterbury Church provoked me, long before I began this work and to the present day, into thinking more deeply about Catholicism; while we have never talked about O'Connor, his ideas have helped me better grasp her attitudes and themes.

Four extraordinary teachers deserve mention. Ronald Christ provided the kind of sharp feedback I first found when I was a student in his undergraduate classes many years ago. I am grateful for his honesty and insight. Robert Weisbuch taught me to think more clearly and deeply about Melville, which, in turn, helped me think more deeply about O'Connor, one of his literary descendants. Jonathan Rose first introduced me to the subject of book history and oversaw an earlier version of this work when he served as my dissertation director at Drew University. His enthusiasm, characterized by his ending many emails with the affirming command "Onward!", meant a great deal to me and still does. Finally, I am forever indebted to William Vesterman, who provided good sense, conversation, and support throughout the writing of this book and throughout my adult reading life. It is no exaggeration to say that he taught me how to read critically when I entered his classroom many years ago at Rutgers; his friendship and approach to literature have made me a better reader, writer, and thinker than I ever would have been had we never met.

A second staple of acknowledgment pages is that the author's family is thanked last. But how could things be otherwise? My children's support of my work was constant and appreciated; their sense of humor always prevented me from taking myself too seriously, and I am grateful to them in ways they will not understand until they are older. My wife, Deirdre, supported this work from its beginning and motivated me to stick with it, especially on those days when I came home from the library empty-handed or with only a few sentences added to the whole. She, as Wordsworth wrote, has had "no slight or trivial influence / On that best portion of a good man's life." And while O'Connor reminds us that a good man is hard to find, I know that Deirdre has made me at least a better one, and it is to her that I dedicate this work.

Permissions

For permission to quote archival material, I thank Hualing Nieh Engle, Caroline Gordon Wood Fallon, and Dr. Robert E. Lee.

Dale Francis's August 12, 1955, letter to the editors of *Commonweal* and the unsigned review of *A Good Man Is Hard to Find* of February 22, 1957, are reprinted with the permission of *Commonweal*, © 1955, © 1957.

Quotations from unpublished letters by Regina O'Connor and Elizabeth McKee are reprinted by permission of the Mary Flannery O'Connor Charitable Trust via Harold Matson Company, Inc. © 1970, 1972 Elizabeth McKee, © 1976, 1977 Regina O'Connor. All rights reserved.

Excerpts from unpublished letters to various recipients and correspondence written by Robert Giroux from 1963 to 1990 are copyright © 2016 by Farrar, Straus and Giroux, LLC. Printed by permission of Farrar, Straus and Giroux, LLC.

Quotations from unpublished letters by Robert Fitzgerald and Sally Fitzgerald are reprinted by permission of Ughetta Lubin Fitzgerald, on behalf of the children of Robert and Sally Fitzgerald.

Introduction

Stamp of Approval

In May 2015 the United States Postal Service announced that the image of Flannery O'Connor would grace an upcoming ninety-three-cent stamp. O'Connor's admirers were understandably pleased that she would join the likes of Hawthorne, Faulkner, Hurston, and the twenty-seven other authors in the USPS's Literary Arts series. She may not have reached the heights of the "Forever" stamp status, a distinction held by only Mark Twain and O. Henry, but at least she had been admitted to the pantheon. In his gracious and appreciative speech at the unveiling that June, Bruce Gentry, editor of the *Flannery O'Connor Review*, called the stamp "very pretty" as he praised the inclusion of peacock feathers—a touch that has become almost de rigueur in depictions of the author. He also noted the appropriateness of O'Connor, a prolific letter writer, appearing on a stamp, even if it were one that would not be used frequently: "I have noticed that the stamp to honor O'Connor is a three-ounce stamp, one that does not go on ordinary correspondence," he said. "But this too seems right, for O'Connor wrote letters that were anything but ordinary."[1] Bloggers, columnists, and everyday readers on social media responded with great enthusiasm for the stamp, naturally feeling that one of their favorite authors was given the respect she deserved.

However, some of O'Connor's admirers expressed their distaste for an airbrushed image of her so seemingly at odds with the content of her work. Writing in the *New York Times*, Lawrence Downes called it, with perfect insincerity, "a pretty picture" and then asked, "Wait—what's Betty Crocker doing on Flannery's stamp?"[2] To Downes, the stamp was a poor representation of O'Connor's singular talent, her matchless ability to look at "the sin-stricken world through cat-eye glasses that are as much her visual signature as Hemingway's beard or Frida's eyebrow." The face should reflect the fiction: "I wish," he stated, "the Postal Service had produced a stamp that was more recognizably the grown-up Flannery, and contained some taste of her strange and majestic artistic vision." This idea was echoed by Joyce Carol Oates, who tweeted, "Not only did portraitist never see a photo of Flannery O'Connor but obviously he/she had never read a word by her."[3] Learning that the artist had actually read O'Connor's work wouldn't have mattered to Oates and others who saw the stamp as a sanitized image they might call "Flannery-lite."

A third (and, to me, the most compelling) way of thinking about O'Connor's stamp was articulated by Ralph C. Wood in *First Things*. Wood, author of the important study *Flannery O'Connor and the Christ-Haunted South*, said nothing of the stamp's denomination or aesthetics but much about its symbolic importance: calling O'Connor an "anomalous candidate for such acclaim," Wood noted, "she would not be honored with a commemorative stamp if she had attuned her faith and her fiction to the national consensus." Moreover, "Precisely in her refusal to assimilate her fiction to the national consensus, she made her most valuable gift to it."[4] The stamp's significance lay not in its appearance but in the acknowledgment, by a nation often practicing what the Jesuit theologian Bernard Coughlin called "antireligious religion," that O'Connor's work challenges the seductive secularism of American life. "Our official authorities may stamp Flannery O'Connor's image on its postage," Wood explained, "but no one can cancel her witness to the Charity that burns with purifying fire."

The artist commissioned to create the stamp, Sam Weber, was not upset by any complaints, nor did he become the least defensive when I asked him about his artistic choices in composing the illustration as he did. Stating that he was sympathetic to other viewpoints, he said that the stamp was designed to celebrate an American literary figure more than offer some comment on her work. Weber also informed me that the photograph upon which he based his illustration—one taken when O'Connor was a student at the Georgia State College for Women, before she acquired her signature spectacles and had written a word of *Wise Blood*—was chosen for him by the USPS, which had negotiated with O'Connor's estate the rights to use it. Financial and legal factors thus played more of a role in the design of the stamp than Joyce Carol Oates may have suspected.

Why should any of this matter? The answer is that the debate illustrates, on a small scale, larger issues of literary reputation. Any opinion on how the stamps in the series should look—indeed, of who should receive this national *imprimatur* of acceptance in the first place—is grounded in a host of assumptions about a writer's character, work, importance, and legacy. But these assumptions do not arise in a cultural vacuum; instead, they are part and parcel of how any author's work, personality, and even image are marketed, packaged, presented, adapted, and received. How this has happened with O'Connor— this creation of her reputation by a number of players in many arenas—is the subject of this book.

O'Connor's Cartoons

Three years before the O'Connor stamp was issued, in 2012, Fantagraphics Books published *Flannery O'Connor: The Cartoons*, a collection of linoleum cuts and uncollected cartoons she made mostly while a high school and college student. The long-established weight of O'Connor's name ensured that the book would be reviewed both widely and well. Most of the reviewers peppered their responses with familiar phrases or what John Rodden calls "watchwords": repeated descriptions that "characterize a figure's radiance and suggest a program of action toward him."[5] Thus, reviewers of *The Cartoons* repeatedly described them as "grotesques,"[6] O'Connor's sense of humor as "darkly funny,"[7] "deft,"[8] and "acidic,"[9] and her work as the epitome of "Southern Gothic."[10] All these phrases serve as critical, and often reductive, shorthand. Readers with more than a casual interest in O'Connor know that such terms only reveal small aspects of her artistic performance. O'Connor knew this as well: when she learned that a friend had secured a professorship teaching "Southern literature," she teased him with the question, "What is that?"[11] As Rodden shows throughout his study of Orwell, watchwords are means by which a writer's image and reputation are fostered over time. By watching the watchwords, one can trace the history of a writer's critical reception and literary identity.

The most trenchant observation on *The Cartoons* came not from highbrow sources but from Daniel Elkin in *Comics Bulletin*. After quoting reviewers who characterized the cartoons as valuable in their early revelation of O'Connor's "perspective of the outsider"[12] or as revealing her early ability to depict "the emotionally fraught relationships between individuals and the institutions that both guide and constrict them,"[13] Elkin argued that, in the case of O'Connor's cartoons, the Emperor had no clothes:

> These reviewers sound like they know what they are talking about. They are able to unearth rather obtuse intellectual understandings from these linoleum prints and crash those concepts into nicely constructed sentences. And it all sounds like it means something, doesn't it? But would they have done so in the absence of the context? Had these very cartoons been done by my grandmother for the *Elmont Gazette* and found in an old box in the attic, would these reviewers still wax so intellectually? Is it the work itself here that is being reviewed, or is it the context?[14]

Elkin's question is worth considering because it raises the issue of how a present literary reputation affects judgments of past work. What is past may be prologue, but the present affects our assumptions about the past. When thinking about *Adventures of Huckleberry Finn*, for example, many modern readers automatically regard the novel as a controversial one that raises troubling issues regarding race—but Twain's original audience worried much more about what they saw as Twain's celebration of juvenile delinquency.[15] A modern reader may be similarly surprised to learn that the original reviewers of *Benito Cereno* did not regard Melville's novella as a treatise on the slave trade; as James Machor explains, "Melville had simply never been read as a writer dealing with political issues, at least not such a highly contentious, national one such as slavery."[16] Reviews of *The Cartoons* suggest that new aspects of writers' continually evolving reputations change the ways in which their past work is regarded—even when, as in this case, that past work seems more of a juvenile curiosity than a prefiguring of later triumphs.

In his essay "Kafka and His Precursors," Jorge Luis Borges shows how, in some texts predating Kafka's, we detect Kafka's "idiosyncrasy to a greater or lesser degree, but if Kafka had never written a line, we would not perceive this quality; in other words, it would not exist."[17] Because of Kafka, Borges argues, we read works by Browning and Kierkegaard differently. Borges's conclusion—that "every writer *creates* his own precursors"—is demonstrated by many reviewers' reactions to O'Connor's cartoons and is the source of Elkins's puzzlement in the above passage. Kelly Gerald's fine essay that accompanies the published cartoons sheds light on their context so that a reader understands all the local jokes about WAVES invading the campus of the Georgia State College for Women, but Gerald also strains to justify the existence of the collection by arguing that O'Connor's "background in the visual arts" led to the "highly visual quality of her prose."[18] Such a claim seems analogous to finding that Shakespeare played the lute and then explaining how such a discovery sheds light on the musical qualities of his verse. Once an author's style, content, and favorite issues—all of which help create his or her reputation—have been agreed upon, anything from his or her previous life can be read as evidence for the dominant critical opinion. What O'Connor's readers have singled out as worthy of their attention—what Peter J. Rabinowitz calls "rules of notice"—and how what has been noticed has changed over time is one subject of this study.

The publication and effusive reception of *The Cartoons* confirms O'Connor's unshakable place in the canon. A look at the number of scholarly articles on O'Connor listed in the MLA Bibliography shows a consistent level of academic interest, with over a thousand articles published since her death in 1964. Collections of her letters and manuscripts are major archives for students of American literature, journals such as the *Sewanee Review* and *Shenandoah* proudly list O'Connor as one of their notable contributors, the University of Georgia

Press has sponsored a fiction award in O'Connor's name since 1983, and the University of Iowa and Georgia College and State University have celebrated O'Connor as among their most notable alumni. One can purchase bumper stickers bearing her remarks ("When in Rome, do as you did in Milledgeville") and wear T-shirts with her likeness or quotations, such as, "Ye shall know the truth and the truth shall make you odd." She has been recommended in the pages of the *New York Times* by authors as different as Dean Koontz, Larry McMurtry, Colson Whitehead, and Richard Price. Musicians have contributed to O'Connor's reputation as well: on the eve of O'Connor's ninetieth birthday, Lucinda Williams performed "Atonement" and mentioned O'Connor by name. On his biblically inspired album *Seven Swans*, Sufjan Stevens adapted "A Good Man Is Hard to Find" as one of the tracks. And Bruce Springsteen has mentioned O'Connor in many interviews, such as when he stated that her stories "contained the dark Gothicness" of his childhood spent not in Faulkner's or McCullers's South, but in Freehold, New Jersey.[19] O'Connor's childhood home in Savannah sponsors an annual birthday parade and street fair; her later home, Andalusia, is a tourist attraction being slowly restored by efforts such as a 2014 campaign announced on Twitter as #FundFlannerysFarm. These examples of interest in O'Connor from sources both inside and outside the academy seem as natural, and deserved, as those of other American authors. Readers today may find nothing surprising about her place in the Library of America, on university syllabi, or in anthologies of American fiction. O'Connor is now so widely known it is hard to imagine that her success was not a *fait accompli*; the publication of a new book on O'Connor—including this one—is as surprising as that of a new one on Poe, Twain, or Hawthorne.

Yet many of O'Connor's original reviewers, like those of *Huckleberry Finn*, failed to recognize what now seems obvious about her work to her many admirers. These original reviewers, however, were neither myopic nor unsophisticated; rather, they were faced with the work of an author who defied easy categorization. In his examination of the critical reception of *The Catcher in the Rye*, Richard Ohmann observes that many of the novel's original reviewers seemed blind to what now seems obvious: part of Holden's rage against "phonies" is the result of the class prejudice he detests and his disillusionment with the values of capitalism. Ohmann notes that early reviewers universalized the source of Holden's angst and argues that the first wave of critics ignored all of the novel's attacks on capitalism because they themselves were part of what was being criticized: "It seems natural," Ohmann states, "for a critical establishment so located in U.S. capitalism to interpret and judge literary works in a way harmonious with the continuance of capitalism."[20] The reception of Salinger's novel reminds us that what seems to be a tacit, general agreement about an author's thematic concerns changes over time and has a history that can be traced. *The Catcher in the Rye* has not changed, but we have. And just as our eyes see elements in Holden Caulfield's angst that may have been invisible to reviewers in 1951, so our eyes now see themes—and talent—in *Wise Blood* that many critics in 1952 did not. How readers' eyes have been opened and refocused as they looked at O'Connor's work is another subject of this study.

O'Connor is not, however, the subject of universal adoration. Consider the following review, posted by a reader on the "social reading" site *Goodreads*:

> How would you feel if you emptied your garbage can on the floor, searching through the contents for a valuable you were sure was lost there, only to end up with muck on your hands? That's how I felt after reading a collection of the author's short stories. . . . I don't find the characters delightful or amusing, as some suggest; the tone of the stories feels as if the author is laughing at me rather than with me. Nor do the stories read as "Gothic" to me; instead, they seem postmodern, a genre whose nihilistic pointlessness leaves me cold. As a result, I could find neither connection nor sympathy with the characters and plots.[21]

Time can damage one's reputation just as often as it can enrich it, as demonstrated by Harold Bloom's 1986 introduction to his *Modern Critical Views* anthology of critical essays: "Her pious admirers to the contrary, O'Connor would have bequeathed us even stronger novels and stories, of the eminence of Faulkner's, if she had been able to restrain her spiritual tendentiousness."[22] Just who is being tendentious here is debatable. However, Bloom's opinions are shared by other readers not in the ivory tower of the academy: as an Amazon .com customer remarked in an online review of O'Connor's *Complete Stories*, "Just remember, the writer being dead doesn't mean their work is great."[23] Some readers regard her in the same light that Rayber, the self-righteous schoolteacher in *The Violent Bear It Away*, views his prophesying uncle: "A type that's almost extinct."[24]

The term "reputation" is a broad one and may encompass elements of an author's personal life, sales, or place in the canon. Each of these elements—and dozens of others—adds one piece to what Robert Giroux called the "total mosaic"[25] of an author's reputation. For the purposes of this study, "reputation" will be used to suggest the shared understandings between critics, publishers, general readers, directors, and other figures about a writer's thematic concerns and artistic performance. Naturally, opinions of O'Connor's work and its meaning will sometimes clash. How the producers of the *Schlitz Playhouse* understood "The Life You Save May Be Your Own" when they adapted it for television did not complement the way that many readers, including O'Connor herself, understood the story; how some reviewers of *The Violent Bear It Away* understood its treatment of Tarwater's life as a prophet—a burdensome yet unavoidable vocation—clashed with how others understood it as the result of a mental disorder.

A recent incident resulting from O'Connor's exploration of racial themes shows how an author's reputation can be a function of current social assumptions. In the summer of 2000 *A Good Man Is Hard to Find* was banned from the Catholic schools of Lafayette, Louisiana; the irony of a Catholic bishop's banning O'Connor's work was not lost on many readers.[26] A similar example of social assumptions affecting her reputation is found in a tendency among her biographers and critics to apologize for her supposed moral failings in terms of race—a trend that began in earnest with the 1979 publication of *The Habit of Being*, the definitive collection of O'Connor's letters. In her introduction, Sally Fitzgerald struggles with the task of addressing O'Connor's views on race in a way that will not put off her readers. Fitzgerald's unease is obvious:

> There was an area of sensibility in her that seems to have remained imperfectly developed, as her letters suggest. . . . I have found myself thinking that her own being would have been likewise raised and perfected, completed, by a greater personal empathy with the blacks who were so important a part of the tissue of the South, and of the humanity with whose redemption she was so truly and deeply concerned.[27]

Yet Fitzgerald soon adds that O'Connor's "will was never in danger on the score of racism." If this were the case—which I believe it to be—why the need for the defense? Or why the need for the phrase "which I believe it to be" in the previous sentence, where I added my own defense of O'Connor? Both Fitzgerald and I, it seems, are attempting to protect O'Connor from a charge that can damage a reputation, just as the charge of anti-Semitism has affected T. S. Eliot's. Terry Eagleton asked, "Why do critics feel a need to defend the authors they write on, like doting parents deaf to all criticism of their obnoxious children? Eliot's well-earned reputation is established beyond all doubt, and making him out to be as unflawed as the Archangel Gabriel does him no favours."[28] Eagleton here points out how readers who feel the need to defend a writer's reputation may engage in an unnecessary and, in the end, ineffective defense.

Readers who find O'Connor's work important and relevant may be irked by encountering a one-star review of *Wise Blood* on *Goodreads* or finding O'Connor lumped together with Erskine Caldwell and Carson McCullers as a niche writer who specialized in southern curiosities. However, such readers should also be aware of what Barbara Herrnstein Smith calls "contingencies of value," what Richard Ohmann calls the "politics of letters," what John Rodden calls "the politics of literary reputation," and what other historians have skillfully revealed in their reception histories of figures such as Faulkner, Hemingway, and Erica Jong.[29] O'Connor is one of our greatest literary artists, but not simply because readers have "caught up" to her or because her genius has become more visible over time. Her admirers' urging her work on their friends and students are far from voices crying in the wilderness. But her reputation and establishment in the canon can be examined not only as the result of her talent but also as the result of a network of events, chance occurrences, personal relationships, media adaptations, cultural institutions, and websites—a network that has affected and continues to affect O'Connor's literary identity.

In 1966, two years after O'Connor's death, Fordham University Press published *The Added Dimension: The Art and Mind of Flannery O'Connor*, the first collection of critical essays devoted to her work. Its preface by editors Melvin J. Friedman and Lewis A. Lawson declares, in its second sentence, that their subject is worth the trouble: "The editors and contributors, however much they may disagree in their interpretation about the work Flannery O'Connor has left behind, are firmly agreed on their estimation of her achievement."[30] This estimation obviously still holds, as the number and scope of works devoted to O'Connor continues to increase. The kind of patient textual analysis practiced by the critics gathered in *The Added Dimension* is still found in contemporary works such as Thomas F. Haddox's *Hard Sayings: The Rhetoric of Christian Orthodoxy in Late Modern Fiction* (2013) and J. Ramsey Michaels's *Passing by the Dragon: The Biblical Tales of Flannery O'Connor* (2013), both of which explicate O'Connor's work in order to increase a reader's appreciation for it. A work such as Jordan Cofer's *The Gospel According to Flannery O'Connor: Examining the Role of the Bible in Flannery O'Connor's Fiction* (2014) takes a similarly expected approach. And scholars working in fields that did not exist at the time of O'Connor's death have also found her work useful for their own purposes and projects. For example, Emily Russell's *Reading Embodied Citizenship: Disability, Narrative, and the Body Politic* (2011) and Timothy J. Basselin's *Flannery O'Connor: Writing a Theology of Disabled Humanity* (2013) examine the theological and political underpinnings of O'Connor's work with the tools of disability studies. Scholars in other specialized fields have examined her work through their own lenses.[31] The last decade has seen the publication of several biographies, most notably Brad Gooch's popular *Flannery: A Life of Flannery O'Connor* (2009) but also Lorraine V. Murray's *The Abbess of Andalusia: Flannery O'Connor's Spiritual Journey* (2009), Eileen Morgan-Zayacheck's *Flannery O'Connor, Hermit Novelist* (2011), and Jonathan Rogers's *The Terrible Speed of Mercy: A Spiritual Biography of Flannery O'Connor* (2012). As of this writing, yet another biography—the authorized one—is being written by William A. Sessions. O'Connor has even appeared as a character in others' works: Carlene Bauer's novel *Frances and Bernard* (2013) imagines an epistolary romance between O'Connor and Robert Lowell, while R. T. Smith's *The Red Wolf: A Dream of Flannery O'Connor* (2013) is a series of poems in O'Connor's voice.

What none of the above authors directly examine, however, is how O'Connor came to her current, often-exulted position as an author, Catholic, southerner, theologian, and woman that scholars and others wish to spend time and energy studying. This is certainly no fault of their work or sin of omission and is mentioned only to highlight the aim of this book, which is less a work of literary criticism than of book history and cultural analysis. *Creating Flannery O'Connor* examines how she became the figure worthy of such study and continued fascination. Sometimes, talent will out, but as the careers of other writers have shown, talent is not the sole factor in forming an author's reputation. Poe died almost literally in the gutter without anyone suspecting that his work would become canonical; Joseph Hergesheimer, the subject of the first PhD in modern American Literature and voted "most important American writer" in a 1922 *Literary Digest* poll, is forgotten today. A number of factors affect an author's reputation, beyond the ways in which he or she manipulates language and holds a mirror up to nature. This book examines and evaluates these factors, telling the story of the understanding and misunderstanding, the reading and misreading, the attacks on and eventual canonization—in the literary sense— of Flannery O'Connor. *Why* O'Connor matters is one story; this story is about *how* she has mattered to publishers, readers, and other artists.

The Two Receptions of *Wise Blood*

Rules of Notice

In 1945 Flannery O'Connor, a twenty-year-old graduate of Georgia State Col-
lege for Women, made a trip north to inquire about admission to the Iowa
Writers' Workshop. Brad Gooch recounts the initial meeting of O'Connor and
Paul Engle, the workshop's director:

> When she finally spoke, her Georgia dialect sounded so thick to his Midwest-
> ern ear that he asked her to repeat her question. Embarrassed by an inability a
> second time to understand, Engle handed her a pad to write what she had said.
> So in schoolgirl script, she put down three short lines: "My name is Flannery
> O'Connor. I am not a journalist. Can I come to the Writers' Workshop?"[1]

This was not the first or the last time that someone would have trouble understanding O'Connor; while Engle, after reading her stories, immediately recognized her talent, literary agents, publishers, screenwriters, editors, and, of
course, reviewers from the first have responded to her work in a number of
ways, often lauding her talent but sometimes puzzled by, or downright hostile to, her work. The reception of *Wise Blood* over the course of two different
publishers' releases of the novel, separated by the span of ten years, reflects the
ways in which an initial befuddlement can be forgotten in the wake of a new
critical understanding.

    In *Before Reading: Narrative Conventions and the Politics of Interpretation*,
Peter J. Rabinowitz charts the actual process of reading and then categorizes
various rules that readers follow when making sense of a text. He knows that
reading is a messy endeavor, a "complex holistic process in which various rules
interact with one another in ways that we may never understand, even though
we seem to have little difficulty putting them into practice intuitively."[2] Rabinowitz calls the first of these "rules of notice": since a text offers an overwhelming amount of data, readers need to privilege certain details at the expense of
others. The notion that every word of a text is as important as any other has
been argued by many, especially in light of the New Critics, whose methods

were mimicked for decades in classroom close-reading exercises. Rabinowitz, however, contends that "the way people actually read and write" is by creating what Gary Saul Morson calls "hierarchies of relevance that make some of [a text's] details central and others peripheral."[3] Rules of notice "tell us where to concentrate our attention" and offer "the basic structure on which to build an interpretation," since "interpretations start, at least, with the most notable details."[4] Rules of notice concerning titles, for example, suggest where a reader should focus his or her attention before reading—hence Rabinowitz's own title, which perfectly illustrates the very phenomena he describes. Knowing the title of *Macbeth*, for example, adds weight to the words of the witches and soldiers in the opening scenes when they mention the title character's name, just as Hemingway's choice of *The Sun Also Rises* as a title instructs readers what to notice in terms of the universality of his thematic concerns. In short, rules of notice help readers begin to make meaning out of a mass of information.

A comparable phenomenon occurs when reviewers tackle a work by an unknown author. A broad survey of representative examples from the original reviews of *Wise Blood*, first published by Harcourt, Brace in 1952, suggests that O'Connor's reputation was initially formed according to critical rules of notice governing what was worth observing about an unknown author, or one at least unknown outside the local scene. In this case, instead of rules of notice governing titles, openings, and closings, reviewers followed rules of notice involving age, gender, and geography. What O'Connor's original reviewers found important—what they noticed about her and her first novel and what they urged their readers to notice in turn—reveals some of the assumptions about authorship shared by these reviewers and how the groundwork for O'Connor's reputation was laid. Nobody today could write a review of a newly discovered manuscript by Joyce or Faulkner without drawing on, directly or indirectly, the complicated reputations of these two figures. Even readers only vaguely familiar with these writers and who have never read a word of their work may already know that they are identified with specific places, that they are prized by the academy, and that they wrote "difficult" novels. Such is one effect of rules of notice being applied to a writer's career as well as his or her work—and how, once established, what is noticed begins to help create a reputation. All the watchwords and phrases that O'Connor's critics would employ for the next fifty years are present in the original reviews of *Wise Blood*, although there is, as we shall see, an important part of O'Connor's current reputation that is almost entirely absent.

The first rule of notice that many reviewers followed was treating O'Connor's age as if it were a definitive quality. The *New York Herald Tribune Book Review*, for example, called O'Connor a "Young Writer with a Bizarre Tale to Tell,"[5] and *Newsweek* called her "perhaps the most naturally gifted of the youngest generation of American novelists."[6] One of the earliest reviews ends, "Her book is dedicated to her mother,"[7] suggesting O'Connor's youth and her first foray into the world of publishing as the little girl striving to please her parent. Other reviewers linked O'Connor's youth to her southern identity, treating her as a type rather than an individual. Noticing geography—and asking readers to notice it, too—would presumably allow a reader to better understand O'Connor and why she wrote about figures as odd as Hazel Motes. The opening sentence of John W. Simons's review in *Commonweal*—"This is the first novel of a twenty-six year-old Georgia woman"[8]—implies that age and region are elements with meanings and associations too obvious to warrant explanation. The reviewer notices them for the reader, who then uses them to begin forming opinions of the subject's work. The original reviews are filled with mentions of O'Connor's southern roots, regardless of whether the review is one that lauds or dismisses the novel. For example, William Goyen's assessment in the *New York Times Book Review* begins, "Written by a Southerner from Georgia, this first novel, whose language is Tennessee-Georgia dialect expertly wrought into a clipped, elliptic, and blunt style, introduces its author as a writer of power."[9] An unnamed critic writing in *Newsweek* praised O'Connor's previous work as original but also revealed his position as a northerner who brought to *Wise Blood* certain assumptions about the South: "In 1946 she attracted the attention of advance-guard critics with a story in a little magazine, *Accent*. In fact, she originated a curious kind of extremely personal fiction, odd little stories about Southerners who were backward but intelligent, brutal but poetic, like hard-boiled Emily Dickinsons."[10] That southerners could be as complex as the Belle of Amherst was, apparently, some kind of revelation. Such an innovation was striking enough to Martin Greenberg, who noted in *American Mercury* that while *Wise Blood* was "full of violence, primitivism, degeneracy, and decay" and "smack in the tradition of Southern fiction," it overleapt the supposed limits of its genre:

> I was astonished to discover as I read along in the story, it is also a philosophical novel, a very rare bird in this genre of writing. I don't mean to imply by this that there are no Big Ideas in the works of Faulkner. There are, but only implicitly and as it were unwittingly, and the reader has to get them out of the story for himself; whereas the elements of *Wise Blood*'s story . . . are manipulated to yield an idea directly.[11]

A writer across the Atlantic offered a similar observation when the novel was first issued by the London publisher Neville Spearman in 1955: "Miss Flannery O'Connor is one of those writers from the American South whose gifts, intense, erratic, and strange, demand more than a customary effort of understanding from the English reader.... Miss O'Connor may become an important writer."[12] Again, the reviewer leads with what he finds worthy of notice: O'Connor as a southern author who, like others from the same place, makes particular demands on readers outside of that region.

One reason for so many mentions of O'Connor as a southerner—why this fact was often emphasized as another rule of notice—had to do not only with the novel's setting of Eastrod, Tennessee, but with an assumption about southern art that had been trumpeted decades before O'Connor began her career. In 1917 H. L. Mencken's famous (or notorious) essay, "The Sahara of the Bozart," appeared in the *New York Evening Mail*; the title (with its phonetic spelling of "beaux arts") reflects Mencken's view of the land of cotton as a cultural wasteland: "Down there a poet is now rare as a philosopher or an oboe-player. The vast region south of the Potomac is as large as Europe. You could lose France, Germany and Italy in it, with the British Isles for good measure. And yet it is as sterile, artistically, intellectually, culturally, as the Sahara Desert. It would be difficult in all history to match so amazing a drying-up of civilization."[13] Mencken further states that James Branch Cabell was the only southern novelist "whose work shows any originality or vitality" and that, in his life as an editor, he has found betting on the appearance of the Great Southern Novel a losing proposition:

> Part of my job in the world is the reading of manuscripts, chiefly by new authors. I go through hundreds every week. This business has taught me some curious things, and among them the fact that the literary passion is segregated geographically, and with it the literary talent.... The South is an almost complete blank. I don't see one printable manuscript from down there a week. And in my more than three years of steady reading the Carolinas, Georgia, Alabama, Mississippi, Florida and Tennessee have not offered six taken together. (493)

Mencken's reason for this dearth of talent—that "the civil war actually finished off nearly all the civilized folk in the South and thus left the country to the poor white trash, whose descendants now run it" (493)—might have been contested at the time, but his assumptions concerning the South were held by many readers and reviewers when *Wise Blood* was first published. Edward S. Shapiro has examined the ways in which the assumptions that undergirded Mencken's essay later motivated the Fugitives and Southern Agrarians, noting,

"The Agrarians were amazed and horrified by these bitter attacks on the South by Mencken and his imitators. Even more shocking was their acceptance by much of the country as an authentic picture of the South."[14] Decades of such acceptance, fostered in part by Frank Tannenbaum's *The Darker Phases of the South* (1924), Walter White's *Rope and Faggot: A Biography of Judge Lynch* (1929), and W. J. Cash's *The Mind of the South* (1941), reinforced many readers' impressions of the region. O'Connor's home state was thus very much viewed as worthy of notice, a key part of her identity, and the cornerstone of her burgeoning reputation. But it was also a part of her newly forming reputation about which the author often complained. In a 1955 interview, O'Connor stated that *Wise Blood* was not "about the South" but about more universal truths: "A serious novelist is in pursuit of reality. And of course when you're a Southerner and in pursuit of reality, the reality you come up with is going to have a Southern accent, but that's just an accent; it's not the essence of what you're trying to do."[15] Still, O'Connor could be defensive of the South when she felt it was being trampled underfoot: in a 1963 letter describing the publication in the *New Yorker* of Eudora Welty's "Where Is the Voice Coming From," a fictional treatment of the murder of Medgar Evers, O'Connor fumed, "What I hate most is its being in the *New Yorker* and all the stupid Yankee liberals smacking their lips over typical life in the dear old dirty Southland."[16] O'Connor accepted the fact that her reputation would always be a function of her being a southerner. What she resented, and what surfaces in some of the early reviews, is how "southern" became a watchword connoting backward, regressive social policies and antimodern attitudes, an assumption that some contemporary readers still bring to O'Connor's work.

Almost as if they had anticipated a response in the urban press that treated *Wise Blood* as a hard-hitting exposé rather than a work of the imagination, southern reviewers used their reviews as occasions to suggest that the South was in fact a place of culture and sophistication. One of O'Connor's first notices in the press was local: the *Milledgeville Union-Recorder* blazoned O'Connor's entry into the literary marketplace with the headline, "May 15 is Publication Date of Novel by Flannery O'Connor, Milledgeville." Noting that *Wise Blood* had been acquired by Harcourt, Brace, "one of the country's leading publishing houses," the piece quotes Caroline Gordon's praise of the novel and revealingly introduces Gordon as a "New York Critic"[17] rather than the wife of Allen Tate. The implication here is that even a Yankee could not deny the talent of this southern artist; the review is more of a press release than a critical evaluation. Like later reviews, the piece mentions O'Connor's age; unlike other reviews, however, the piece mentions O'Connor's southern roots as part of her artistic pedigree and indicators of an implied future success. Similarly, the *Atlanta Journal and Constitution* used the upcoming publication of *Wise Blood* as an example of southern cultural superiority: its headline, "Miss O'Connor Adds Luster to Georgia," suggests that O'Connor was worthy of praise for defeating the very assumptions articulated by writers like Mencken. The opening sentence, "Georgia's vitality in the field of literature continues, a fact which is brought to our attention by an autograph party being given by the Georgia State College for Women for Miss Flannery O'Connor,"[18] reveals the true subject of the article to be the worthiness of southern writers and their importance to the national literary scene. The article ends praising O'Connor's individual talents and those of Georgians as a whole: "We congratulate her as another in the list of Georgians who by production of first-rate writing keep Georgia's name before the nation in a favorable and commendable light."[19] Upon the novel's release, the *Atlanta Journal and Constitution* again touted O'Connor as a local hero: "In a novel whose overtones are chilling and whose horror is undiluted, Georgia introduces an extraordinary talent."[20] But even this piece of puffery contains a moment where the writer indulges in the fostering of a southern stereotype, noting that "the very same goblins" that plague the characters "might 'git' you!"[21] In general, the publication of *Wise Blood* was likened in the southern press as akin to the debutante's entrance at a cotillion. The reviewers also implied that critics in the North were not the unquestionable arbiters of artistic quality.

If O'Connor's age and address proved surprising to some reviewers, her gender proved more so. The *Newsweek* piece compounds clichés about the South with those concerning young, female novelists: "In her personal life," it states, "Miss O'Connor is warm and pleasant, with a soft Southern drawl, but nobody will ever guess it from her stories."[22] Such an assumption about what one might "guess" about an author's gender informs Martin Greenberg's review in *The American Mercury*—the journal founded by Mencken in 1924—in which he offers what stands as the most left-handed compliment in O'Connor's early reception: after declaring that "the author of *Wise Blood* clearly has great gifts," he qualifies his praise by adding, "You would never guess from the vigor and boldness of the writing that Flannery O'Connor is a woman."[23] Such a backhanded compliment was also given by Evelyn Waugh, who, when asked for a blurb for the dust jacket, responded, "If this really is the unaided work of a young lady, it is a remarkable product."[24] Greenberg's parting shot, that some of the novel's strained humor might be "chalked up to the writer's youthfulness,"[25] allows his review to stand as a representative example of the initial positive response to *Wise Blood*: a noteworthy first novel, especially when one considers the age and gender of its source.

O'Connor herself had little concern with her identity as a female author: she once dismissed the entire topic by cracking, "I just never think, that is never think of qualities which are specifically feminine or masculine. I suppose I divide people into two classes: the Irksome and the Non-Irksome without regard for sex."[26] Her reviewers, however, thought otherwise—as did O'Connor's mother, Regina, who asked her daughter to write an introduction to the novel so that Katie Semmes, the novelist's eighty-four-year-old cousin and a social doyenne, would not be upset by the novel's content. O'Connor soon complained to Sally and Robert Fitzgerald, "This piece has to be in the tone of the Sacred Heart Messenger"[27] and never composed it. In his biography of O'Connor, Brad Gooch recounts the horrified Cousin Katie (as she was called) "penning notes of apology to all the priests who had received copies" and reacting, like O'Connor's aunt Mary Cline, in a "horrified and theatrical" manner to *Wise Blood*'s frank portrayal of the whore, Mrs. Leora Watts, and Sabbath Lily Hawks, the fifteen-year-old whom Motes also beds during the course of his twisted pilgrimage. O'Connor's college writing instructor was shocked by her student's first work for its inclusion of such objectionable material, and other "ladies who lunch in Milledgeville" were horrified by what they read because it came from the pen of one who they thought should have known better. Even a contemporary admirer of *Wise Blood*, an editor for the *Alumnae Journal* of the Georgia State College for Women who knew O'Connor and had once commissioned her cartoons, noted, "What to do? Everybody liked the child. Everybody was glad that she'd gotten something published, but one did wish it had been something ladylike."[28]

The original reviews are also notable for establishing one of the most widely used pieces of critical shorthand, the antithesis of "ladylike," which would be used by both critics and O'Connor herself for the rest of her career. Anyone who studies O'Connor at any length cannot avoid encountering the word "grotesque," frequently used as a noun to describe O'Connor's characters and as an adjective to describe her style; the word has gained such currency that a *Los Angeles Times* article on what would have been her ninetieth birthday was headlined, "Happy birthday Flannery O'Connor, avatar of the Southern grotesque." Derived from the Italian *grottesca*, the word originally described the fantastic and highly ornamental visual style of Nero's *Domus Aurea*, discovered in the Renaissance. Literary critics employ the term more often than they de-

fine it. In his edition of Montaigne's *Essays* (1603), John Florio translated the
opening of "On Friendship" as follows:

> Considering the proceeding of a Painters worke I have, a desire hath possessed
> mee to imitate him: He maketh choice of the most convenient place and middle
> of everie wall, there to place a picture, laboured with all his skill and sufficien-
> cie; and all void places about it he filleth up with antike Boscage [ornament] or
> Croteske [grotesque] works; which are fantasticall pictures, having no grace, but
> in the variety and strangenesse of them. And what are these my compositions in
> truth, other than antike workes, and monstrous bodies, patched and hudled up
> together of divers members, without any certaine or well ordered figure, having
> neither order, dependencie, or proportion, but casuall and framed by chance?

Two hundred years later, William Hazlitt lectured, "Our literature, in a
word, is Gothic and grotesque; unequal and irregular; not cast in a previous
mould, nor of one uniform texture, but of great weight in the whole, and of
incomparable value in the best parts."[29] In American literature, the word's most
notable appearance is in the title of Poe's 1840 story collection, *Tales of the
Grotesque and Arabesque*, which does not explicitly define the term, the author
more interested in rhyming than defining. Almost sixty years later, Sherwood
Anderson would title his introductory episode in *Winesburg, Ohio* "The Book
of the Grotesque." In all these examples, the word suggests variety, contradiction, asymmetry, and strangeness, and a tension between form and content:
qualities that theorists of the grotesque have illuminated for centuries.[30] These
examples lack any of the negative connotations the term might carry in casual,
contemporary conversation, but some reviews of *Wise Blood*, critics used it as
a means to express their disapproval of O'Connor's style and subject.

The watchword "grotesque" makes its first appearances in conjunction with
O'Connor in these reviews and has only gained momentum as a means by which
critics explore her work: a 2015 search of the MLA International Bibliography
reveals over eighty books, articles, and dissertations concerning O'Connor and
the grotesque. It first appeared in a short, unsigned, and dismissive review in
the pages of the *Bulletin from Virginia's Kirkus's Book Shop Service* in May 1952.
After describing each of *Wise Blood*'s characters and recounting Hazel Motes's
fate, the reviewer states: "A grotesque—for the more zealous avant-gardists;
for others, a deep anesthesia."[31] Here, the term is used disparagingly, suggesting
that *Wise Blood* is not a novel but some other, lesser form appealing to only a
small part of the reading public. However, this reviewer's attitude toward the
grotesque was not dominant among the initial reviewers, most of whom used

the term, even when not defining it, to describe what they found difficult to characterize. For example, the *Savannah Morning News* described the "excruciating directness" and "graphic manner" of the novel before stating that the novel works by "sweeping the reader from one grotesque and baffling situation to another."[32] The *New York Herald Tribune Book Review* praised the novel as "a tale at once delicate and grotesque,"[33] the critic here expressing surprise at O'Connor's care in creating a novel featuring raw emotion and violence.

Other reviewers used the term to suggest the extremes to which O'Connor took her characters and readers: one noted that, in the course of the plot, "occasional comedy yields to the grotesque, and the grotesque to horror"[34] while another noted, "Grotesques, to hold interest, must be extra convincing" and complained that O'Connor's "outrageousness" is "mere sordidness."[35] R. W. B. Lewis wrote, "The characters seem to be grotesque variations on each other" while complaining about the novel's "horridly surrealistic set of characters,"[36] revealing his assumption that if a novel's characters are grotesques, the putatively normal reader is unable to share in their struggles. Perhaps—but again, the watchword "grotesque" is used here as if it illuminated, rather than obfuscated, O'Connor's artistic performance; the same can be said for "horridly surrealistic," a phrase that does not accurately describe *Wise Blood* or any of O'Connor's work. Calling O'Connor's characters "grotesques" is a way of sounding specific while sidestepping the critical challenge of describing such figures as the dimwitted Enoch Emery or the penitent Hazel Motes. As we shall see with those who labeled *Wise Blood* a "satire," many reviewers responded to the strangeness of O'Connor's work by trying to quantify that strangeness and bring it to heel. Like Justice Potter Stewart when faced with the challenge of defining "obscenity," critics did not define "grotesque" but spoke as if they knew it when they saw it.

Only Carl Hartman, writing in the *Western Review*, gave the grotesque its due. His review begins with a quick manifesto on the grotesque that is perhaps the single most useful approach to O'Connor's use of grotesque characters and situations. His explication of what constitutes the grotesque and the artistic challenges it presents can be read as a corrective to his fellow reviewers, who used the term indiscriminately:

That which is merely distorted or merely horrible or merely funny is not grotesque; that which *is* grotesque must, to exist as such, remain always on a very fine line somewhere in between the divergent forces which comprise and orient its grotesqueness. The grotesque must be held in its artistic place, so to speak, through the tensions of its own almost diametrically opposed qualities—through, for example, the juxtaposition and combining of ugliness with beauty, reality with unreality, normalcy and abnormality, humor with the distinctly unfunny. And these conflicting elements, whatever they may be, must be synthesized in such a way that their final emphasis is that of a true and special amalgam, not a hodgepodge. A slight push too far in any single direction . . . will send the whole structure toppling.[37]

The Misfit and Hugla, Rayber and Old Tarwater, Rufus and O. E. Parker are all prefigured in these remarks. Hartman knew and articulated what others did not: that O'Connor was an artist who perfected the use of such striking combinations, of which the human and the divine make the ultimate example.

Finally, the original reviews of *Wise Blood* offer an array of allusions: by examining the writers to whom she was compared, a contemporary reader can better understand the original reviewers' difficulty in characterizing a writer as singular as O'Connor. Again, many responded to her strangeness by attempting to limit it, often by comparing her to more widely known authors. Unsurprisingly, her work was frequently compared to that of Faulkner and Carson McCullers, and her characters were compared to those of Erskine Caldwell—the last comparison mere cultural shorthand and surely not any great compliment to O'Connor. Other comparisons were more attuned to the values and assumptions that informed O'Connor's art: her debt to Dostoevsky, for example, was mentioned by several reviewers.[38] Others perceptively noted the thematic similarities between the novel and "The Hound of Heaven," Francis Thompson's poem about a Christ-haunted renegade, as well as the characters' similarities to those created by (predictably) Poe, (interestingly) O'Neill, and (improbably) Steinbeck.[39]

Wise Blood was also placed—in its very first and many subsequent reviews—"in the tradition of Kafka,"[40] both as a means of praise and of attack: one of the most cutting remarks about the novel was that it reads "as if Kafka had been set to writing the continuity for *Lil' Abner*."[41] Perhaps Caroline Gordon, whose instincts O'Connor trusted absolutely, fostered such a notion, since she described and praised the novel as "Kafkaesque" in her original dust-jacket blurb, surely to do her friend a favor and place the novel in the realm of the respectable. But does such a term truly reflect the novel? "Kafkaesque" suggests a world filled with great struggles and questions, but few results and fewer answers. The world of *Wise Blood* is just the opposite: there is a narrative center that ultimately gives meaning to Motes's struggles and without which the novel is a series of escalating and empty horrors. The Haze who stumbles in darkness at the end of the novel, wrapped in barbed wire and knowing that he can no longer flee the Hound of Heaven, would never compare himself to Joseph K. or Gregor Samsa. As Motes tells his landlady, "There's no other house no nor other city" to which he intends to flee.[42] His actions are filled with a degree of meaning that even the blind can see.

The question remains what the original reviewers thought of the book's themes and what they identified as *Wise Blood*'s important issues. The very first of O'Connor's reviewers, writing in *Library Journal*, remarked that the novel "is about the South" and "southern religionists,"[43] as if the complicated definition of the first topic was readily understood by all readers and the types mentioned as the second topic were obvious and recognizable at first glance. Another reviewer stated that Motes's struggle becomes "the vehicle for some wry commentary on life"[44]—a statement only slightly less vague than the one previously quoted but of a piece with a number of reviews that spoke of the novel's themes in only the most general terms. Other reviewers, dodging their duty of evaluating the work and justifying their opinions, simply retold the plot, scene for scene, including the shocking surprise of Motes's self-blinding and death. A reader of *Wise Blood*'s original reviews will be struck by how often reviewers gave away these crucial moments in the novel, seemingly stymied by O'Connor's form and content. Surely, Motes's self-blinding is meant to shock the reader as much as it does his landlady—and the effect of such shock on the reader is part of what makes O'Connor's art so disconcerting and power-ful. To inform the reader of such an event makes an indirect admission that *Wise Blood* had proven too strange for some readers, who responded to the strangeness by exposing it and robbing it of its bite. As she later remarked, "To the hard of hearing you shout, and for the almost-blind you draw large and startling figures."[45] Reviewers who gave away the twists of the plot were tam-ing the fiction, making the "startling figures"—however grotesque—less large and less startling by depriving them of their shock, affecting O'Connor's early reputation by portraying her as a writer who offered gruesome grotesques for their own sake rather than one who employed such characters with the goal of dramatizing complex spiritual issues.

Most surprising is that only a single original review of *Wise Blood* mentions O'Connor's Catholicism or the Catholic themes of the novel—a rule of notice and defining aspect of her reputation that today seems impossible to forget or avoid. O'Connor is as identified as a Catholic novelist today as automatically as Philip Roth is labeled a Jewish one—so automatically, in fact, that one must be reminded that this was not always the case. Even more surprising, the single review that does mention her Catholicism does so in an incidental manner, as if the religion that informed every word she wrote and is perhaps the most frequent and prominent watchword of her present reputation was a bit of interesting, but not crucial, information: the *Newsweek* piece notes, "She is a Catholic in her religion, and at present is trying to read all the works of Henry James, but not making much headway with them, and writes every morning from 9 to 12, finding it hard work."[46] Soon after the novel's publication, O'Connor wrote to Betty Boyd Love, "The thought is all Catholic, perhaps overbearingly so,"[47] but almost none of the original reviewers thought the same. Of course, literature is not simply a subcategory of any creed, nor is Catholicism the only meaningful avenue into O'Connor's work. But the fact that her Catholicism was simply not an issue to many original reviewers reminds us that what seems like an obvious part of her reputation was not always so. Perhaps the notion of an author's being southern, female, and Catholic was too improbable a combination for O'Connor's initial reviewers to consider.

As if not noticing O'Connor's Catholic themes were not surprising enough, many of the original reviewers assumed that her approach to Motes's struggle was satirical and sarcastic rather than sincere. Again, some reviewers' responses to the issues O'Connor raised—issues as thorny as sin, redemption, and the reality of Christ—were based on the assumption that her aim was ironic; an examination of the original reviews reveals an effort to contain or neutralize O'Connor's Catholic themes and assume that she was mocking Motes rather than presenting him as a person worthy of sympathy. Descriptions of *Wise Blood* as a novel treating "the difficult subject of religious mania"[48] or one about which "we may assume, if we wish, that Christ has gained a wordless victory"[49] both miss the mark, for Motes is not subject to any "mania" but the call of Christ who moves like "a wild ragged figure" from "tree to tree in the back of his mind."[50] Similarly, noting that we "may assume" Christ's victory "if we wish" suggests that making such an assumption is purely a matter of opinion, when O'Connor's text portrays Christ's victory as absolute. Motes's troubles are spiritual, not psychological, and if Christ has not gained a victory in him, the novel is an empty gallery of horrors. Such a response to her work, which suggests O'Connor is satirizing "religious mania" rather than dramatizing the encounter of the human with the divine, hints at what would come later in her career, when some readers of *The Violent Bear It Away* suggested that Tarwater's eventual acceptance of his vocation to become a prophet was the result of his being "brainwashed" by his great-uncle. Granted, Isaac Rosenfeld (in the *New Re-*

public) did note that "the theme of *Wise Blood* is Christ the Pursuer, the Ineluc-table," but he also complained that O'Connor fails to fully explore this theme because "Motes is plain crazy, and Miss O'Connor has all along presented him this way."[51] His remarks here resemble those made in another review, where a critic calls Motes "completely insane"[52] before his death—although every word of *Wise Blood* depicts Motes's movement *toward* a kind of Catholic sanity, albeit with some shocking reversals and a horrifying cost. "Plain crazy" and "com-pletely insane" are reminiscent of reviews that characterize *Wise Blood* as being "about the South" and filled with "grotesques" but barely illuminate O'Connor's thematic concerns and artistic performance. Brad Gooch describes the review-ers' dilemma by stating that the novel "was obviously satiric, but the object of the satire could be a question mark."[53] Even this misses some of the point, never explaining why he finds *Wise Blood* satiric nor suggesting any possible targets of O'Connor's satire. Without identifiable targets, "satirical" becomes, like "grotesque," more vague than illuminating.

The most complete initial treatment of O'Connor's thematic concerns and artistic performance appeared not in one of the major outlets, but in *Shenan-doah*, the literary magazine of Washington and Lee University founded in 1950, two years before the publication of *Wise Blood*. When its editor, Tom Carter, asked Andrew Lytle, O'Connor's instructor at the Iowa Writers' Workshop, for a review, Lytle declined, acknowledging O'Connor's talent but feeling that the theological basis for her themes was limiting her art.[54] O'Connor had not writ-ten the book that Lytle wanted her to write, and his refusal to review *Wise Blood* reflects how some other reviewers and readers responded to the novel's urgent and unapologetic religious themes: by dismissing or avoiding them.

Carter next asked Brainard Cheney, the Agrarian novelist, to review the novel. Cheney proved to be a reader O'Connor deserved; his review warrants attention because of how it articulated the style and issues that today strike readers as unquestionably and automatically hers but which many readers in 1952 failed to recognize. His six-page-long review, which seems even longer juxtaposed with Faulkner's single-paragraph review of *The Old Man and the Sea* immediately preceding it, is both a recognition of O'Connor's unique voice and praise for how she surpassed other southern writers who had explored ways in which the nation's "Patent Electric Blanket"—its sense of security—had short-circuited in the South. Like other reviewers, Cheney compared O'Connor to Caldwell and Faulkner but argued that Caldwell was merely a "dull pornogra-pher" and that Faulkner, "one of the great visionaries of our time," could write about religion in *As I Lay Dying* but had still not "been granted the grace of vision."[55] Cheney noted that Caldwell and Faulkner described the hungers of the southern soul but missed the artistic mark by ascribing that hunger to social class (as in *Tobacco Road*) or naturalistic forces (as in *As I Lay Dying*):

> *Wise Blood* is not about belly hunger, nor religious nostalgia, but about the persistent craving of the soul. It is not about a man whose religious allegiance is a name for shiftlessness and fatalism that make him degenerate in poverty and bestial before hunger, nor about a family of rustics who sink in naturalistic anonymity when the religious elevation of their burial rite is over. It is about man's inescapable need of his fearful, if blind, search for salvation. Miss O'Connor has not been confused by the symptoms.[56]

Like other reviewers, Cheney revealed surprises in the plot but did so in the spirit of appreciation and analysis, noting, for example, that when Motes's car is pushed down the hill by the policeman, the scene is "the first apparent clue to Haze's reembodiment of the Christ-myth, this ironic *temptation* from the mountain-top."[57] Whether or not a reader finds Cheney's analysis here convincing, he or she can appreciate Cheney's taking the novel on its own terms and not assuming it to be a series of cruel jokes about its protagonist.

O'Connor wholly appreciated Cheney's review, writing him that she had been "surprised again and again to learn what a tough character I must be to have produced a work so lacking in what one lady called 'love.' The love of God doesn't count or else I didn't make it recognizable."[58] O'Connor's words here reflect the general idea that a reviewer, like Motes himself, can only see what his or her eyes can behold. She also thanked Cheney for considering the novel "so carefully and with so much understanding" and joked about her local reputation among her "connections," who thought "it would be nicer if I wrote about nice people."[59] Cheney replied, "I am not surprised that your novel did not find popular acceptance" and clarified one source of his enthusiasm: "I'll have to confess that I was set up for your story: an ex-Protestant, ex-agnostic, who had just found his way back (after 10 or 12 generations) to The Church."[60] Perhaps, in this case, it took one to know one: Cheney and his wife were baptized into the Roman Catholic Church a week before he wrote to O'Connor.

Wise Blood Ten Years Later

In 1962, prompted by the success of *A Good Man Is Hard to Find* (1955) and *The Violent Bear It Away* (1960), Farrar, Straus and Cudahy released a second edition of *Wise Blood*, again in hardcover and this time featuring a short introductory note by O'Connor. While she was pleased by the second edition, O'Connor was not thrilled at what she called the "repulsive"[61] prospect of writing any kind of explanation: "The fewer claims made for a book," she noted, "the better chance it has to stand on its own feet. 'Explanations' are repugnant to me and to send out a book with directions for its enjoyment is terrible."[62] However, O'Connor eventually justified her writing of the introduction on the grounds that doing so would "prevent some of the far-out interpretations,"[63] perhaps those found in the original reviews suggesting that she was mocking the very themes to which she was committed. Her concern that an introduction would rob readers of the benefit of a "naïve" reading further reminds us that one of O'Connor's artistic aims was to shock her readers by the very events (such as Motes's murder of Solace Layfield, his self-blinding, and his wrapping himself in barbed wire) that so many of the novel's original reviewers described.

O'Connor's single-paragraph introductory note is a corrective to what she viewed as misreadings of the novel and a reflection of her by-then established reputation as a Catholic writer. Her description of *Wise Blood* as "a comic novel about a Christian *malgré lui*, and as such, very serious" responds to the critical assumption that her aim was satirical or that her goal was to simply report on the South.[64] Her statement, "That belief in Christ is to some a matter of life and death has been a stumbling block for some readers who would prefer to think it a matter of no great consequence," addresses those original reviewers who dismissed Motes as insane and who tried to force the square peg of *Wise Blood* into the round hole of modern secularist values. The final sentences of O'Connor's note are an admonition to those reviewers and future readers who would use her work—or the work of any novelist—to explain away spiritual matters (such as one's free will contesting with God's) in an effort to make them less troubling: "Freedom cannot be conceived simply. It is a mystery and one which a novel, even a comic novel, can only be asked to deepen." What she saw as the tendency of contemporary thinkers to reduce the mysteries she explored eventually became one of her artistic subjects, epitomized by Hulga in "Good Country People" and Rayber in *The Violent Bear It Away*, who is warned by his uncle, "Yours not to grind the Lord into your head and spit out a number!"[65] To O'Connor, art could only "deepen" spiritual questions, not solve them.

However, reviews of the second edition of *Wise Blood* suggest that O'Connor's worries about "far-out interpretations" were not entirely justified since fewer critics in 1962 attempted to grind O'Connor into their own heads and spit out a number for their readers than did their counterparts a decade earlier.

The text of *Wise Blood* was exactly the same, but the critical community was not: *A Good Man Is Hard to Find* (1955) and *The Violent Bear It Away* (1960) had readjusted the critical focus so that the very issues puzzling *Wise Blood's* initial reviewers now appeared clearer. O'Connor's talent now also seemed obvious.

Before many reviewers even discussed the novels' merits, they noted the unusual practice of releasing it in a second, hardback edition, a move that reflected Farrar, Straus and Cudahy's investment in her as source of financial and cultural returns. For example, the *Chicago Sun-Times* noted, "Miss O'Connor's novel, reissued now not in paperback but in hard covers and at a hard cover price, was not a best-seller when it appeared 10 years ago, but it was and is a good novel and should be kept in print."[66] Other reviewers noted that the "happily reissued"[67] edition of *Wise Blood* was "a literary event,"[68] that the reissue "confirmed the arrival on the American literary scene of a novelist of importance,"[69] and that "Anyone who missed *Wise Blood* when first published 10 years ago should not fail to read it in this new edition."[70] Such a reissue was "an unusual event in the publishing world—and one of not little significance."[71] The critical community's endorsement of the reissue reflected a new critical belief, articulated in the *Oakland Tribune*, that *Wise Blood* "unquestioningly repays a second reading."[72] "Unquestioningly" now, but not so ten years earlier.

One review of the second printing demonstrates a shift in critical attitudes toward O'Connor and how previous rules of notice governing what was worth mentioning about O'Connor had changed. Writing in *Christian Century*, Dean Peerman began his review, "An ardent Roman Catholic who is sometimes mistaken for a diabolist or a demoniac, young Georgia novelist Flannery O'Connor is a master of Gothic grotesquerie, but at bottom her stories are far too complex, far too concerned with fundamentals, ever to be mere typifications of that genre."[73] O'Connor's age, region, and use of the grotesque are still offered as worthy of notice, but here they have become secondary to O'Connor's "ardent" Catholicism. Noting that O'Connor was a Catholic reflected how her reviewers had learned, over the course of the intervening decade, to read *Wise Blood* in a different light. Time and the publication of two additional titles had illuminated *Wise Blood* in ways that the book by itself seemingly could not.

Several reviews from British periodicals, written four years after O'Connor's death and after the reissue of *Wise Blood* in the United Kingdom, echo their American counterparts. The *Times Literary Supplement* called the reissue "an event warmly to be welcomed" and declared that O'Connor's Catholicism, "never intrusive in the stories, for once is dominant."[74] What was originally only noticed once, in passing, had now become "dominant." And while the

Manchester Guardian Weekly noted that O'Connor's reputation in the United Kingdom was "subterranean, a bit special, limited to those who can appreciate the peculiar flavor of religious violence that pervades her work," the reviewer did note O'Connor's "passion for ravaging a few souls."[75] The South also rose again here, although this time in qualified terms: "It is a work of strange beauty, totally original, set in a South as far removed from Tennessee Williams and his lachrymose cripples as it is possible to be. A tougher writer, O'Connor invested her human relics with a ferocious dignity."[76] Geography had become less a way to pigeonhole O'Connor than a way to help account for the "strange beauty" of her work, a beauty with which critics were still coming to terms.

Reviews are not, of course, the only means by which an author's reputation is created and established. The visual artists responsible for illuminating the themes of an author's work also affect one's reputation, if, again, by "reputation" we mean the ways that an author's artistic performance and thematic concerns are apprehended by various readers. People do judge books by their covers, and covers are a means by which a writer's reputation is built over time, since the artwork on them can reflect contemporary understandings of a writer's style and themes. In his examination of the dust jackets of William Styron's *The Confessions of Nat Turner*, James L. W. West III argues convincingly that the design of the novel's dust jacket and typeface influenced readers and critics—and while he admits that "It is impossible to get at such things empirically,"[77] his essay as a whole serves as a convincing case for the effects of what Gérard Genette calls "paratexts" on readers and critics. Genette defines "paratexts" as the accessories that accompany a text, such as the author's name, the work's title, and introductory matter that precedes it. A book's cover and artwork are also paratexts, ones that advise a reader on how to approach the text and that attempt to "ensure for the text a destiny consistent with the author's purpose."[78]

The history of *Wise Blood*'s various covers reveals a number of attempts to suggest O'Connor's thematic concerns, some more consistent with these than others. The history of the covers parallels that of the novel's critical reception: like the reviews, the covers range from vague to misleading to eventually representative of O'Connor's thematic concerns. The early covers suggest that those charged with initially packaging the novel felt some of the same unease experienced by the original reviewers. The first edition of *Wise Blood* in 1952 features the title surrounded by warped concentric circles (fig. 1); all a reader might infer about the novel is that it is strange or, perhaps, concerns hypnosis. O'Connor regarded the design as "very pretty" but also noted, "The jacket is lousy with me blown up on the back of it, looking like a refugee from deep

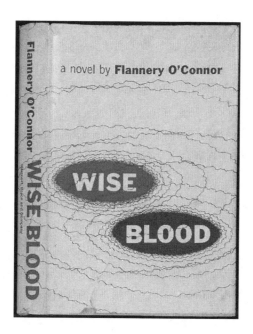

Figure 1. Cover of *Wise Blood*, first edition, 1952.

thought."[79] The British edition of *Wise Blood*, published by Neville Spearman in 1955, featured a cover designed by Guy Nicholls representing Hazel Motes wearing his enormous preacher's hat, looking heavenward and seemingly praying for his car. The bright pink hues of the background offer no indication whatsoever of the novel's violence or dark comedy: the cover would, according to O'Connor, "stop the blindest Englishman in the thickest fog."[80] Such visual misrepresentation continued when the paperback was issued by Signet in 1953: its cover featured an illustration of Motes attempting to nap in the forest while Sabbath—looking older than her fifteen years of age—removes what certainly does not resemble the preacher's hat that reminds Motes of his struggle (fig. 2). The illustration looks more like a scene from a traveling salesman joke than one from O'Connor's novel. The comments on the back also obfuscate the book's content, as they describe *Wise Blood* as "A richly humorous story of strangers in a lazy Southern town who become enmeshed in a conflicting web of earthly and spiritual desires" and "a compassionate, ironic, and warmly human novel of frustrated hopes and loves." Such description, better suited to a saccharine romance, misrepresented O'Connor's novel because more accurate phrases would never have sold it. Ace Books used a similarly misleading cover in 1960 (fig. 3), which O'Connor despised, noting, "Sabbath is thereon turned into Marilyn Monroe in underclothes."[81] Such covers were blatant attempts to sell O'Connor's work in a way that eliminated any hint of its theological content: the "sin" mentioned over each title is not implied to be blasphemy, but one more immediately recognizable and salacious. One can imagine how disappointed the readers who purchased *Wise Blood* on the strength of these covers must have been.

The 1962 reissue of the novel featured cover art by Milton Glaser (fig. 4) and better reflected the novel: anyone noticing this edition, with its shadowy portrait of either Asa Hawks or Motes himself, would have a much better idea of the novel's grim content than could be discerned from earlier editions. Glaser later famously defined the logo as "the point of entry to the brand"; such a definition applies to his cover of *Wise Blood*, which serves as a point of entry to the novel's theme of spiritual blindness. Two years later saw Signet's publication of *Three by Flannery O'Connor*, a collection that included *Wise Blood*; its cover, featuring a cartoon of Motes in his Essex with Sabbath's legs hanging over the side and a "CHURCH WITHOUT CHRIST" sign cleverly replacing the expected "JUST MARRIED" (fig. 5). That Motes never hangs such a sign on his rat-colored Essex is beside the point of the illustrator's attempt to convey a sense of wackiness. A later Signet reprint (fig. 6) emphasized the rural setting of O'Connor's

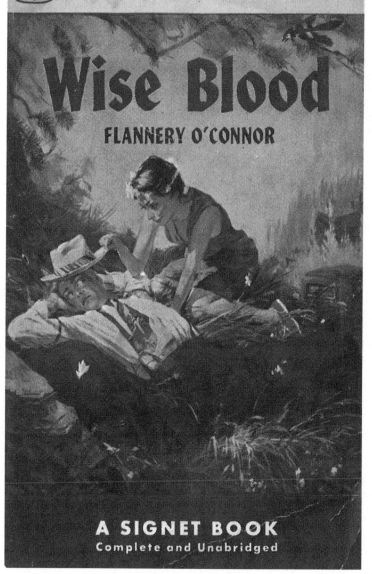

A Searching Novel of Sin and Redemption

Wise Blood

FLANNERY O'CONNOR

A SIGNET BOOK
Complete and Unabridged

Figure 2. Cover of *Wise Blood*, Signet, 1953.

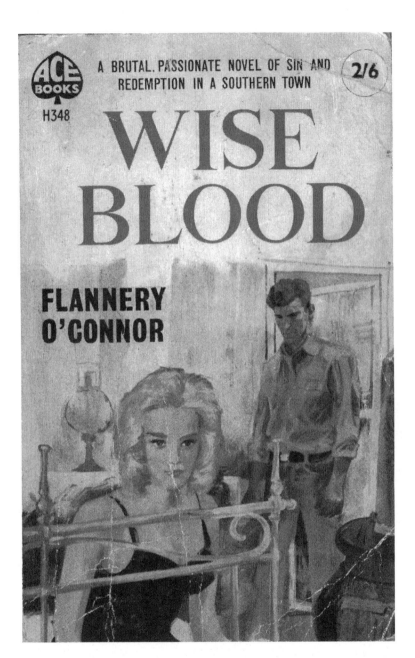

Figure 3. Cover of *Wise Blood*, Ace, 1960.

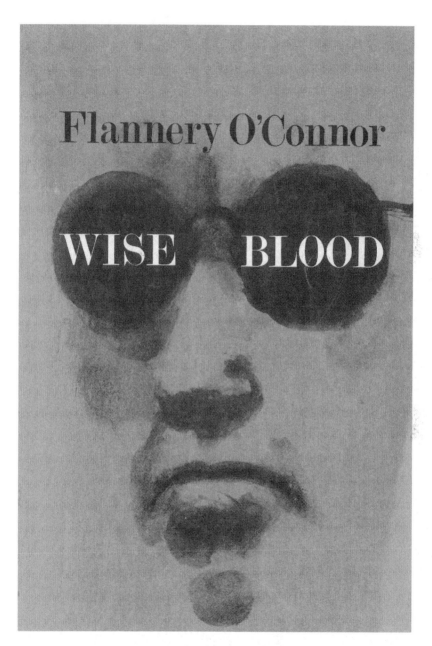

Figure 4. Cover of *Wise Blood*, Glaser illustration, 1962.

3 by
FLANNERY
O'CONNOR

Now complete and unabridged in one volume:

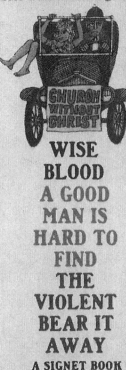

WISE
BLOOD
A GOOD
MAN IS
HARD TO
FIND
THE
VIOLENT
BEAR IT
AWAY
A SIGNET BOOK

Figure 5. Cover of *Three by Flannery O'Connor*, Signet, 1964.

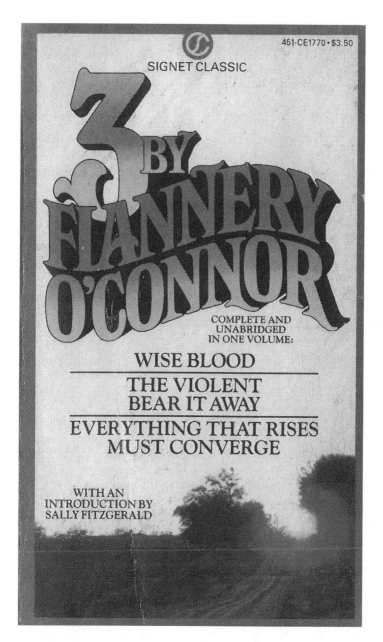

Figure 6. Cover of *Three by Flannery O'Connor*, Signet, 1983.

works and implied, with a font reminiscent of saloon signs or roadside diners, a cheerfulness and "down-hominess" that her work totally lacks. The road on this cover seems not to be the one promising endless persecution that Tarwater knows he must walk in *The Violent Bear It Away*.

In 1990 Farrar, Straus and Giroux reissued paperback editions of several of O'Connor's works and hired Canadian illustrator Roxanna Bikadoroff to illustrate their covers. Her illustration for *Wise Blood* stands as ideally representative of O'Connor's thematic concerns and artistic performance and most indicative of O'Connor's reputation as an author of shocking *and* spiritual fiction (fig. 7). When asked about her design, Bikadoroff explained how she arrived at her choice of image and why she felt it to be appropriate for the novel:

> I wanted the covers to have simple, iconic images. Symbolic imagery is very much like an arrow or key that allows instant entry to the unconscious or collective unconscious; it is a different language than writing, but together they work on both sides of the brain at once and bring a union/understanding. O'Connor uses so much symbolism, too, it was only appropriate. So I chose symbols that were universal, powerful. They had to have a twist which made them particular to the stories, though, and convey the essence of the work or the main character. The heart with barbed wire is pretty obvious for *Wise Blood*. It echoes the crown of thorns and the sacred heart of Jesus, but also the barbed wire Motes wraps around his chest in his religious self-flagellation/penance.[82]

Bikadoroff's cover, coupled with a blurb on the back by Brad Leithauser declaring, "No other major American writer of our century has constructed a fictional world so energetically and forthrightly charged by religious investigation,"[83] demonstrates the degree to which the understanding of *Wise Blood* in particular and O'Connor in general had changed over time. Her spiritual concerns, now blazoned on the cover of her first novel, had become more worthy of notice than the violence of her plots. Further indication of this change appears in a transcript of one of the 2008 Open Yale courses on American literature. The professor, Amy Hungerford, begins by directing her students to look at Bikadoroff's cover and then asking, "What does it look like to you?" When a student responds, "Is it the Sacred Heart?" Hungerford responds:

> It's the Sacred Heart, yes. It's the Sacred Heart of Jesus. In Catholic iconography of a certain kind, the figure of Christ is shown usually parting His clothes and His flesh and showing you His Sacred Heart, which is usually crowned with flame and often encircled with thorns. So it's an image of Christ the suffering

Figure 7. Cover of *Wise Blood*, Bikadoroff illustration, 1990.

godhead: the very human, fleshly person who will part His own flesh in order to connect with, in order to redeem, the believer. So right in the packaging of this novel that we have today—this cover has changed over time—nevertheless, even today, that very Catholic iconography is right on the front of the cover. And when you see *Wise Blood*, that title, right below the Sacred Heart, you can't help but think of: well, this blood is somehow the blood of Christ. That's the kind of blood we're talking about. It's already entered a sort of metaphorical register, religious register, in the way this book is packaged.[84]

O'Connor's reputation as a Catholic writer has taken root so firmly that it can be mentioned at the start of a lecture. The "register" Hungerford mentions is one that has been reshaped by criticism, publishers, and graphic designers since 1952.

The Farrar, Straus and Giroux paperback edition (2007) features a golden cross against a black background with the novel's title written in stately capitals (fig. 8), Leithauser's blurb at the bottom, and the FS&G logo on the side as an indicator of the book's literary pedigree; the 2008 Faber & Faber cover features a cross-topped church. O'Connor's reputation as a Catholic novelist is now taken for granted, but publishers, like reviewers, took their time before they allowed themselves to acknowledge—rather than hide or avoid—this fact. And, in a final example of how cover art can reflect different approaches to a work at different points in time, June Glasson's illustration for the 2015 FSG Classics edition recalls Milton Glaser's 1962 portrait of Motes and emphasizes the book's religious themes less than the previous edition did (fig. 9).

In an angry letter to John Selby, her original editor at Rinehart who held an option on *Wise Blood* and who, according to O'Connor, wanted to "train it into a conventional novel," O'Connor declared, "I think that the quality of the novel I write will derive precisely from the peculiarity or aloneness, if you will, of the experience I write from. . . . The finished book will be just as odd if not odder than the nine chapters you have now. The question is: is Rinehart interested in publishing this kind of novel?"[85] O'Connor knew what it took many readers ten years (and two other works by O'Connor) to learn: "this kind of novel" could simply not be read as a conventional one in which issues are neatly resolved, where geography is artistic destiny, or where violence was more sensational than suggestive of a spiritual *agon*. But one must not accuse these reviewers of benighted judgment: like Motes, they needed to be jolted out of their figurative blindness, a jolt supplied by O'Connor herself with the publication of *A Good Man Is Hard to Find* in 1955 and *The Violent Bear It Away* in 1960.

WISE
BLOOD

A NOVEL

FSG
CLASSICS

"No other major American writer of our century
has constructed a fictional world so energetically and
forthrightly charged by religious investigation."
—BRAD LEITHAUSER, *The New Yorker*

FLANNERY O'CONNOR

Figure 8. Cover of *Wise Blood*, Bikadoroff illustration, 1990.

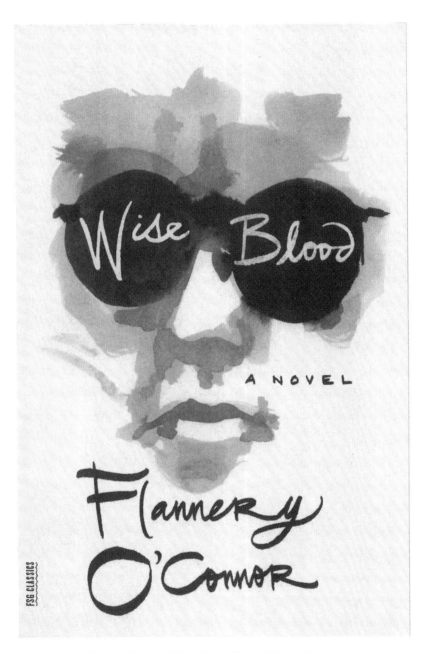

Figure 9. Cover of *Wise Blood*, Glasson illustration, 2015.

The "Discovery" of O'Connor's Catholicism

Authorial Audiences

Near the end of *The Life of Samuel Johnson* (1791), James Boswell offers one of many scenes in which Johnson expresses his fear of death:

> Dr. Johnson surprised [Mr. Henderson] not a little, by acknowledging with a look of horrour, that he was much oppressed by the fear of death. The amiable Dr. Adams suggested that God was infinitely good. *Johnson:* "That he is infinitely good, as far as the perfection of his nature will allow, I certainly believe; but it is necessary for good upon the whole, that individuals should be punished. As to an *individual*, therefore, he is not infinitely good; and as I cannot be *sure* that I have fulfilled the conditions on which salvation is granted, I am afraid I may be one of those who shall be damned" (looking dismally). *Dr. Adams:* "What do you mean by damned?" *Johnson* (passionately and loudly): "Sent to Hell, Sir, and punished everlastingly." *Dr. Adams:* "I don't believe that doctrine." *Johnson:* "Hold, Sir; do you believe that some will be punished at all?" *Dr. Adams:* "Being excluded from Heaven will be a punishment; yet there may be no great positive suffering." *Johnson:* "Well, Sir; but if you admit any degree of punishment, there is an end of your argument for infinite goodness simply considered; for, infinite goodness would inflict no punishment whatever. There is not infinite goodness physically considered; morally there is." *Boswell:* "But may not a man attain to such a degree of hope as not to be uneasy from the fear of death?" *Johnson:* "A man may have such a degree of hope as to keep him quiet. You see I am not quiet, from the vehemence with which I talk; but I do not despair." *Mrs. Adams:* "You seem, Sir, to forget the merits of our Redeemer." *Johnson:* "Madam, I do not forget the merits of my Redeemer; but my Redeemer has said that he will set some on his right hand and some on his left." He was in gloomy agitation, and said, "I'll have no more on't."[1]

A reader may empathize with the Adamses, trying to console the Great Cham in the final year of his life. But Boswell chooses to emphasize Johnson's clear thinking about damnation and refusal to entertain what he saw as spiritual sophistry. To Johnson, all who believe in "damnation" know, or should know, exactly what it entails. As O'Connor would note in a 1955 letter, "The Truth does not change according to our ability to stomach it."[2]

Like Dr. Adams when asking Johnson about damnation, many reviewers, even after *Wise Blood*, could not believe O'Connor took the spiritual issues she explored in her work as seriously, as definitively, and as absolutely as she did. But in the ten years between the two editions of *Wise Blood*, many readers came to recognize that O'Connor did take her subjects—such as sin, grace, and salvation—quite seriously and was as steadfast in her moral reasoning as Johnson was in his. The "satire" of which reviewers spoke when reviewing *Wise Blood* was replaced with a growing awareness (and, sometimes, unease) that, like Johnson, O'Connor viewed the truth as fixed, absolute, and beyond human equivocation. In his biography of O'Connor, Jonathan Rogers notes, "As shocking as the grotesqueries in her fiction are, none is so shocking as the realization that they are marshaled in the service of a Catholic orthodoxy that the author submits to—or, in any case, wishes to submit to—without the least trace of ironic detachment."[3] As O'Connor cracked when Mary McCarthy described the Eucharist as a "pretty good" symbol of Christ, "Well, if it's a symbol, to hell with it."[4]

As seen in the previous chapter, Peter J. Rabinowitz has cataloged what he calls "rules of notice": ways in which readers highlight various pieces of data in order to begin making sense of a text. But the author, Rabinowitz argues, also needs to make assumptions about her readers' understanding of what is significant in a text:

> An author has, in most cases, no firm knowledge of the actual readers who will pick up his or her book. Yet he or she cannot begin to fill up a blank page without making assumptions about the readers' beliefs, knowledge, and familiarity with conventions. As a result, authors are forced to guess; they design their books rhetorically for some more or less *hypothetical* audience, which I call the *authorial audience*. Artistic choices are based upon these assumptions—conscious or unconscious—about readers, and to a certain extent, artistic success depends on their shrewdness, on the degree to which actual and authorial audience overlap.[5]

In other words, the authorial audience is the hypothetical reader to whom a work of fiction is addressed; this reader will often be imagined by writers as one who shares a number of his or her values and assumptions. John Bunyan assumed that he and his authorial audience shared a number of opinions regarding the journey from this world to that which is to come, just as Dashiell Hammett assumed that, to engineer the surprise at the end of *The Maltese Falcon*, he could exploit his authorial audience's opinions about the dangerous nature of beautiful women, especially when they appeared in pulp novels. Of course, the actual audience might be different from the authorial one and is not bound in any way to read the work as the author imagined (or didn't imagine) it would be. One could imagine, for example, a reader breaking from Melville's authorial audience, wholly unsympathetic to Ahab and regarding him as the villain of *Moby-Dick*. The authorial audience is as much a creation of the writer's imagination as the fiction itself, but the actual audience can read and respond however it chooses.

When Rabinowitz states that "artistic success" depends on "the degree to which actual and authorial audience overlap," he is suggesting that one mark of artistic success is the degree to which an author has managed to provide his or her readers with a vision of the world that complements how they imagine their own and that this vision is built upon at least some shared assumptions between author and reader. For example, those whose opinions of Gary Gilmore resemble Norman Mailer's will be more likely to label *The Executioner's Song* an "artistic success" than those whose opinions of Gilmore are directly opposed to Mailer's. Of course, one of Mailer's goals is to change his readers' assumptions on this subject, but if the reader does not budge in his detestation of Gilmore, it is difficult to imagine him or her applauding Mailer's work as anything more than biased—however engaging—reportage. Rabinowitz's work is a heuristic for investigating why certain works are praised and others are not: the degree to which readers' experiences mirror those of the authorial audience, the collection of "presuppositions upon which a text is built,"[6] may suggest the degree to which readers will praise or condemn a writer's artistic performance.

Applying Rabinowitz's ideas to a reception study is useful because doing so enables the historian first to discern and describe his or her subject's authorial audience and then to determine the degree to which readers in the actual audience accepted or resisted reading in an authorially imagined manner. Proceeding this way can allow the critic to write a reception history that accounts for changes in reading habits, rather than one that simply records who-liked-what-when. Creating a sketch of O'Connor's authorial audience is a particularly useful method for examining the shift in critical opinion that occurred between the first (1952) and second (1962) editions of *Wise Blood*. An examination of the reception of *A Good Man Is Hard to Find* and *The Violent Bear It Away* suggests that critics gradually began reading her work as she imagined members of her authorial audience doing. Once they did, the Catholic themes of her work, previously obscure, became apparent.

So who comprised O'Connor's authorial audience? What hypothetical readers did she have in mind as she wrote? To what values and assumptions, for example, did she hope to appeal when deciding that, in "The River," Harry Ashfield would seek a place where he "counted"? One way to determine O'Connor's authorial, imagined audience is to examine its opposite: a collection of readers too-clever-by-half who sought to explain away her fiction's mysteries, many of them spiritual, with "psychoanalytic" readings or a hunt for symbols. One reviewer of *The Violent Bear It Away*, for example, relied on jargon to help him defeat the mysteries of the plot, diagnosing Mason, Tarwater, and Rayber as "an obsessive psychotic, a paranoiac delinquent, and a fanatical monomaniac."[7] When O'Connor was asked by a professor at Wesleyan about the "significance" of the Misfit's hat, she replied, "To cover his head."[8] Mason Tarwater rails against his nephew for trying to reduce God to a number; O'Connor had little patience for readers who tried to read in any similarly reductive manner and who viewed fiction as an intellectual parlor game in which the players won by offering the most edgy interpretations. Readers approaching the work "as if it were a problem in algebra," seeking to "find X [so] when they find X they can dismiss the rest of it,"[9] outraged O'Connor's assumptions about fiction and the life it reflected. Those who concocted outlandish interpretations, such as the reviewer for *Commentary* who found *The Violent Bear It Away* a novel about homosexual incest,[10] were, to O'Connor, beyond the critical pale: "When you have a generation of students who are being taught to think like that, there's nothing to do but wait for another generation to come along and hope it won't be worse."[11] The phrase "think like that" suggests O'Connor's imagined audience by describing its opposite. O'Connor never saw her works as being enclosed in irony-bestowing quotation marks.

To complicate matters, a writer may have more than one authorial audience in mind as he or she creates a work of fiction. A reader unfamiliar with O'Connor might initially assume that her authorial audience was composed of other Christians and that O'Connor imagined herself writing to them in the spirit of confirming what they already believed. However, O'Connor also imagined a second authorial audience defined by what its members did *not* believe, rather than what they did. "My audience," she wrote shortly after the publication of *A Good Man Is Hard to Find*, "are the people who think God is dead. At least these are the people I am conscious of writing for."[12] O'Connor understood that her fiction would often be read by "a public with a predisposition to believe the opposite"[13] and viewed one of her primary challenges as dramatizing the action of grace and redemption for readers who denied their existence: as she articulated her artistic challenge in a 1955 letter, "How are you going to make such things clear to people who don't believe in God?"[14] O'Connor thought her stories and novels were sometimes met with confusion or scorn because readers had dismissed their themes as archaic: she sympathized with John Hawkes's task of "speaking to an audience which does not believe in evil"[15] and complained to her former teacher, Andrew Lytle, that "The River" would be panned because "baptism is just another idiocy to the general reader."[16] O'Connor imagined her audience as composed not only of others who shared her convictions but also of those who found these convictions ridiculous. "Part of the difficulty of all this," she explained, "is that you write for an audience who doesn't know what grace is and who doesn't recognize it when they see it."[17]

For a reader to fully appreciate the degree to which her fiction reflected reality, O'Connor assumed that he or she had to be capable of at least entertaining the ideas of grace and God; such readers might be called the "genuine" authorial audience. But also at hand was this second audience that can be called the "ironic" authorial audience. This matter of rival audiences made all the difference in the building of her literary reputation: for example, the "genuine" authorial readers of *The Violent Bear It Away* responded to the subject of prophecy in a way almost uniformly opposed to that of the "ironic" authorial audience. As one reviewer noted with regard to that novel, "Those to whom anything less than total commitment is anathema will find this novel a searching study of that engulfing power," while "The more detached may well find the novel hinges on a doubtful premise."[18] Both of these audiences were present in O'Connor's mind as she wrote, and both affected the course of O'Connor's reputation.

While O'Connor lamented of many readers that "the religious sense has been bred out of them in the kind of society we've lived in since the 18th century" and that they had lost any "sense of the power of God,"[19] she never viewed her art as a means of preaching to the choir. She had as little regard for unskilled Catholic readers, even when they were members of the genuine authorial audience, as she did for secular ones: she once described the "average Catholic reader" as a "Militant Moron."[20] To O'Connor, fiction was not a means to proselytize. In 1957 she told a group of students at Emory University, "The type of mind that can understand good fiction is not necessarily the educated mind, but it is at all times the kind of mind that is willing to have its sense of mystery deepened by contact with reality, and its sense of reality deepened by contact with mystery."[21] To O'Connor, the mystery of the world was as much a part of it as its physicality, and the writer's aim was to make his or her readers contemplate the mystery that she viewed the "modern world" as trying to "eliminate."[22] "I'm always highly irritated," she explained in the same lecture, "by people who imply that writing fiction is an escape from reality. It is a plunge into reality and it's very shocking to the system."[23] O'Connor believed T. S. Eliot's claim that "human kind cannot bear very much reality" and explored this in her fiction. Some of her more resistant, ironic readers proved the claim with their reactions to her work.

Lest quotations from O'Connor, such as those above, make her seem only annoyed by or even contemptuous of her readers, three points should be reviewed. First, the ironic audience who "thinks God is dead" was, again, not the only one O'Connor had in mind as she wrote; she obviously imagined readers who would recognize that Mr. Head experiences the gift of divine mercy or that the smooth-talking stranger who speaks to Tarwater is the devil and not, as some ironic readers assumed, a projection of his schizophrenic state. O'Connor did not imagine herself writing *only* to those who thought God was dead. Second, the existence of an ironic audience was seen by O'Connor as a spur to producing higher-quality work. As she wrote in "The Church and the Fiction Writer," "The Catholic who does not write for a limited circle of fellow Catholics will in all probability consider that, since this is his vision, he is writing for a hostile audience, and he will be more than ever concerned to have his work stand on its own two feet and be complete and self-sufficient and impregnable in its own right."[24] Finally, O'Connor knew that an author without readers was playing solitaire: "Success means *being heard.* . . . You may write for the joy of it, but the act of writing is not complete in itself. It has its end in its audience."[25] The original audiences of *A Good Man Is Hard to Find* and *The Violent Bear It Away* responded to these works along fault lines that revealed their approach—genuine or ironic—to O'Connor's work.

A Good Man Is Hard to Find

Reviews of O'Connor's 1955 collection of stories reveal many of the same approaches, observations, and "rules of notice" that surfaced three years earlier with *Wise Blood*. O'Connor's age was still worthy of notice, as when James

Greene in *Commonweal* described her as "scarcely thirty years old"[26] or when Granville Hicks stated, "If there is a young writer—Miss O'Connor is 30— who has given clearer power of originality and thinking, I cannot think who it is."[27] Likewise, the southern accents of her work were highlighted and, as earlier, made an object of fun: one reviewer described her fiction as "*Grand Guignol* with hominy grits"[28] while others observed, less playfully, "The chance of lower middle-class Southerners reading anything at all between hard covers is pretty slim"[29] and that O'Connor was not of "the mint julep circuit,"[30] noting a distinction of class as well as geography.

But other reviewers also noted that the South was more than a regionalistic Skinner box and thought that the highest praise to give a southern writer was to say that her work transcended its setting, as in the compliment, "Here in rural miniature are the primary intuitions of man."[31] A reviewer from *Harper's Bazaar* stated, "Flannery O'Connor writes of the South, but 'regional' is not the word for her writing,"[32] and Fred Bornhauser, in *Shenandoah*, stated that O'Connor's stories take place in a "terrifyingly familiar" world that is not Georgia as much as "microcosmically The Universe."[33] And in the *Savannah Morning News*, Ben W. Griffith Jr. stated, "One feels as if the incidents of these stories occurred in any region on earth they would immediately be absorbed into the folklore of that area and be told and retold eternally on front porches and back fences. These stories, in short, have universality and depth in their narrative elements alone. . . . These stories have humor, characterizations, freshness, and universality."[34] O'Connor's South was still viewed by reviewers as a place "where vision and understanding often extend hardly beyond one's individual fence rails,"[35] but there was a growing consensus that "the Southern locale in no way gives the stories a provincial bias."[36] Critical recognition of O'Connor's fiction as not confined to the South was important because it developed both her growing reputation as more than a local hero and widened her appeal to her authorial audiences, both genuine and ironic.

A surprising feature of *A Good Man Is Hard to Find*'s original reviews is that the title story—frequently anthologized and universally viewed as her signature work—was often disparaged, misread, or simply ignored.[37] One reviewer stated that the story "has serious artistic defects,"[38] while another made a pedestrian stab at interpreting the title by claiming, "The 'good man' of the title story" is "an escaped murderer who casually dispatches six people."[39] Critics often described the story as "one of multiple tragedy"[40] and pointed out that the Misfit and his men kill all six members of Bailey's family. Counting the bodies was apparently easier than wrestling with the Misfit's ideas about whether or not Jesus should have raised the dead. Many reviewers could say nothing more about the story than that it was "tragic and terrible,"[41] as if the gunshots, and not the painful and complicated reasons behind them, were at the heart of O'Connor's thematic concerns. (The repeated use of "tragic" in these reviews shows that critics were responding to the ages and number of the victims, rather than the meaning of their deaths.) The unnamed reviewer for *Time* simply condensed the plot, noting that the characters "run into three escaped convicts who rob and shoot the lot, the babbling old featherwit last of all."[42] This reviewer saw no significance in the grandmother's last action and words, nor in the application of the Misfit's sardonic eulogy for her ("She would have been a good woman if it had been someone there to shoot her every minute of her life"[43]) to every reader of the story. O'Connor was right in her assumptions about some members of her ironic authorial audience and their unwillingness to acknowledge the mystery she thought necessary for fiction; she remarked that this particular review "nearly gave me apoplexy."[44]

Many reviewers instead found "The Displaced Person" to be the collection's strongest work. The *New York Herald Tribune Book Review* called it "the finest in the book,"[45] *Today* called it "the most successful story,"[46] the *Virginia Quarterly* called it the "most complex story"[47] in the collection, and the *Sewanee Review* called it the "most ambitious story"[48] of the lot. Others praised it even more highly: a reviewer for *Best Sellers* called it "the nearest to a classic tragedy of all the collection of ten,"[49] and another called it "a classic-tragedy of a man who disturbed his neighbors by minding his own business."[50] Reviewers' praise of "The Displaced Person" is the closest thing to a critical consensus of O'Connor's artistic performance to be found in her early career. That "A Good Man Is Hard to Find" is now much more widely anthologized and associated with O'Connor is a fact that modern critics may take for granted, but upon its first release in this collection, the story did not strike many reviewers as superior to its nine companion pieces.

The question remains why so many of the collection's initial readers viewed "The Displaced Person" as having "greater strength and deeper implications than any of the others."[51] The most obvious reason is that displaced persons were of contemporary concern in 1955, with the 1948 Displaced Persons Act still in readers' memories. Another possibility is that, unlike the title story, "The Displaced Person" is more neatly allegorical. The links between the title character, Mr. Guizac, and Christ are obvious: O'Connor even has Mrs. McIntyre remark, "Christ was just another D.P.,"[52] almost as a means to prompt the reader. Similarly, Guizac's horrifying death—and Mrs. McIntyre's complicity in it—

smacks more of the story of the Paschal lamb, especially since Guizac had been an advocate of loving one's neighbor when dealing with the blatantly racist Mrs. McIntyre. The allegory of the sacrificed innocent is not only effective, it is also easily accessible to first-time readers. "A Good Man Is Hard to Find," on the other hand, is a story more difficult to categorize. It seems to begin as a social comedy, with the stock character of the irritating, know-it-all grandmother presented as an easy target—but once Bailey's car flips on its back, the characters and the reader are no longer in the driver's seat. What began as a recognizable story about a meddling old lady becomes a serious disquisition on Christ, punishment, sin, and grace, and the grandmother becomes not merely an object of social ridicule. The Misfit and O'Connor challenge and unsettle both the delirious grandmother and the unsuspecting reader. In "The Displaced Person," the reader is flattered into recognizing Guizac's goodness; in "A Good Man Is Hard to Find," the reader's assumptions are dramatically upended in a moment of violence. This technique of luring her reader into making a number of literary and moral assumptions, only to have them violently shaken, was one that O'Connor would use again and again in her best work: one only needs to recall the endings of "Everything That Rises Must Converge" or "Revelation" as later examples. In the *Sewanee Review*, Louis D. Rubin Jr. noted that while writers like Erskine Caldwell had social aims and axes to grind, "Flannery O'Connor has no such intention, no such simple approach to people."[53] But a simple approach may have been what many reviewers wanted and took, which is why they had more difficulty with the Misfit than with the displaced person.

Still, some readers did argue—in what were becoming longer and more sophisticated evaluations of O'Connor's work—that the title, as Thomas H. Carter observed, "states quite literally the burden of the book."[54] As with *Wise Blood*, a reviewer for *Shenandoah* offered perhaps the most lucid explanation of O'Connor's technique: Fred Bornhauser claimed that the collection's title would be perfect even without the eponymous story and that titles such as "A Good Man Is Hard to Find," "The Life You Save May Be Your Own," and "Good Country People" help "illuminate in inverse situations the ethos which is the absolute center of gravity"[55] in O'Connor's stories. Yet it was Robert Giroux—not O'Connor—who named the collection after the work that had impressed him most as he readied O'Connor's stories for publication.[56] O'Connor regarded "The Artificial Nigger" as "my favorite and probably the best thing I'll ever write,"[57] but she trusted Giroux and followed his instincts. Of course, one cannot imagine a collection named after O'Connor's favorite story selling well or without great controversy in 1955 or today. When the collection was published in the United Kingdom two years later under the title *The Artificial Nigger*, O'Connor was upset about the title change.[58] Giroux's naming of the collection has helped cement the title story as O'Connor's most representative work and O'Connor as a writer who, in the words of one reviewer, relies on "ironic violence"[59] or, in the more colloquial words of Granville Hicks, leaves a "nasty taste in the reader's mouth."[60]

Indeed, the early reviews are marked by general critical unease in responding to the nastiness of O'Connor's plots. One of the first reviewers warned that O'Connor "is not the kind of writer who caters to people who want what is commonly called escape stuff" and stated, "If you are one of those who 'read for entertainment,' skip Miss O'Connor."[61] What the reviewer means by "escape stuff" can be vaguely defined as the material of potboilers—but potboilers feature as many, if not more, criminal characters and scenes of lust, murder, and mayhem as O'Connor's fiction. *A Good Man Is Hard to Find* differs from page-turners because O'Connor presents sensationalistic elements as a means to explore complicated theological issues. Orville Prescott warned his readers in the *New York Times* that "*A Good Man Is Hard to Find* is not a dish to be set before most readers"[62] while another reviewer noted that the collection "is hardly to be recommended for light reading."[63] Critics seemed to define "light reading" and "escape stuff" as fiction in which the killer does his or her business for clear and recognizable aims: money, revenge, or sex. A killer whose acts reflect a spiritual crisis and who undermines the announced motives of his own actions with the remark "It's no real pleasure in life"[64] was more difficult to categorize. Thus the content and themes prompted one reviewer to recommend the book only for "adult readers,"[65] and Caroline Gordon noted that "many people profess to find her work hard to understand."[66] O'Connor was as rough on the senses as she was on the soul. As with *Wise Blood*, many critics pointed out the horrors and violence of O'Connor's work but fell short of further comment; they saw the "large and startling figures" but did not examine their meaning, as if the strangeness and violence of her stories were gratuitous rather than thematic. "When I see these stories described as horror stories," O'Connor wrote to Betty Hester, "I am always amused because the reviewer always has hold of the wrong horror."[67]

By this point in her career, O'Connor recognized her reputation as an author whose work was described in ways akin to the films of Quentin Tarantino forty years later. In a letter in which she spoke of a squib in the *New Yorker* that characterized her work as superficial and characterized by "brutality,"[68] O'Connor remarked, "I am mighty tired of reading reviews that call *A Good*

Man brutal and sarcastic. The stories are hard but they are hard because there is nothing harder nor less sentimental than Christian realism."[69] O'Connor uses "hard" here to mean "hard" to stomach but also "hard" on one's easy assumptions about God and man, another part of her reputation that is today taken for granted. For example, in a 2009 PBS interview, Ralph Wood commented on her reputation in unequivocal language: "Flannery O'Connor is the only great Christian writer this nation has produced. Now, that's an astonishing fact. Emerson, Thoreau, Hawthorne, Melville, Twain, Emily Dickinson, Frost, Stevens—not one of them Christian, at least not orthodoxly Christian. She's a Southerner and a Catholic, she's not at the center of American culture, and yet she is our only great Christian writer."[70] However, as with *Wise Blood*, the original reviewers of *A Good Man Is Hard to Find* did not, as a whole, emphasize what Wood states as obvious and the current critical community generally believes, as reflected in the amount and focus of scholarly and popular examinations of O'Connor and her work. Some readers immediately noticed what O'Connor and Wood both state about her work, but most did not. The reviewers who immediately recognized the Christian themes of *A Good Man Is Hard to Find* deserve attention here because their reviews are important mile markers on the road of O'Connor's reputation, a road that began as a dirt track with small signposts calling *Wise Blood* an odd, minor, "ingrown"[71] book about a specific region and which has become a highway marked by billboards (such as Wood's remarks) declaring her importance as a Christian writer. When O'Connor's *Complete Stories* was published in 1971, seven years after her death, a critic for the *National Catholic Reporter* could, without pause, call her "the most deeply committed Christian writer of her day,"[72] and while one could note that "Christian" is a less-defining term than "Catholic," such an appreciation of her spiritual themes was not obvious to all who read her work in that day's first light.

In fact, the first notice that firmly and irrevocably contributed to O'Connor's reputation as a Christian writer was not a scholarly examination in a peer-reviewed journal or an extended appreciation in a literary magazine but a two-paragraph letter to the editor of *Commonweal*. Dale Francis, who would later found the *Texas Catholic Herald* and serve as director of the University of Notre Dame Press, responded to James Greene's review of *A Good Man Is Hard to Find* in which Greene praised O'Connor's work for demonstrating the "rustic religiosity" of her characters and for the ways in which she "lifts a 'comic' device to complex dimensions."[73] Francis shared Greene's admiration for O'Connor's work but argued that Greene was not seeing what informed it:

To the editors: I couldn't be more in agreement with James Greene in his praise
of the talents of Flannery O'Connor (July 22). But I would like to suggest that
it is the Catholicism of Miss O'Connor that gives her the viewpoint from which
she writes. There is compassion in her writing, there is understanding of reality;
she belongs to neither the school of writing about the South that sees only deca-
dence nor to the school that sees only magnolias.

Miss O'Connor—who despite the Irish name is a convert to the Church—is
an important addition to the list of American Catholic writers. And make no
mistake, although her stories have not touched on Catholic subject matter, she is
not just a writer who is a Catholic, but a Catholic writer.[74]

Francis's need to "suggest" that O'Connor's Catholicism was the thematic
foundation of her work might strike a modern reader as akin to a critic's need
to "suggest" that Orwell's political thinking informed *1984*. However, the very
word "suggest," used by a reader like Francis who was well versed in contemporary Christian writing, proves that regarding O'Connor as a writer interested
in Catholic mysteries was, at this point, a novel idea. Also worth notice here is
that even Francis seems not to realize the depth of his own insight: the statement "her stories have not touched on Catholic subject matter" seems difficult, at this point in time, to make. One only needs to examine the collection's
table of contents to see that the stories abound in "Catholic subject matter,"
such as baptism ("The River"), redemption ("A Good Man Is Hard to Find"),
the sacrifice of innocents ("The Displaced Person"), divine mercy ("The Artificial Nigger"), and, most obviously, the Eucharist ("A Temple of the Holy
Ghost"). Scholars can now begin their books with sentences such as "Flannery
O'Connor's religious faith engages the interest of nearly every critic or reviewer
who considers her fiction,"[75] but this interest was not found in the initial reception of those critics who could not see the Catholic forest for the grotesque and
southern trees.

Francis's letter is also worth notice because of an error that reveals how
Catholic writers were sometimes received. His claim that O'Connor was "a
convert to the Church" was untrue: O'Connor's parents were prominent Catholics in both Savannah and Milledgeville, and she was raised in that faith. Why
Francis described her as a "convert" is unknown, but in a letter to Frances Neel
Cheney, written a month after Francis's piece, O'Connor noted, "I must say
Mr. Dale Francis' communication didn't rejoice me any. I wrote him a real
polite letter though and *thanked* him for his high opinion and told him I was a
born Catholic. I thought maybe after that he would write them and correct it

but he didn't even answer my letter. It doesn't make any difference except that people do believe that if you have been brought up in the church, you write ads if you write anything."[76] Three years later, O'Connor's reputation as a convert still surfaced with enough frequency to make O'Connor complain to Cecil Dawkins, "They always insist on calling me a convert" and to blame Francis's letter to *Commonweal* for the mistake: "He thought somebody told him so, or some such thing, and ever since anybody that writes anything announces I am a convert."[77]

This error illuminates the ways that some critics—even admiring ones, like Francis—regarded writing that explored spiritual themes: presumably only one with all the sound and fury of a convert would want to explore these themes in her work or be unabashed in her enthusiasm for doing so.[78] Just as assumptions about the South were epitomized in Mencken's "The Sahara of the Bozart," those about the pedestrian qualities of Catholic writing were reflected in an essay by George Orwell composed fifteen years before the publication of *A Good Man Is Hard to Find*: "The atmosphere of orthodoxy is always damaging to prose, and above all it is completely ruinous to the novel, the most anarchical of all forms of literature. How many Roman Catholics have been good novelists? Even the handful one could name have usually been bad Catholics. The novel is practically a Protestant form of art; it is a product of the free mind, of the autonomous individual."[79] The idea that a free mind cannot coexist with a Catholic soul is one still found in some circles today and was present in O'Connor's crack about writers of faith being assumed to write only ads. To O'Connor, the danger of being labeled as a Catholic writer was that readers "assumed that you have some religious axe to grind"[80] and that "no one thinks you can lift the pen without trying to show somebody redeemed."[81] Spiritual propaganda disguised as fiction was never her aim: as she explained to a priest, "being propaganda for the side of the angels only makes it worse."[82]

The second important notice of *A Good Man Is Hard to Find* that marked O'Connor's growing reputation as a Catholic writer appeared two months after Francis's letter. Writing in *Today*, a Catholic periodical published in Chicago, John A. Lynch used the occasion of *A Good Man Is Hard to Find* to comment on O'Connor but also on what he viewed as the timid state of Catholic publishers and the readers to which they catered. Baldly stating that O'Connor "is a Catholic writer, or, a Catholic who is a writer, or, a writer who is a Catholic," Lynch laments that she "remains outside the literary fraternity."[83] Her status as outsider, according to Lynch, was the result of assumptions held by readers such as Orwell, which O'Connor addressed when mentioning that too many

readers assumed that Catholics could write only propaganda: "In this enlightened day, Flannery O'Connor, for all her ability, is faced with a formidable
congregation of audience and critics who would decide a writer's merits on
his Catholicism, and his Catholicism, in turn, on his expressed piety."[84] "Expressed" is the key word here, for Lynch further complains that O'Connor has
been ignored by more mainstream Catholic outlets because "Miss O'Connor's
orthodoxy is not their orthodoxy," an orthodoxy "co-existent only with sweet-
ness and light."[85] The violence and what Lynch calls the "macabre tightening"
of O'Connor's stories was here viewed as an asset and as crucial to an understanding of her work. Lynch's review is significant for proclaiming that one
could explore Catholic themes in a way directly opposite those found in the
Catholic Home Journal, which Lynch notes solicited "snappy love stories with
a light Catholic touch."[86] Indeed, Lynch's assertion that little magazines and
other secular sources provided a more welcome forum for O'Connor and her
work than Catholic outlets seems well founded: reviews that emphasized the
moral and Catholic foundations of O'Connor's collection were found in the
pages of the *Kenyon Review,*[87] the *Sewanee Review,*[88] and the liberal and social-
ist *New Leader,* where Granville Hicks noted that O'Connor writes from "an
orthodox Christian point of view."[89]

The third significant notice that marks O'Connor's growing reputation as a
Catholic writer is so short that its insight seems all the more surprising. Less a
review than a squib, this unsigned notice in *Commonweal* of the 1957 paperback
edition of *A Good Man Is Hard to Find* encapsulates two years' worth of critical
evolution in fewer than fifty words: "Astonishingly adult and profound short
stories by one of the most seriously theological and competent of women novelists. These earthy stories of the South are by a talent who bids fair to be a
Catholic Turgenev. (Recently reissued as a paperback.)"[90] All the early history
of critical engagement with O'Connor's collection surfaces in this unsigned notice. "Astonishingly adult" recalls the reviews that emphasized the stories' violence and nastiness. "Profound" recalls the increased attention to ways that this
violence suggests deeper, spiritual themes. "Women novelists" and "stories of
the South" are predictable in their appearance, but they are used here as means
of praise: O'Connor is "seriously theological and competent," and her South is
"earthy" or realistic. And O'Connor is again compared to another author, but
now the comparison is not to an American author but to a Russian writer in the
most complimentary way and on grounds of form rather than subject matter.
That a number of assumptions about O'Connor could all be compressed into
such a short space suggests the degree to which, in only two years after the ini-

tial publication of *A Good Man Is Hard to Find*, they had become established in a general critical consciousness. A "genuine" authorial audience, it now seemed, was forging O'Connor's reputation, although these readers would soon be challenged by a different kind of opposition upon the release of her next work.

The Violent Bear It Away

In 1960, five years after the publication of *A Good Man Is Hard to Find* and only four years before O'Connor's death, Farrar, Straus and Cudahy published *The Violent Bear It Away*, O'Connor's second novel and the last of her fiction to be published during her lifetime. Granted, eight years after *Wise Blood*, some reviewers were still amazed by O'Connor's gender and prone to left-handed compliments such as, "There is strength and a gustiness in her which is rare in any woman writer."[91] O'Connor's southern sensibilities were still a part of many reviews and almost as much of her reputation as the work itself: Faulkner still occasionally cast his shadow, as when one reviewer noted that the book "smelled of Faulkner."[92] But O'Connor was now regarded as different from other southern writers because of what critics had come to recognize about her spiritual themes: writing in the *Arizona Quarterly*, for example, Donald C. Emerson stated that O'Connor was often called a "Southern Writer" but noted that O'Connor could not be so easily labeled, since "Her values are Christian, and the horrors with which she deals have meaning where the witless violence of Caldwell's *Tobacco Road* does not."[93] Emerson's remark recalls the earlier point made about the level and meaning of violence in *A Good Man Is Hard to Find* compared to that found in pulp fiction. As with *A Good Man Is Hard to Find*, other critics discovered O'Connor's South as a potential staging ground for fiction exploring transcendent themes. One of the novel's early and enthusiastic reviewers stated, "Tarwater is one of the most challenging symbols of modern man who tries to see only the part of reality that he wants to see,"[94] while another noted that O'Connor's works "are not regional, but are of the people whose special conflicts with life could happen anywhere."[95] Such praise marks how far responses to O'Connor had come from remarks claiming that *Wise Blood* was strictly "about the South" and "southern religionists."[96] The *Times Literary Supplement* recognized *The Violent Bear It Away* as a novel that transcended even the category of American fiction and explored mankind on a "universal scale."[97] O'Connor's reputation had come a long way from the days of *Wise Blood* when she was viewed as a southern oddity: her work was now regarded as possessing "a note of universalism,"[98] and although she would still be labeled a "southern girl," the same critic could describe O'Connor as "universal in her work."[99] Orwell did not have the final word on orthodox authors, nor was the Sahara of the Bozart now as dry as some had once assumed.

Reviewers were quick to point out the difficulty of *The Violent Bear It Away*, remarking, "many readers will prefer the pabulum of slick best sellers"[100] and noting that "all but the most careful readers are likely to be misled."[101] These warnings to potential readers about the horrors of O'Connor's plots became more frequent: one reviewer stated that the novel's "strong flavor will be too much for the taste of most fiction readers,"[102] while another noted that the book would "not appeal to the average reader; nor can it be recommended for teenagers or the immature."[103] Not surprisingly, "grotesque" remained a watch-word, appearing in almost every review of the novel and more strongly tied to O'Connor's reputation than ever before.[104] But by now the term, despite its usefulness, was starting to show its age and limitations: writing in the *Jackson Clarion-Ledger*, Louis Dollarhide denied the power and accuracy of the term by arguing, "Here is characterization as incisive and clean-cut as stone images, yet of characters, not mere grotesques, who live and breathe."[105] A critic for the *Catholic World* similarly found "grotesque" and its usual companions inadequate: writing of Tarwater's simultaneous drowning and baptism of his cousin, Bishop, the reviewer cast aside two specific (and important) critical voices and all those who followed their lead: "This time it is doubtful if any reviewer will refer to Tarwater's action as a 'garish climax,' as the *Saturday Review* once did to the climax of her story 'Greenleaf'; or as an act of 'sardonic brutality,' as *Time* did the action of 'A Good Man Is Hard to Find.' It is now obvious that there is nothing 'garish,' 'gratuitous,' or 'grotesque' about this novel, or about any of her other works for that matter."[106] The words "It is now obvious" remind us of the degree to which literary reputations evolve over time. One way to gage a watchword's power is to note when voices rise against it and complain of its inadequacy.

Reviewers also noted O'Connor's humor but did not regard it as "satiri-cal" as so many did when they first encountered *Wise Blood*. Perhaps the most representative example of the ways many readers regarded O'Connor's humor at this point in her career is found in a review for the *Chicago Sunday Tribune Magazine of Books*, where Fanny Butcher (a critic whose very name might have been created by O'Connor) noted that her work was "shot through with hu-mor, but of a menacing kind" and compared O'Connor's comic sense to "a poke in the ribs made with a poison barb."[107] Descriptions of the humor in

The Violent Bear It Away followed suit: critics called the novel's humor "rueful,"[108] "merciless,"[109] "mirthless,"[110] and, of course, "grotesque,"[111] but they also noted that O'Connor's humor was a means by which she illuminated human nature—something that she always did but which was now noticed by her readers as part of her complex art. Thus Tarwater's struggle was described by Paul Engle as "hilarious and touching,"[112] and Thomas F. Gossett stated that O'Connor possessed "a mordant humor which is extremely perceptive."[113] Not surprisingly, Brainard Cheney—as much a member of her genuine authorial audience as O'Connor could wish—noted that O'Connor's humor was not simply sarcastic or dark but philosophical and, ultimately, affirming:

> Her original achievement, her genius, is that she has restored to humor the religious point of view. That is, man looking at himself not in the presence of time and space, however great, and certainly not this humanly-conceived time and space looking at man. But man, looking at himself, in the Presence of Infinity— Infinity for Whom there is no unknown, no unknowable, from Whom there are no secrets. But an Infinity of Love and Compassion as well as Awfulness.[114]

Cheney's opinions apply to *Wise Blood* and *A Good Man Is Hard to Find* as much as they do to *The Violent Bear It Away*, but they took eight years to make their way into print. The history of how critics characterized O'Connor's humor—which remained unchanged in tone and style throughout her career— demonstrates the ways in which they struggled to describe a humor they found unsettling. Should a reader laugh with or at these characters? Eventually, her combination of ethical issues and dark humor would become another part of O'Connor's reputation that was taken for granted, as in Walter Clemons's 1971 *Newsweek* review of *The Complete Stories*: "To read *The Complete Stories* is to see, better than before, the development of her profound moral vision. This doesn't change the fact that Flannery O'Connor is one of the funniest American writers."[115] When Clemons subsequently notes, "It takes some readers (I was one) a while to understand that it's more than a superb Punch-and-Judy show,"[116] he could be speaking for his critical colleagues.

The most notable and complex issue that arises from an examination of *The Violent Bear It Away*'s initial reception is the way in which critics responded to the prophet Mason Tarwater in particular and to the possibility of prophecy in general. Part of the novel's tension arises from two strong, opposing characters vying for the loyalty of the fourteen-year-old protagonist. Old Mason Tarwater, Francis's great-uncle, regards prophecy as a trial and a burden but knows that he must follow his calling and raise his great-nephew to assume the prophet's mantle; Rayber, Francis's uncle, regards prophecy as a psychological aberration and seeks to save his nephew from what he views as the insane manipulations of the old man. Tarwater's struggle between these two conflicting accounts of "prophecy" drives the plot of the novel and brings Tarwater to a revelation, the acceptance of his vocation, and his march to the hellish city, where "the children of God lay sleeping."[117] His role will not be an easy one, but his charge to awaken the sleeping souls is one that he cannot deny. A first-time reader's questioning Tarwater's vocation is expected and even, at times, courted by O'Connor as a means of drawing the reader into Tarwater's own struggle. But in the final analysis, the implications of O'Connor's form, content, and title work to confirm the reality of Tarwater's vision. Like Hazel Motes, Tarwater ends the novel in surrender to a force that O'Connor identifies and depicts forcefully and without humor. Prophecy is a deadly serious business.

O'Connor's letters repeatedly reflect her concern about this topic but also her unwillingness to compromise her own vision of prophecy. She knew that her treatment of the subject would generate misunderstanding, even attacks, from a large segment of the critical community. Before the novel's publication, she wrote to Maryat Lee, "There is nothing like being pleased with your own work—and this is the best stage—before it is published and begins to be misunderstood."[118] Days later, she wrote to Cecil Dawkins, "I dread all the reviews, all the misunderstanding of my intentions, etc. etc. Sometimes the most you can ask is to be ignored."[119] To Ted Spivey, she stated, "A lot of arty people will read it and be revolted, I trust"[120]; to Sally and Robert Fitzgerald, she joked, "I await the critical reception with distaste and unanticipation."[121] O'Connor knew that many readers would attack her just as the sleeping children of God, mentioned in the novel's final sentence, will attack Tarwater. "I am resigned to the fact that I am going to be the book's greatest admirer,"[122] she remarked and steeled herself against what she assumed would be a wave of "nothing but disappointed reviews."[123]

The initial critical reception proved O'Connor half-right. There were a number of vehement attacks featuring what she would label as misreadings of both the novel and her artistic intentions in writing it, but there were also enthusiastic reviews that praised the novel as O'Connor's best work to date. The critical split occurred along the fault line of her ironic and genuine authorial audiences. With some important exceptions I will examine later, the genuine authorial audience—many writing in Catholic outlets—assumed the reality of Mason's prophecies and Tarwater's vocation; the ironic authorial audience assumed Mason to be a lunatic and Tarwater a victim of brainwashing. However, the audience from which a critic approached the novel was not always a guarantee

of how he or she would respond: there were members of the genuine authorial audience who accepted the possibility of Mason's vocation but panned the
novel and members of the ironic authorial audience who mocked the idea of
prophecy yet praised O'Connor's work.

Most of the novel's original reviewers, however, split along these "lines of
audience," and that split affected how readers regarded O'Connor's thematic
concerns. A reviewer could assume the novel was, to those in the genuine authorial audience, an examination of what O'Connor called "the nobility of
unnaturalness"[124]; to those in the ironic authorial audience, it was a chilling
portrayal of the manipulation of a vulnerable youth. Mason Tarwater would
surely endorse the first theme, while Rayber might affirm the second, although
even this assertion about Rayber is problematic, since he physically and mentally collapses after realizing that he has sacrificed his humanity for the sake
of a spiteful philosophical stance. O'Connor anticipated this response as well:
to Betty Hester, she wrote, "Many will think that the author shares Rayber's
point of view and praise the book on account of it,"[125] and to John Hawkes
she declared, "The modern reader will identify himself with the schoolteacher
[Rayber], but it is the old man who speaks for me."[126]

Those in the genuine authorial audience, often writing in Catholic periodicals, took Mason and O'Connor at their word. For example, an unnamed reviewer for the Catholic weekly journal *America* stated that the novel depicts the
ways in which "contemporary man gropes toward God through a miasma of
self-deception that can be enlightened only per *Christum Dominum nostrum.*"[127]
In *Today*, another Catholic periodical, Sister Bede Sullivan stated (at the end
of her opening paragraph) that O'Connor "sees more clearly than her fellow
mortals do, and proclaims more surely the Kingdom of God,"[128] implying that
O'Connor was prophetic in her own way, an idea Sullivan emphasized in the
Catholic Library World, where she ended her praise of the novel with the Catholic antiphon, "O wisdom who proceeded from the mouth of the Most High."[129]
Less effusive praise in Catholic quarters came from Bud Johnson in the *Catholic Messenger*, who stated that O'Connor had "written about the great struggle
that has engulfed the world since the Fall of Man,"[130] and from Eileen Hall,
who, in the Archdiocese of Atlanta's *Bulletin*, referred to Tarwater's prophetic
visions as his "gift" and argued that the novel's conclusion "demonstrates that
God will not be denied nor, in lesser degree, even dictated to."[131] In the Catholic
magazine *Jubilee*, Paul Levine described the novel as a portrait of "those who
seek to be their own Salvation, only to lose it, and those who grapple with
their Redemption, only to accept it."[132]

In one of the longest reviews of the novel, P. Albert Duhamel, writing in

Catholic World, praised O'Connor's ability to "see things as they really are,"[133] which to him meant through a Christian lens. Duhamel's examination, however, is much more than a glowing review; it is a watershed moment in the story of O'Connor's reputation, for Duhamel notes the ways in which O'Connor had been regarded and how, from this moment onward, he imagined she would be:

> Until [1959], critics had disguised their uncertainty over just what she could be up to by falling back on the condescending categories of the over-worked reviewer and labeling her "an interesting Southern stylist," or "promising young woman writer." With the publication of her third book there is now the very real possibility that they will go to the opposite extreme and disregard her art and concentrate excessively on her ideas.[134]

Duhamel reminds his readers of the power of watchwords, the allure of easy phrases for reviewers faced with deadlines, and how the pendulum of an author's reputation can swing in new directions.

However, reading as a member of the genuine authorial audience did not guarantee praise: some critics accepted the reality of O'Connor's themes but faulted her handling of them. For example, one early reviewer called the novel a "dark allegory touched by the clear light of Christian theology" yet found it "weighted, sometimes too heavily, with symbolism."[135] Walter Sullivan, writing in the *Nashville Tennessean*, flatly stated that O'Connor explored the "sense of paradox" that lies "at the heart of the Christian faith" but complained that the novel "thins out at the end, and the pace is perhaps too slow there."[136] Similarly, Paul Pickrel, writing for *Harper's Magazine*, accepted the genuine authorial assumptions, describing Tarwater as a young man who "assumes the mantle of prophecy" but also calling O'Connor's novel "too schematic," since "every incident neatly advances the scheme, every character illustrates it, and every symbol is exactly in place."[137] Even a member of the genuine authorial audience writing in a Catholic periodical was not a guarantee of praise: a reviewer for *Ave Maria*—a major Catholic magazine published for over one hundred years—stated that O'Connor wrote "lovely prose" but that *The Violent Bear It Away* would "not appeal to the average reader" because of O'Connor's "habit of jumping from present to past and back again in a manner readers may find tedious and annoying." This same reviewer also found Tarwater's defilement by the man in the lavender-colored car near the end of the novel to be "unfortunate and unnecessary to the story."[138] O'Connor's friend and fellow Catholic, Thomas F. Gossett, noted, "The trouble is that the religious insight of the great-uncle is so explosive that it often comes through as mere bigotry and does not seem an adequate foil for the smug scientism of Rayber."[139]

While such reviews may have done little to boost O'Connor's sales, their authors did demonstrate that members of the genuine authorial audience— even when they disparaged the novel—were the most ready to judge it by aesthetic criteria, rather than simply react (as Duhamel feared) to her "ideas." Her thematic concerns, these readers argued, were worthwhile but suffered because of her artistic performance. O'Connor herself might not have objected to such a manner of reading: her letters sometimes reveal her own doubts about her artistic handling of the theme she had chosen, as when she wrote to John Hawkes, "Rayber, of course, was always the stumbling block,"[140] to the Fitzgeralds, "Rayber has been the trouble all along,"[141] or to her editor, Catherine Carver, "Rayber has been the difficulty all along. I'll never manage to get him [as] alive as Tarwater and the old man."[142] At least the members of the genuine authorial audience who faulted the novel on aesthetic grounds were not reacting to O'Connor's "ideas" but to her skills as a writer. O'Connor may have found such an approach justified, even if she was not pleased with the critical verdicts.

O'Connor had in mind members of the ironic audience as she wrote, but those readers rarely spoke of *The Violent Bear It Away* as an aesthetic object. They instead reacted, almost reflexively and as Duhamel had predicted, to O'Connor's "ideas" of prophecy. O'Connor herself jokingly prophesied the critical reaction to be almost uniformly negative but did not foresee how similar so many of the negative reviews were in focus of attack: old Mason's status as a prophet. The very first published review of the novel mentions "the old man's fanaticism,"[143] and this label appears throughout the reviews, used as casually as if it were an obvious fact instead of pejorative opinion. Dozens of critics repeatedly referred to Mason as "fanatically fundamentalist,"[144] a man "warped by fanaticism,"[145] a "Baptist fanatic,"[146] and, over and over, a "religious fanatic."[147] Close behind "fanatic" in the watchword race were terms suggesting that Mason's prophetic gifts were signs of insanity: in a review entitled "Mad Tennessee Prophet Casts Backwoods Shadow," a reviewer for the *Chattanooga Times* described Mason as "twice as mad as the proverbial March hare,"[148] and many other critics argued the same. Mason's status as a prophet was also routinely undermined by the use of irony-bestowing quotation marks, as in a Massachusetts reviewer's remark that "The old man was a 'prophet' who believed he was appointed by the lord."[149] Emily Dickinson's coupling of madness and divinest sense was not a notion informing the ironic audience's opinion of Mason

Tarwater. The many unquestioned references to Mason's "madness" suggest this audience's fundamental split with its genuine authorial counterpart.

These same members of the ironic audience who assumed Mason's insanity also assumed O'Connor's great theme to be what Granville Hicks described as Tarwater's attempt to break "out of the darkness of superstition into the light of reason."[150] One review can stand as a representative example of many: writing in the *Boston Herald*, Ruth Wolfe Fuller praised the novel as "very moving" and "superbly written"—but praised it according to a set of values that the novel repeatedly questions and ultimately attacks:

> The pitiful and true theme of the book lies in the inhumanity to a child, the little boy Tarwater who has been brought up, if it can be called bringing up, in his dreadful old shack in the woods.
>
> It would spoil the story to tell how the boy's courage and initiative finally provide his escape. Yet the escape is only temporary, for the tragedy lies in the hurt and harm, so long inflicted.[151]

Her calling Tarwater a "child" and "little boy" despite his age (fourteen) and temperament (sarcastic, spiteful) is an attempt to portray him as a victim; her emphasis on his social condition instead of his spiritual one brings to mind O'Connor's jibe that southern readers "still believe that man has fallen and that he is only perfectible by God's grace" while those north of the Mason-Dixon line view spiritual crises as "a problem of better housing, sanitation, health, etc."[152] Fuller's speaking of O'Connor's "true theme" reflects her inability to imagine—like Dr. Adams when trying to console Dr. Johnson—that her subject takes these ideas seriously. Further, Fuller's characterization of Tarwater's profound struggle recalls similar reviews of *Wise Blood* in which Motes is viewed as heroic for attempting to break free from the Christ-haunted South; her calling the novel a "tragedy" of "hurt and harm" seems like something that might be said by Bernice Bishop, the "welfare woman" who marries Rayber and who, like him, assumes that spiritual struggles are rooted in social inequities. As a reviewer for the *Springfield (Mass.) Republican* soberly instructed, "She seems to be giving us an indirect but worthwhile reminder that we are all shaped by our environments"[153]; while another reviewer fumed, "Young Tarwater deserved better of life."[154] Fuller never mentions—despite her apparent concern over "the inhumanity to a child"—Rayber's attempt to drown his own mentally retarded son as a means to prove his own superiority over the emotional commitment that the child demanded.

Other readers spoke of Rayber in similar terms: Orville Prescott referred to Rayber as a "kindly and well-intentioned schoolteacher,"[155] while a reviewer for

the *Houston Chronicle* called him "well-meaning" and "placed in juxtaposition
to the irrational youth."[156] Tarwater was often characterized by ironic reviewers as an "impressionable young boy"[157] or a "corrupted child"[158]; they never
considered that the novel explores Tarwater's delivery from the corruption of
Rayber, nor, as with Fuller, did they mention Rayber's attempted murder of his
own son. That Mason is a fanatic is never questioned; that Rayber might be
one is never considered. Rather, he was seen by these critics as the novel's hero,
"bent on saving the boy from the seeds of destruction he knows the old man
has planted"[159] in Tarwater and as a rational figure attempting to undo "the
fanatic's brainwashing"[160] from which he has freed himself and which he seeks
to reverse in his nephew. The ironic audience's siding with Rayber suggests
G. K. Chesterton's argument about the modern cult of "logic" and his remark
that an excess of reason—not spirituality—breeds insanity: "Poets do not go
mad," he wrote, "but chess-players do."[161] While these critics are surely not mad,
their categorical dismissal of Mason reflects their refusal to take the novel on
its own terms.

Certain members of the genuine authorial audience accepted O'Connor's
themes but faulted her artistic performance; conversely, members of the ironic
audience, like Fuller, categorically denied the reality of O'Connor's overarch-
ing theme of prophecy yet still praised the novel, viewing her artistic performance as supporting their argument for Mason's insanity. They assumed that
O'Connor, despite what later readers might see as the pronounced Catholic
themes of *Wise Blood* and *A Good Man Is Hard to Find*, was mocking the old
man in her novel just as they were in their reviews. They had viewed *Wise Blood*
as a bitter "satire" of religion rather than an examination of a man's deathly
serious struggle with Christ; they now viewed *The Violent Bear It Away* as "a
bitter denunciation of faith based solely on emotion."[162] For example, a writer
for the *Omaha World-Herald* stated, "That the old man is insane is obvious" but
praised the "character drawing" as "magnificent" and declared, "If there were
more books like this one, television would have fewer viewers."[163] Many members of the ironic audience praised the novel not as one depicting Tarwater's
struggle against the fate chosen for him by God, but against what one reader
called the "chains of fanaticism"[164] forged by his great-uncle. Again, reading
as a member of the genuine authorial audience did not guarantee praise, nor
did reading as a member of the ironic audience guarantee condemnation. The
original reviews of *The Violent Bear It Away* recall the novel's portrayal of the
"perfidy" Rayber works upon Mason: many reviews from the ironic audience
read as if they were written by Rayber himself, who, of course, does write a long
analysis of his uncle's "mania" for a magazine, noting, "He needed the assurance

of a call, and so he called himself."[165] Rarely has the critical reaction to a novel so perfectly mirrored one of the novel's own themes.

Reviews that may surprise a modern reader are those that came relatively late in the novel's reception and questioned the single most prominent aspect of her reputation that readers note today: her Catholicism. The novelist Robert O. Bowen, one of O'Connor's contemporaries and a professor of literature at Cornell, offered the single greatest attack in print thus far and serves as an indicator of how much O'Connor's reputation as a Catholic writer had developed. His 1961 review, "Hope vs. Despair in the Gothic Novel," appeared in *Renascence*, a journal of Marquette University that, according to its website, acts as "a Christian witness to literature for promoting the study of values" and "includes essays which incorporate Christian perspectives as a way of looking at literature."[166] In his examination of *The Violent Bear It Away* for *Renascence*, Bowen complains that contemporary critics accept literary reputations *prima facie* and, in the case of O'Connor, assume that her work is laden with "religious profundity."[167] Yet Bowen asks, "Must we accept her work as 'Catholic' because she is Catholic?" This is a fair enough question, and Bowen answers it in his long review by arguing that the novel reflects the "relentlessly deterministic pattern" of contemporary works. Ultimately, Bowen finds the novel flawed on both aesthetic and Catholic grounds. While Tarwater's vocation is, to Bowen, "a true one," O'Connor's artistic performance in presenting him as unable to engage in any choice—his lack of what modern theorists might call "agency"—makes him O'Connor's puppet rather than a recognizable person. To Bowen, O'Connor's inescapable and pessimistic determinism belies her Catholicism:

> Since this novel has been widely spoken of as "Catholic," it seems imperative that one point out that like so much current negative writing, this book is not Catholic at all in any doctrinal sense. Neither its content nor its significance is Catholic. Beyond not being Catholic, the novel is distinctly anti-Catholic in being a thorough, point-by-point dramatic argument against Free Will, Redemption, and Divine Justice, along with other aspects of Catholic thought.[168]

O'Connor was previously compared to Faulkner and McCullers because of their common regions, but Bowen compares her to Bellow, Nabokov, and Salinger as writers who "can tear down but not build up, who will not tolerate faith or hope."[169] Such alleged intolerances on O'Connor's part result in Bowen's final judgment of her as "an enemy of literature and of life."[170] This objection to O'Connor's alleged anti-Catholic determinism is also found in a review by Frederick S. Kiley, who complained that O'Connor offered only extremes of rationalism and fanaticism and that her characters, in deterministic dazes, "go places and do things without ever quite realizing why or how."[171]

Two years after Bowen's attack, Thomas F. Smith reevaluated the novel for the *Pittsburg Catholic* newspaper and directly addressed the subject of O'Connor's reputation as a Catholic author: "I'm pleased as anyone that she's a member of the Church, but it is regrettable that her Catholicity has complicated discussion of her literary merits in some quarters."[172] In these responses we see that the once invisible had now become too pronounced and even subject to attack. Only a few years earlier, critics were informing their readers of O'Connor's Christian and Catholic themes as if they had made an important discovery; now, some reviewers were pushing back against her Catholic reputation, arguing that a label such as "Catholic novelist" needed to be evaluated as much as the work itself. Smith's review is a moment in the development of O'Connor's reputation where her status as a Catholic author had trumped her status as a female or even southern and was accepted widely enough to warrant attention and require correction.

In 1960, four years before O'Connor's death, Eileen Hall looked back at the initial reception of *Wise Blood* and predicted the ways in which *The Violent Bear It Away* would complicate O'Connor's reputation:

> It is an interesting aspect of Miss O'Connor's career that when her first work was being published in the early fifties she was gleefully identified by many as her own antithesis. At a great distance, grappling antagonists often have a confusing way of looking like lovers. . . . Now that the sixties are here and the author has published her third book, she is not misunderstood. This does not mean, however, that she is yet properly appreciated. On the contrary, now that many of her erstwhile admirers have learned that she means precisely the opposite of their original assumption, she may, in some corners at least, be even less appreciated.[173]

Hall's remarks characterize the early reviewers of *Wise Blood* who claimed the novel was satirical and that O'Connor was "gleefully" presenting Motes as a paranoid schizophrenic, as well as those original reviewers of *The Violent Bear It Away* who dismissed Mason as a fanatic or objected to the very label of "Catholic author" when used to describe O'Connor. However, her claim that O'Connor was finally "not misunderstood" is, to again invoke Samuel Johnson, the triumph of hope over experience. The decades following the publication of *The Violent Bear it Away* would see many more examples of O'Connor being misunderstood as her reputation gathered momentum.

Chapter 3

O'Connor's Posthumous Reputation

The Death of the Author

The years between the publication of *The Violent Bear It Away* (1960) and *Mystery and Manners* (1969) saw the deterioration of O'Connor's health and her death in 1964. But her death did not slow her works' rate of publication nor quiet the readers and reviewers who were working, however unknowingly and certainly not in concert, to construct a reputation that would finally earn O'Connor the first posthumously awarded National Book Award for fiction, an early place in the Library of America, and a collection of associations and assumptions about her fiction that accompanies O'Connor's name to the present day.

After *The Violent Bear It Away*, O'Connor continued publishing short stories in quality fiction magazines (such as *New World Writing* and *Sewanee Review*) as well as in one with greater, national readership: the opening chapter of her third, unfinished novel, *Why Do the Heathen Rage?*, appeared in the July 1963 *Esquire*, which, at the time, had its own impressive reputation for publishing fiction. "Everything That Rises Must Converge" won the 1962 O. Henry Award; "Revelation" won it in 1964; her work was well received in France thanks to the efforts of Maurice Coindreau (who translated *Wise Blood* in 1959 and *The Violent Bear It Away* in 1965) and the Éditions Gallimard versions of her work; and O'Connor received honorary degrees from Smith College and from Saint Mary's, the women's college of Notre Dame. Her name on a book's cover—as opposed to a lurid or intriguing illustration—was now given greater prominence than the title: in 1963 the New American Library released *A Good Man Is Hard to Find* and the two novels in a single volume entitled *Three by Flannery O'Connor*.

In 1961 O'Connor composed an introduction to *A Memoir of Mary Ann*, written by the Dominican nuns who staffed the Our Lady of Perpetual Help Free Cancer Home in Atlanta; although this introduction is read and discussed more by O'Connor's ardent admirers than by her casual fans, its composition and reception offer a glimpse into her reputation at this time. The memoir's titular figure arrived at the home when she was three and remained there until her death, at the age of twelve, from a cancerous tumor that dominated her face. The nuns who cared for Mary Ann found her an inspiring example of God's grace and asked O'Connor to compose the memoir herself, but O'Connor demurred, instead agreeing to edit the work and write an introduction, which today reminds readers of her unflinching style (its opening sentence, for example, states, "Stories of pious children tend to be false"[1]) and favorite themes, such as the idea that all human life is like Mary Ann's, filled with mystery and preparation for death. In terms of O'Connor's reputation, the introduction suggests, even by virtue of O'Connor's having been asked to write the memoir herself, how her literary stock had risen. Some of the memoir's reviewers cited the introduction and described O'Connor as a "brilliant Southern novelist"[2] and "a professional writer by stature and a Catholic."[3] O'Connor was also regarded as the perfect antidote to the potential mawkishness of the subject: writing in the *Boston Pilot*, Edward F. Callahan admitted that the subject matter "gives the reader the fear that the book will be an orgy of saccharine equal to the mid-Victorian tearjerkers," putting one in the mind of Little Nell, but then stated, "In the editing of this memoir, Miss O'Connor has obviously used a broad, blue pencil with the end result being a book of a much greater power than its subject or its literary predecessors might suggest."[4] This reviewer's emphasis on O'Connor's lack of sentimentality cropped up in a review for the *Savannah Morning News Magazine* that described the Dominican nuns approaching O'Connor and asking her to write the book herself: "We can imagine Miss O'Connor's dilemma," the reviewer states, "for all who know her gothic style would know that this was not exactly her medium."[5] O'Connor's thematic concerns and artistic performance were so well recognized that reviewers could imagine, with confidence, how she would respond to a text. Such is one effect of an established reputation and an effect found in much of the subsequent critical reaction to *Everything That Rises Must Converge*. O'Connor's name on the cover of both the hardcover and paperback reprints (fig. 10) thus lent the nuns a literary air without which the initial release may have been ignored or, in the case of the paperback, dismissed as being as sentimental as its cover art.

On August 3, 1964, three years after the publication of *A Memoir of Mary Ann*, O'Connor died of kidney failure brought on by the lupus that she had battled for over ten years. The news of O'Connor's death as reported by the AP wire and reprinted in hundreds of newspapers offered a bare-bones summary of her career: "MILLEDGEVILLE, GA (AP)—Flannery O'Connor, short-story writer and novelist who suffered from a chronic crippling illness, died Monday at the

Figure 10. Cover of *A Memoir of Mary Ann*, 1961.

age of 39. In 1959, Miss O'Connor was one of 11 American writers to receive a Ford Foundation grant."[6] The UPI obituary added, "Many of her characters, Southerners, were freak prophets, men of limited background who felt a super-natural call to preach."[7] (The characterization of figures such as Tarwater here suggests that the author of this obituary was a member of O'Connor's ironic audience.) The *New York Times* obituary, "Flannery O'Connor Dead at 39; Novelist and Short-Story Writer; Used Religion and the South as Themes in Her Work; Won O. Henry Awards," erased any tension between the ironic and genuine authorial audiences or between those who found her unreadable and those who found her prophetic: "In Miss O'Connor's writing were qualities that attract and annoy many critics: she was steeped in Southern tradition, she had an individual view of her Christian faith and her fiction was often peopled by introspective children. But while other writers received critical scorn for turning these themes into clichés, Miss O'Connor's two novels and few dozen stories were highly praised."[8] The author elaborated on the UPI writer's impression of O'Connor's characters, describing them as "Protestant Fundamentalists and fanatics."[9] Again, as with the case of Mason Tarwater, we see a reviewer tip his or her hand through the use of the word "fanatic." And *Time* magazine, ever ironic toward O'Connor and her fiction, described her in its "Milestones" section as an "authoress of the Deep South, an impassioned Roman Catholic from the Georgia backwoods who . . . explored the South's religious curiosities, finding among them . . . an appalling collection of lunatic prophets and murderous fanatics."[10] O'Connor and members of her genuine authorial audience would certainly object to this description of the prophets she had "found" while writing her fiction: even the terrifying hoodlums in "A Circle in the Fire" who, in their burning of the woods, prophesy to Mrs. Cope are not lunatics.

After her death, the student editors of *Esprit*, the University of Scranton's literary magazine, devoted the entire Winter 1964 issue to O'Connor. This may not, at first, seem like a major tribute. However, this issue of *Esprit* is invaluable to anyone examining the history of O'Connor's reputation because its faculty advisor, the Rev. John J. Quinn, S.J., solicited opinions about and reminiscences of O'Connor from dozens of critics, scholars, and authors, many of them established names. O'Connor had a friendly relationship with Quinn and *Esprit*: she had judged the magazine's first short-story contest and published her essay "The Regional Writer" in its pages. Quinn maintained a correspondence with O'Connor and also visited her mother after O'Connor's death, which he noted in the issue's foreword, thanking "Mrs. Edward F. O'Connor and her charming family for the gracious hospitality extended *Esprit* on the occasion of its unforgettable week-end (Oct. 30–Nov. 2, 1964) visit to Andalusia."[11] One of the student editors, John F. Judge, described Quinn as "the drive and inspiration" for O'Connor's presence in the university's courses and revealed, "Although he knew it would be impossible for any northern university to be even considered, Quinn actually made an effort to establish the University of Scranton as the Flannery O'Connor Library."[12] The relationship between the magazine and O'Connor was thus a substantial one; that the University of Scranton is a Jesuit institution certainly did not prevent O'Connor's ideas and art from receiving a fair hearing. The eighty-eight-page issue invaluably traces the history of O'Connor's reputation.

The tribute begins with Quinn's preface proclaiming the magazine's mission to extol O'Connor's artistic and personal virtues, "Lest the Prophet be without honor in her own terrestrial country."[13] This declaration is followed by "The Achievement of Flannery O'Connor," in which University of Scranton professor John J. Clarke argues that O'Connor's importance lay in her readjusting general notions of Catholic literature. Noting that "we have had too narrow a notion of what Catholic art might embrace," Clarke states that O'Connor "has expanded our view, even if it should be the verdict of time that the sensational situations of her stories transgress artistic limits" and that, regardless of how one reacts to the content of her work, "In the persisting paucity in America of Catholics who are good fiction writers, her absence will be sorely felt."[14] The issue also contains three extended critical analyses of O'Connor's work as well as a comparison of her work with Dostoevsky's, line drawings inspired by scenes and characters from her fiction, six poetic responses to O'Connor (among them "A Celt Sleeps," an excruciating imitation of Robert Burns), and two pieces of short fiction. The issue, for the most part, attempts to serve as an instruction manual for O'Connor's work, with a number of professors offering declarative statements such as, "The theme of Flannery O'Connor's fiction is free will,"[15] or "The significance of Flannery O'Connor is to be found . . . in her insistence upon the primacy of ideas."[16] One aim of the issue was to help readers appreciate what the editors, with their fingers on the pulse of O'Connor's reputation, had already discovered.

The heart of this issue of *Esprit*, however, is "Flannery O'Connor—A Tribute," a collection of reminiscences and testimonials that Quinn solicited in the days following her death. Of the forty-nine pieces of commentary gathered here, nine were previously published in such periodicals as the *New Yorker* and the *New York Times*. All are arranged alphabetically, save one: a reminiscence of O'Connor made, via telephone, by Katherine Anne Porter, which appears last in the collection, interspersed with photographs of Andalusia. To emphasize the value of Porter's words, the editors gave them their own title ("Gracious Greatness") and noted, "*Esprit* expresses its special gratitude to Miss Porter for telephoning—from her sick bed in her Washington home—the following reminiscence of Miss O'Connor."[17] Other notable contributors of original commentary included Elizabeth Bishop, Kay Boyle, Cleanth Brooks, Caroline Gordon, Elizabeth Hardwick, John Hawkes, Granville Hicks, Frank Kermode, Robert Lowell, Andrew Lytle, Robie Macauley, Thomas Merton, Allen Tate, Robert Penn Warren, and Eudora Welty. Some of the authors gathered here suggest the importance of O'Connor's work by their presence as well as their actual words, as in the case of Saul Bellow, whose contribution, in full, reads, "I was distressed to hear of Miss O'Connor's death. I admire her books greatly and had the same feeling for the person who wrote them. I wish I were able to say more, but it isn't possible just now."[18] J. F. Powers, another Catholic whose faith informed his fiction, supplied a similarly brief yet meaningful set of remarks: "Flannery O'Connor was an artist blessed (and cursed) with more than talent. In a dark and silly time, she had the great gift—the power and the burden—of striking fire and light. She was one of those rare ones, among writers, whose life's work was not in vain."[19]

An examination of "Flannery O'Connor—A Tribute" reveals the trends in O'Connor's reputation later surfacing in reviews of *Everything That Rises Must Converge*. The first of these trends was the interest in treating O'Connor's reputation as a subject as worthy of comment as her work itself and the desire to correct presumed prevailing notions of her place in American letters. Those who rose to this challenge of setting the record (as they saw it) straight were the professors. Charles Brady, of Canisius College, noted, "One of the biggest difficulties in assessing contemporary literary reputations is the tendency to praise an emerging writer for the wrong reasons"[20] and that praising O'Connor as another McCullers or Capote was off the mark (and, in fact, far from actual praise). Robert Drake, of the University of Texas, similarly complained that labels such as "Southern Gothic novelist" or "a Roman Catholic Erskine Caldwell"[21] were inadequate and inexact. James F. Farnham, at Western Reserve University, wrote, "Miss O'Connor is an artist, and Catholicism is one of her 'circumstances,'"[22] just like her southern address. Sr. Mariella Gable, of the College of St. Benedict, complained that O'Connor was "carelessly lumped with other outstanding Southern writers as another purveyor of the gratuitously grotesque."[23] Louis D. Rubin, then professor at Hollins College, insisted that O'Connor "did not write in the shadow of Faulkner, or of anyone else."[24] Nathan A. Scott Jr., of the University of Chicago, called "Southern Gothic" a "foolish rubric"[25] to use when thinking about O'Connor. And Robert Penn Warren, then at Yale, noted, "She is sometimes spoken of as a member of the 'Southern school' (whatever that is), but she is clearly and authoritatively herself."[26]

Other authors included in *Esprit* argued that O'Connor's reputation initially suffered because her first readers were not ready for a voice as original as hers. For example, Elizabeth Hardwick stated that O'Connor was "indeed, a Catholic writer, also a Southern writer; but neither of these traditions prepares us for the oddity and beauty of her lonely fiction."[27] Caroline Gordon accurately summarized much of O'Connor's early reception when she noted, "We do not naturally like anything which is unfamiliar. No wonder Miss O'Connor's writings have baffled the reviewers—so much so that they have reached for any *cliché* they could lay hold of in order to have some way of apprehending this original and disturbing work."[28] The description "Southern Gothic Catholic female novelist" seemed to carry less weight than it did the previous decade and was now regarded as misleading.

One soon-to-be cliché that was just gaining ground in O'Connor's reputation was that her illness was somehow responsible for her art—an idea that, in the wake of her death, proved irresistible to many readers and would gain traction a few months later in the reviews of *Everything That Rises Must Converge*. In what might be the most presumptuous of the appreciations gathered in *Esprit*, Brother Antonius (the poet and critic William Everson) noted, "Doubtless the facts of her personal life enabled her to confront the problem of violence in the search for understanding." After acknowledging about these facts that "I do not know what they were," Everson explained, "there was in her work an affinity to the humanity of her characters that could only have come from deep suffering."[29] As Caroline Gordon noted, many readers would reach for any cliché—here, the one of the Suffering Artist—to make sense of O'Connor's work. Elizabeth Hardwick mentioned O'Connor's "secluded life,"[30] an untrue characterization that, we will see, gained ground in the coming years but does not illuminate O'Connor's work; others mention what one author calls a "beautiful soul in an afflicted body,"[31] which similarly illuminates very little of O'Connor's actual character in anything but saccharine terms. Robie Macauley, then editor of the *Kenyon Review* and an acquaintance of O'Connor, stated, "Much of her life must have been a torment. She wrote hard and re-wrote even more painfully; her terrible affliction was with her for many years. It is no wonder that her great subject was the anti-Christ—the fierce and bestial side of the human mind. She treated it with a confused and emotional hatred."[32] That O'Connor experienced great physical pain is not debatable; that "much of her life must have been a torment" certainly is. Macauley's desire to account for O'Connor's art as the result of her "terrible affliction" rather than her imagination or intelligence is the kind of thinking that Caroline Gordon protested and which, a year later, would surface in reviews of *Everything That Rises Must Converge.*

Other contributors to "Flannery O'Connor—A Tribute" offered their opinions of O'Connor's character as a means of accounting for the moral courage they assumed she required to tackle her chosen subjects. Cleanth Brooks's comment, "I find it hard to separate the person from the artist" since "the character of both was an invincible integrity,"[33] reflects the ways in which many other contributors praised O'Connor's "enduring courage,"[34] "toughness,"[35] and "bravery."[36] Robert Lowell described O'Connor as "a brave one, who never relaxed or wrote anything that didn't cost her everything."[37] Laurence Perrine, a professor at Southern Methodist University whose literature textbooks became standard-issue in thousands of English courses, related an anecdote in which he wrote to O'Connor, asking her why, in "Greenleaf," she had named Mrs. May as she did. His description of O'Connor's reply emphasizes the image of the playfully teasing O'Connor found throughout the pages of *Esprit*:

> Miss O'Connor's reply, dated June 6, 1964, was written from a hospital in Atlanta, Georgia, a bare two months before her death. She answered, in a kindly letter that must have given her trouble to write at all, "As for Mrs. May, I must have named her that because I knew some English teacher would write and ask me why. I think you folks sometimes strain the soup too thin." I still feel a pleasant ache where my wrist was thus lightly slapped by so gallant a lady.[38]

The general effect of such testimonials is the continued fostering of O'Connor as a stoic figure and an intertwining of the artist's personality and subject matter. In the hopes of illuminating O'Connor's strength, Katherine Anne Porter engaged in a kind of physiognomic appreciation that would resurface in reviews of *Everything That Rises Must Converge*: in her description of O'Connor's self-portrait, Porter states that "the whole pose fiercely intent gives an uncompromising glimpse of her character."[39] The assumption that underlies so much of "Flannery O'Connor—A Tribute" is that O'Connor faced the truth and the truth had made her tough.

There are, however, some voices included in the tribute that balance the overwhelming portrayal of O'Connor as similar in temperament to old Mason Tarwater. The novelist John Hawkes emphasized that O'Connor closed all her letters with "Cheers," a word that, he argued, "represents the attitude she took towards life" and suggested the "economy, energy, pleasure and grace" she infused into her fiction. Mindful of O'Connor's reputation as a firebrand, Hawkes noted, "So now it seems important to stress the sprightly warmth and wry, engaging, uninhibited humanity of a writer commonly described as one of America's coldest and most shocking comic writers."[40] In a short offering, critic and professor Francis L. Kunkel similarly stressed the importance of O'Connor's "often overlooked" humor, noting that she resembled Waugh and Powers but demonstrated "the ability to treat religious matters with humor."[41] Not all readers viewed the ability to explore deep spiritual matters and make a reader laugh as mutually exclusive. Mason Tarwater was humorless, but O'Connor was not.

This issue of *Esprit* is also important to O'Connor's reputation because it reflects the growing connection between the peacock and O'Connor's image. The peacock, as O'Connor knew, has had a long association in Catholic art with immortality based on the legend that, after death, the bird's flesh does not decay. In "Living with a Peacock," a lighthearted essay appearing in the September 1961 issue of *Holiday* magazine and later reprinted in *Mystery and Manners* as "The King of the Birds," O'Connor described her interest in collecting peafowl. *Esprit*'s cover reinforced the association between O'Connor and the peacock (fig. 11), as does the issue's final selection, a poem titled "The Peacock and the Phoenix," which depicts a maudlin peacock lamenting, "Fair Authoress, only thirty-nine, / You died before your finest line."[42] The peacock is now as much a part of O'Connor's reputation as butterflies are of Nabokov's or the French poodle, Charlie, is of Steinbeck's—perhaps even more so, since one can hardly find a modern work by or about O'Connor that does not, on its cover, depict her favorite fowl (figs. 12–13). Combining elements of her life on a farm, her religious themes, personal eccentricities, and outsider status, the peacock has proved the perfect icon for O'Connor's readers, critics, and biographers, a form of reputation-shorthand that has only grown more ubiquitous over time—a phenomenon the editors of *Esprit* could not have predicted but which they certainly helped accelerate.

Everything That Rises Must Converge

In April 1965, nine months after O'Connor's death, Robert Giroux published *Everything That Rises Must Converge*, O'Connor's second collection containing

ESPRIT

UNIVERSITY OF SCRANTON

Figure 11. Cover of *Esprit*, Winter 1964.

FLANNERY

A LIFE

of

FLANNERY O'CONNOR

BRAD GOOCH

Figure 12. Cover of Gooch biography, 2009.

THE
TERRIBLE
SPEED
OF
MERCY

A Spiritual Biography of
Flannery O'Connor

JONATHAN ROGERS

Figure 13. Cover of Rogers biography, 2012.

nine stories, all of which had been previously published individually except for
"Judgment Day," a reworking of her first story, "The Geranium." Many of the
original reviewers understandably wrote of O'Connor's recent death, making
their reviews sound like eulogies as much as critical assessments. In the *New
York Times*, for example, Charles Poore noted that O'Connor "died at the height
of her promise,"[43] while a reviewer for the *Cleveland Plain Dealer* lamented the
death of a writer "so young and with so much more to tell a world which
needed to hear it."[44] A writer for the *Arizona Republic* reasoned that "since most
of what she wrote was an improvement over what had gone before, there is no
knowing how far she might have progressed had she been allowed more than
39 years on this earth."[45] *Newsweek* described her death as "a measureless loss,"[46]
and, in what may be the most flattering (or hyperbolic) comparison thus far in
the story of O'Connor's reputation, the novelist and editor R. V. Cassill stated,
"Miss O'Connor did not die quite as young as Keats, but she will keep, in our
minds, a place reminiscent of his."[47] In the twelve years since the publication
of *Wise Blood*, reviewers felt comfortable in speaking of O'Connor's work as a
"permanent part of American literature"[48] or agreeing with Alan Pryce-Jones's
assessment—now found as a blurb on the back covers of paperback editions
of O'Connor's work—that "There is very little in contemporary fiction which
touches the level of Flannery O'Connor at her best."[49] Indeed, the assertion
that "Flannery O'Connor's is a voice that time will never still"[50] is representative of her postmortem reputation. Earlier in her career, O'Connor's reputation as a southern and, especially, a Catholic writer was gradually developed
to the point where these terms gained critical currency; now, after her death,
she was being eulogized as a southern and Catholic writer who escaped "either
catalogue through her own genius."[51] The old watchwords that had seemed so
perfect and so strong were beginning to show their seams.

However, there was not a seismic shift in the way O'Connor was perceived
by her critics: a number of issues found in the reviews of O'Connor's previous
works surfaced, even more strongly, in those of *Everything That Rises Must Converge*. The South as a setting for universal themes was again noted by many
reviewers: the *National Observer* stated that O'Connor's setting and characters
"take on the dimensions of every time, every place, and every man,"[52] while the
Wall Street Journal called O'Connor "truly a writer for all seasons and times."[53]
Even the *New Yorker*, which had panned *A Good Man Is Hard to Find* a decade
earlier, begrudged in a mixed review that "her province is Christendom rather
than the South."[54] Other reviewers argued much the same,[55] but, in a moment
that recalls the action of those writers for *Esprit* who began commenting on
O'Connor's reputation as much as her work, a reviewer for *Georgetowner* maga-

zine remarked, "It is unfortunate that Flannery O'Connor has been tagged as a Southern writer and/or a Catholic writer, for what she has to say has universal significance."[56] She was still routinely compared to Faulkner, Welty, and McCullers, but also now to Dante, whom one reviewer named as O'Connor's "classical mentor."[57] In *Jubilee*, fellow-Catholic and best-selling author Thomas Merton topped even this superlative when he compared her to Sophocles in a quotation that became the blurb featured on the book's dust jacket.[58] Her work was again recommended (as in *Booklist*) for "the discriminating reader,"[59] and her gender was still worthy of notice: "Though feminine in spirit," a reviewer in Atlanta remarked, "Miss O'Connor writes with a firm masculine hand. No story would identify her sex."[60] Finally, one can still find the theme of local-girl-makes-good: an article in the Milledgeville *Union-Recorder* spoke proudly of the fact that the collection was introduced by "Harvard professor"[61] Robert Fitzgerald and then offered readers a series of laudatory selections from major newspapers and magazines, sometimes (as in the case of *Time*) judiciously selecting only those sentences that would read as unmitigated accolades.

While praise for the new collection was strong and widespread, the reviews also contain a common complaint that could only be leveled against a writer with an already-established reputation and known body of work: specifically, the charge that O'Connor's talents were, however striking, essentially limited. Writing in *The Nation*, for example, Webster Schott stated, "Artistically her fiction is the most extraordinary thing to happen to the American short story since Ernest Hemingway," but he also called O'Connor "myopic in her vision."[62] Schott's assessment represents a judgment seen in this period that marked and sometimes marred O'Connor's reputation: what many reviewers gave with one hand—the praise of her artistic performance—they took away with the other by complaining of her "limited" subject matter. The assumption underlying many critical complaints was that strictly proscribed thematic concerns somehow devalued an author's career as a whole. However wrong such an assumption might be, it informed much critical discussion of *Everything That Rises Must Converge* and O'Connor's subsequent reputation. Walter Sullivan stated that O'Connor's "limitations were numerous and her range was narrow,"[63] assuming that one mark of literary success was the tackling of a number of different themes; writing in *Jubilee*, Paul Levine described O'Connor's achievement as "austerely limited."[64] Both of these reviewers, however, felt that what O'Connor did, she did very well, Sullivan acknowledging that "her ear for dialogue, her eye for human gestures were as good as anybody's"[65] and Levine similarly describing O'Connor's "vision" as "deep rather than wide."[66]

This simultaneous faulting of O'Connor's lack of breadth while praising her depth is found in many of the collection's original reviews. Writing in *Commentary*, Warren Coffey argued that O'Connor "would not go wider than her ground" but that "nobody could have gone deeper there."[67] Richard Poirier, in the *New York Times Book Review*, stated, "Miss O'Connor's major limitation is that the direction of her stories tends to be nearly always the same," yet lent his considerable support to O'Connor's art with the bold statement that "Revelation," the story which earned O'Connor the 1964 O. Henry Award, "belongs with the few masterpieces of the form in English."[68] This notion of O'Connor's limits—what amounts to a new aspect of her reputation at this time—was durable enough to survive an Atlantic crossing: a long but unsigned review in the *Times Literary Supplement* cautioned against "sentimental exaggeration" when judging O'Connor and described her as a "*provincial* writer in the truest sense"—and while her provincialism need not be regarded as a fault, the reviewer regarded it as a "major handicap," which "meant that she *knew* only half the world she lived in and wrote about."[69] Faulkner, this reviewer argued, possessed both the talent and thematic treasure to earn him the reputation he enjoyed: he "had a powerful enough imagination to supply a great deal of vicarious experience. Miss O'Connor, we must acknowledge, lacked this power: her imagination worked excellently within her experience but did not rise above its limitations."[70] A reviewer for the London *Observer* similarly stated that "within her limits, Miss O'Connor brings off some notable feats of impersonation."[71] Ironically, another author whose reputation was forever linked to the violence in one of his early works offered a complete counterstatement to this prevailing idea: writing in *The Listener*, the weekly publication of the BBC, Anthony Burgess noted of the stories, "The range is astonishing."[72]

Some reviewers found O'Connor limited in her thematic concerns; others found her wanting in her artistic performance. Irving Howe detected in O'Connor's work "a recurrent insincerity of tone" in the ways she portrayed characters that he assumed she despised, most notably Julian, the failed writer and smug intellectual in the collection's title story: "Miss O'Connor slips from the poise of irony to the smallness of sarcasm, thereby betraying an unresolved hostility to whatever it is she takes Julian to represent."[73] Similarly, in the *Southern Review*, Louis D. Rubin argued that "Miss O'Connor loads the dice" and "makes her sinners so wretchedly obnoxious one can't feel much compassion for their plight."[74] Such a complaint about O'Connor's limiting the three-dimensionality of her characters is one that would later appear elsewhere, most notably in Harold Bloom's introduction to his *Twentieth Century Views*, where he argues that O'Connor's detestation of Rayber, the smug and secular schoolteacher in *The Violent Bear It Away*, is so strong that she "cannot bother to make him even minimally persuasive."[75]

However, at the time of O'Connor's death, such reviews about the limitations of both her form and content were outnumbered by those proclaiming her to be "a remarkable artist"[76] and "one of the most gifted artists of our time."[77] But while O'Connor's admirers argued that the praise she earned was wholly justified, the undercurrent of critical thought regarding her limitations suggested that much of the praise needed to be qualified. Writing in *Ave Maria*, Thomas Hoobler noted that many reviewers were anxious to not speak ill of O'Connor because of the circumstance of her recent death:

> The reviewers thus far seem reluctant to take on the book as a work of art to be critically reviewed. Miss O'Connor's growing reputation . . . and possibly the fact of posthumous publication, has produced a kind of awe, even among normally skeptical reviewers. . . . Needless to say, this reviewing-by-assent is a high compliment to Miss O'Connor's gift, but hardly, I think, an appropriate comment on her work.[78]

Hoobler's words accurately capture the spirit of many of the reviewers of this period, who came to praise O'Connor as they buried her.

O'Connor's reputation had developed to the point where it was examined by critics alongside the work upon which that reputation was presumably based, as if the critics began gazing upon themselves. A single review can be examined as representative of this greater phenomenon. In one of the first reviews of *Everything That Rises Must Converge*, Stanley Edgar Hyman, whose words carried as much weight in the *New Leader* as Poirier's did in the *New York Times Book Review*, offered a long appreciation of O'Connor's career and death, "the cruelest loss to our literature since the death of Nathanael West."[79] After a mostly positive assessment of the collection, Hyman expanded the scope of his review by identifying what he regarded as O'Connor's chief themes, among them the presence of evil and the gulf between the human and divine. He also corrects what he viewed as the prevailing misconceptions about her work: "Few contemporary writers have been as much misunderstood, wrongly praised, and wrongly damned as Miss O'Connor."[80] Hyman argues that while readers spoke of her violence as excessive and that O'Connor "did come to rely on death too often to end her stories,"[81] her problem was a reliance on melodrama more than on the violence with which her work was associated. Hyman similarly discriminates between the ways in which O'Connor's work was labeled "grotesque" and what it actually was: "Grotesque her fiction is," Hyman states, "but it is never gratuitous . . . it is perfectly functional and necessary."[82] Hyman ends his review by introducing an idea about O'Connor that would take root and flourish as one of the most striking blooms of her current reputation:

> To judge Miss O'Connor by any criteria of realism in fiction, let alone natural-ism, is to misunderstand her. . . . The writer she most deeply resembles in vantage point is West. He saw deeply and prophetically because he was an outsider as a Jew, and doubly an outsider as a Jew alienated from other Jews; she had a com-plete multiple alienation from the dominant assumptions of our culture as a Ro-man Catholic Southern woman.[83]

This is not the first time in print that O'Connor and West were linked: re-viewers of *Wise Blood* saw stylistic affinities between these two writers' work.[84] Hyman was, however, the first to link O'Connor and West as outsiders, a part of O'Connor's reputation that endures. For example, a 1991 appreciation of *The Complete Stories* in the *Times Literary Supplement* begins with the often-told tale of how the five-year-old O'Connor trained a chicken to walk backward, a feat captured on film by Pathé News and regarded as representative of O'Connor's future focus on "freakish creatures" with "their sense of direction all askew."[85] In the opening pages of his biography, Brad Gooch employs this anecdote to suggest how it reflects ways in which O'Connor produced work "running counter to so much trendy literary culture."[86] Other biographers have employed the same anecdote for the same reason: in Paul Elie's 2003 joint biography of O'Connor, Thomas Merton, Dorothy Day, and Walker Percy, Elie describes the chicken as "a freak, a grotesque" that resembled O'Connor's characters and the author herself.[87] Unsurprisingly, O'Connor also described herself as "an ob-ject of considerable curiosity, being a writer about 'Southern degeneracy' and a Catholic at oncet [*sic*] and the same time."[88]

This notion that O'Connor's reputation deserved attention and, at times, needed correcting appears in other reviews besides Hyman's; the frequency with which this notion appears suggests a desire among many of O'Connor's readers to "fix" her reputation, in the sense of "repair" but also "make perma-nent." As we have seen in other chapters, sometimes a small, seemingly un-important notice in an easily overlooked source illuminates greater issues as effectively as the pronouncements of critics in major periodicals: in this case, an unsigned review in the *Emporia (Kans.) Gazette* states, "Already a Flannery O'Connor legend is taking shape."[89] This legend was one that many critics ad-dressed in their reactions to *Everything That Rises Must Converge*. Reviewers took O'Connor's talent as a given, calling her "one of the truly skilled, original, and polished talents of our time"[90] or claiming that the "superb craftsmanship" of her work is such that O'Connor "can match any American writer of the century."[91] A reviewer for the *Nashville Banner* stated, "Her reputation is one of the largest among Southern writers, and she is considered 'must' reading on many college campuses,"[92] but other reviewers argued that O'Connor's reputation needed clarification: writing in the *New York Times*, Charles Poore noted that O'Connor was "mindlessly categorized as a 'Southern writer,'"[93] just as an unsigned review in *Newsday* states, "A Southern writer, a Catholic writer, Miss O'Connor escapes either catalogue through her own genius."[94] Again, a reader sees how the watchwords "Southern" and "Catholic," once used as if they were the Rosetta stone to decoding the secret of O'Connor's strange art, were now, barely a decade later, proving inadequate to the task of accounting for the creation of characters such as Rufus Johnson. She was still predictably compared to Faulkner, but unpredictably not in terms of geography: "It was not too long ago that Flannery O'Connor's production was thought by some to be satisfactorily categorized by the flip label of 'Southern Gothic.'... Early criticism of another Southern writer, William Faulkner, was frequently as uncordial, but in the case of both, time showed them to be something other than practitioners of Gothic horrifics."[95] Lawrence H. Schwartz's 1988 *Creating Faulkner's Reputation: The Politics of Modern Literary Criticism* has proven Farnham correct: while the story of Faulkner's reputation contains more drama (such as the ways in which the publishing of popular fiction changed during the Second World War) and cultural reverberations (such as the ways in which an "elitist aesthetic" arose that demanded literature be "difficult"), Faulkner's reputation, like O'Connor's, first reinforced the notion that he was a writer with specific regional concerns and later fostered the sense that his art transcended time and space.

O'Connor had signed a contract for the collection with Robert Giroux in 1964, in between visits to the hospital. Realizing she was too ill to revise the stories, she decided that their previously published magazine and journal versions would have to suffice, although she did revise "Revelation" and "Parker's Back" while in Piedmont Hospital in Atlanta, initially hiding the manuscripts under her pillow for fear of being told that such activity was forbidden and then working on them for two hours a day in her room.[96] After she died, Giroux arranged for the quick publication of the collection, which featured Thomas Merton's previously quoted comparison to Sophocles on its dust jacket. He also solicited the assistance of Robert Fitzgerald, O'Connor's close friend, to introduce the collection; this introduction is a perfect example of an author attempting to shape the reputation of another.

O'Connor first met Fitzgerald and his wife, Sally, in 1949, when O'Connor was living in New York City and revising *Wise Blood*. Their friendship was immediate; that same year, O'Connor left New York to live at the Fitzgeralds' farm in Connecticut, where she paid sixty-five dollars a month for rent, lived in furnished rooms above the garage, worked on *Wise Blood* each morning, and babysat the Fitzgeralds' children each afternoon. Such an arrangement worked well for O'Connor, giving her a set time in which to write, but also forged a relationship that both the Fitzgeralds and O'Connor prized for the rest of their lives. In a 1954 letter to Sally, O'Connor informed her that she was dedicating *A Good Man Is Hard to Find* to her and Robert "because you all are my adopted kin and if I dedicated it to any of my blood kin they would think they had to go into hiding."[97] She and the Fitzgeralds, also Catholic, spent many nights discussing writers, their own families, and their works-in-progress. While her stay with them was short—within a year she had moved to Milledgeville because of her health—her relationship with them only grew stronger: she served as godmother (with Giroux as godfather) to their third child, met them in Italy during her trip to Lourdes, and named Robert as her literary executor.

Robert Fitzgerald was thus an O'Connor insider, and Giroux's choosing him to introduce the collection permitted a steering of the reader's understanding of O'Connor's character by an approved intimate. Fitzgerald's introduction is no blurb or general impression; it is, instead, a seventeen-page combination of biography, criticism, and reminiscence—the kind of introduction modern readers might expect but that, as Jean W. Cash notes, "gave readers the first significant biographical information about O'Connor."[98] The introduction sustained many aspects of O'Connor's reputation at that time and gave reviewers guidance on how best to assess the work of a writer so strange and seemingly at odds with many aspects of literary modernity. An analysis of Fitzgerald's activity here reveals an act of reputation-engineering motivated by insight, admiration, and friendship.

Fitzgerald establishes his *bona fides* early in his introduction by describing all the O'Connor-related places he has visited and the people with whom he has shared his memories of the writer. He had visited O'Connor's grave with her mother and spent afternoons at the Cline house (where O'Connor's mother, Regina, was raised) and Andalusia many times: he states, "I have been in the dining room looking at old photographs with Regina"[99] and "I have also been in the front room of the other side of the house, Flannery's bedroom, where she worked" (x). Such moments, combined with his description of how he and Sally first met O'Connor in 1949, are ones in which Fitzgerald downplays his own career as a professor of English at Princeton and Harvard and fosters the ethos of a friend more than a critic. However, his desire to instruct and, at times, redirect the course of O'Connor's reputation is evident from the number of assertions he makes about her art. He counters the complaint that O'Connor's work lacks "natural and human beauty" by asking the reader to consider how, in "A Good Man Is Hard to Find," Bailey's attempts to reassure his mother and his wife's volunteering to follow him into the woods are "beautiful actions ... though as brief as beautiful actions usually are" (xii). He also calls "The Life You Save May Be Your Own" a "triumph over Erskine Caldwell and a thing of great beauty" (xx), correcting any readers who may have still regarded O'Connor's setting as confined to Tobacco Road and alluding to Keats in emphasizing the "beauty" of O'Connor's work. The idea that O'Connor's work contained any "human beauty" was one that ran counter to earlier notions of her as a writer whose characters are (as an earlier reviewer described them) "devoid of honor, loyalty, and for the most part, decency"[100] or simply, as the chorus of reviewers often sang, "grotesque."

Unlike dozens of critics before him, Fitzgerald compares O'Connor not to the usual figures but instead to T. S. Eliot, the first time in print that such a comparison was made (but not the last). Fitzgerald argues that both Eliot and O'Connor raise "anagogical meaning over literal action" and even remarks that Eliot "may have felt this himself, for though he rarely read fiction I am told that a few years before he died he read her stories and exclaimed in admiration of them" (xxx). (Time has proven Fitzgerald's story correct: in 1979 Russell Kirk wrote of his recommending her work to Eliot, who read it and responded in a letter, "She has certainly an uncanny talent of a high order but my nerves are just not strong enough to take much of a disturbance."[101]) The number of readers who understood Eliot's work well enough to grasp Fitzgerald's notion of the poet's "analogical meaning" in relation to O'Connor's is impossible to determine; still, one senses Fitzgerald's desire to bolster O'Connor's reputation through such a comparison. More accessible to the general reader is Fitzgerald's argument about O'Connor's "limits"—a topic seized upon by many of the collection's reviewers that Fitzgerald may have anticipated by discussing it in his introduction. After pointing out the similarities between O'Connor's previous work and the stories in this collection, Fitzgerald admits that "the critic will note these recurrent types and situations," how "the setting remains the same" and how "large classes of contemporary experience ... are never touched at all" (xxxii). But he also warns that those who find this a weakness are themselves limited in their understanding of O'Connor's work:

In saying how the stories are limited and how they are not, the sensitive critic will have a care. For one thing, it is evident that the writer deliberately and indeed indifferently, almost defiantly, restricted her horizontal range; as pasture scene and a fortress of pine woods reappear like a signature in story after story. The same is true of her social range and range of idiom. But these restrictions, like the very humility of her style, are all deceptive. The true range of the stories is vertical and Dantesque in what is taken in, in scale of implication. (xxxii)

Many reviewers either ignored Fitzgerald's advice here or simply did not read it, complaining of O'Connor's repetitive plots, character types, and themes. Fitzgerald's assertion that the supposed limits were actually a deliberate restriction, the better to focus on a "scale of implication" akin to Dante, is his attempt to fix O'Connor's reputation in a manner that he, as her friend, fellow author, and admirer, could approve. His long-term success in this regard can be seen in *Understanding Flannery O'Connor*, a 1995 book that outlines O'Connor's work and concerns for general readers in which the author points out the similarities among O'Connor's stories but urges that "the significant focus" is "a vertical relationship, the individual with his or her Maker, rather than a horizontal involvement, individuals in community with each other."[102] Others may have faulted O'Connor for not creating more three-dimensional characters, but to Fitzgerald, this was not a deficiency.

Most of the original reviews of *Everything That Rises Must Converge* noted Fitzgerald's introduction but simply mentioned it as a feature of the text. Even those who lauded it as "wise and intelligent,"[103] "gentle and objective,"[104] or "valuable and perceptive"[105] did not say much else about it. A minority of critics mentioned the same elements of O'Connor's life and art as Fitzgerald did, making them star pupils in his imaginary classroom. A few reviews offered more specific praise and, more importantly, a measure of Fitzgerald's influence by echoing his themes and assertions. Writing in *Best Sellers*, John J. Quinn, the force behind the Winter 1964 issue of *Esprit*, stated that Fitzgerald's "penetrating introduction to the artist as a person and as an artist qualifies him as the expert curator of the O'Connor Gallery,"[106] while another noted Fitzgerald's "valuable" introduction, stating, "he gives a gratifyingly clear portrait, and it is apparent that he understands fully what she was about in her writing."[107] Only one of the original reviewers found fault with Fitzgerald, arguing that the strength of O'Connor's art was that while it was "Catholic, but not obtrusively or aggressively so," Fitzgerald's introduction was "obtrusively Catholic, unfortunate and misleading."[108] This assessment, however, was the exception to the general rule. The inclusion of an introduction, the choice of Robert Fitz-gerald to compose it, and the timing of such an essay all converged to steer O'Connor's reputation to an even more prominent place. In his biography, Paul Elie describes Fitzgerald's introduction as "mannered and overwrought" yet acknowledges that it "served many readers that year as the first portrait of the artist" and secured her reputation more firmly: "No longer would Flannery O'Connor be mistaken for a gentleman or a rural primitive. She was a woman, and a literary saint."[109]

Despite his friendship with O'Connor—or perhaps because of it—Fitz-gerald was not above engaging in some revisionist reputation history. When describing the publication of *Wise Blood*, Fitzgerald states, "The reviewers, by and large, didn't know what to make of it. I don't think anyone even spot-ted the bond with Nathanael West. Isaac Rosenfeld in *The New Republic* ob-jected that since the hero was plain crazy it was difficult to take his religious predicament seriously. But Rosenfeld and everyone else knew that a strong new writer was at large" (xviii). Indeed, not "everyone" knew that "a strong new writer was at large," not even Rosenfeld himself, who dismissed O'Connor's talents and complained that O'Connor's novel suffered from a lack of clar-ity, confused religious ideas, and a style that he found "inconsistent" with the idea that "there is no escaping Christ."[110] That none of this is mentioned by Fitzgerald is hardly shocking and perhaps understandable: Joyce Carol Oates noted in 1965 that O'Connor's early death had "perhaps obscured critical judg-ment."[111] Perhaps—but it is certain that O'Connor's death obscured, for some, the memory of how she was first received, as may be seen in a review appearing in *Newsweek:* "With her first novel, *Wise Blood*, it was clear that a major writer had arrived; and this conviction was confirmed by the first collection of stories, *A Good Man Is Hard to Find.* With her second novel, *The Violent Bear It Away*, nearly all doubters were converted to passionate belief."[112] The very phrasing of the *Newsweek* reviewer echoes Fitzgerald's style and content, as it does his tendency to speak in absolutes. O'Connor's status as a "major writer" may have been clear to the reviewer, but not to all who first encountered her work, such as Katherine Scott, O'Connor's first writing instructor at Georgia State Col-lege for Women, who reflected the sentiments of many original reviewers when she said of *Wise Blood*, "A character who dies in the last chapter could have done the world a great favor by dying in the first chapter instead."[113]

How the cause of her death—her eventual succumbing to the systemic lupus erythematosus with which she was diagnosed in 1951—added its own aura to "the O'Connor legend" claims legitimate attention. Had she died in an automobile accident, her death might still have affected her reputation; that she died because of a slowly working disease about which relatively little was known allowed critics to link her illness with her art in ways they found fascinating but that O'Connor found repulsive. Writing to Maryat Lee in 1960, O'Connor fumed, "I don't want further attention called to myself in this way. My lupus has no business in literary considerations."[114] The occasion was a review in *Time* of *A Good Man Is Hard to Find* that described her as a "bookish spinster" and one whose suffering could have seemed to prevent her from writing: "She suffers from lupus (a tubercular disease of the skin and mucous membranes) that forces her to spend part of her life on crutches. Despite such relative immobility, author O'Connor manages to visit remote and dreadful places of the human spirit."[115] The reviewer is incorrect in both his description of lupus and his assumption that O'Connor's medical condition was somehow responsible for her subject or thematic concerns. The "relative immobility" of which the reviewer speaks was never experienced by O'Connor at this time. She did need a cane and, eventually, two crutches to walk, but she was far from a bedridden victim: from 1955 (the year *A Good Man Is Hard to Find* was published) to 1963 (the year before her death), O'Connor flew to New York City to appear on television, toured Europe for seventeen days with her mother, gave dozens of talks at universities as far as Notre Dame and the University of Chicago, and visited a number of states as far from Georgia as Texas, Louisiana, and Minnesota. Granted, she did much of this traveling with the assistance of her crutches, and sometimes found it trying, but she was no Emily Dickinson shut off from the world or, as V. S. Pritchett inaccurately described her in the *New Statesman*, "an invalid most of her life."[116] Still, O'Connor's lupus and its imagined psychological effects became a large part of her reputation and proved irresistible to many reviewers seeking, once again, to explain away O'Connor and to account for the strangeness of her art. To many critics, her illness had become her muse, an explanation for her choice of themes and manner of exploring them. And despite the disdain that O'Connor would have shown for it, this part of her reputation still holds: in the mid-1990s, Chelsea House published a series of books for young readers, *Great Achievers: Lives of the Physically Challenged*. O'Connor had a volume devoted to her and joined the ranks of Louis Braille, Stephen Hawking, Itzhak Perlman, Roy Campanella, Julius Caesar, and Franklin D. Roosevelt, all subjects of other volumes.

One particularly mawkish reviewer of *Everything That Rises Must Converge* wrote that O'Connor's "personal awareness of death" was so strong that her readers could "sense the shock of identification that Flannery O'Connor must have felt when one of her characters succumbed to his grisly fate. It is as if the author is telling the same story over and over in the hope that it will go away."[117] As he complained of O'Connor's bitter portrayal of "weak humans," Louis D. Rubin ascribed what he viewed as O'Connor's artistic failings to her illness: "Any human being who had to endure what Flannery O'Connor did for the last years of her all-too-brief life . . . would certainly have tended to view the human condition with more than the customary amount of distrust."[118] A reviewer for the *British Association for American Studies Bulletin* attempted to account for the power of O'Connor's stories on medical and psychoanalytic rather than artistic grounds:

> It is a book conceived of by a dying woman who is not afraid of going to hell: she's been in it too long and has begun to find it cozy and dull. Flannery O'Connor was imprisoned in a wracked body for most of her creative life. Hopelessly sick, bald, and deformed, she writes with a vengeance. . . . Her books are impartial, un-sparing, and hilariously beyond despair. She is the only true ghost writer. Having lost all, she invited you to join her in the realm of the hopeless.[119]

Anyone who reads O'Connor with even a modicum of charity will recognize the falseness of these claims, for her fiction as a whole dramatizes the folly of what she viewed as a trendy, modern nihilism: consider Hulga in "Good Country People" as one of many examples of O'Connor's attack on what she viewed as a hollow hopelessness. Without the hope of a place where he "counts," Bevel (in "The River") is simply a drowned boy; without the hope of Heaven, men turn into Misfits. The reviewer for the *Times Literary Supplement* also engaged in perpetuating the idea of lupus-as-muse, noting, "She is writing of death, of its meaning to life, from the depths of her experience of gradually dying."[120] This idea that O'Connor was motivated by her "experience of gradually dying" is one that O'Connor would have mocked, perhaps arguing that she had been engaged in this "experience," like everyone else, since birth: as Old Mason Tarwater says to his great-nephew, "The world is made for the dead. Think of all the dead there are. . . . There's a million times more dead than living and the dead are dead a million times longer than the living are alive."[121] Few American writers were as aware of our "gradually dying" than the creator of the Misfit; to suggest that O'Connor's lupus, more than her imagination, was responsible for her fiction is another example of the continual desire to account for the sources of O'Connor's uncanny art, a desire that affected her reputation with the publication of each new book.

Mystery and Manners

If the testimonials collected in *Esprit* illuminate a general critical and national belief in the importance of O'Connor's fiction and in her admirable character, the publication of *Mystery and Manners* in 1969 marked an even greater jump in O'Connor's critical stock. This volume of occasional prose was assembled by Robert and Sally Fitzgerald, who collected and reshaped a number of O'Connor's talks and lectures on the nature and practice of writing fiction; the collection also includes an essay that had originally appeared in *Holiday* magazine on raising peacocks as well as the previously mentioned introduction to *A Memoir of Mary Ann*. Published by Robert Giroux four years after *Everything That Rises Must Converge* and five years after O'Connor's death, *Mystery and Manners* marked a continuation of the course O'Connor's reputation was taking from local oddball to respectable literary oracle. The specialist in regional grotesques had become a critic to be discussed in the same hushed tones used when discussing Keats, Eliot, Sidney, Wordsworth, Coleridge, Pope, and Aristotle—all of whom reviewers used as comparatives when describing O'Connor's insights into literature.[122]

However, at this point, the author to whom reviewers most frequently compared her was Henry James, whom O'Connor herself referenced throughout her speeches and letters. An unsigned review in the *New Yorker* complained of the essays' repetitiousness yet ended by describing the book as "truer and sounder and wiser about the nature of fiction and the responsibilities of reader and writer than anything published since James's *The Art of the Novel*."[123] Clearly, this was high praise. As James's readers did when they read the Master's collected prefaces, many of O'Connor's readers viewed her pieces here as guides to her overall approach. Like James, O'Connor understood literature as a faithful record of life—"faithful" suggesting both O'Connor's desire to re-create the physical world of the senses and a world that gave form to her own Catholic values and assumptions. And just as James's prefaces illuminate more than the specific novels they precede, many reviewers found the pieces in *Mystery and Manners* to likewise illuminate more than their author's own work: in the words of John J. Quinn, the collection should "rank with the precious few classical studies on the art of fiction ever to be published."[124] A critic for *Publishers Weekly* described *Mystery and Manners* as "practically a handbook" on the art of writing fiction,[125] and other reviewers exhorted "anyone interested in the craft of writing"[126] to read this "lucid and satisfying comment on the art of the short story and the nature of the storyteller's gift."[127] Writing in the *New York Times*, D. Keith Mayo described his immediate reaction to the collection as one of "gratitude": "It seemed to me, it still seems, that I had never read more sensible and significant reflections on the art of writing."[128] A writer for *Kirkus Reviews* described the book as "obligatory in understanding the quintessential aspects of the short story."[129] Many other reviewers echoed these sentiments. O'Connor's opinions on art, like her themes, were now seen as transcendent, an aspect of her reputation that remains today.

But there was more to the reaction to *Mystery and Manners* than praise for O'Connor's Jamesian insights into the art of fiction. Critics viewed the collection as a means to understanding what they still regarded as her strange and challenging fiction, a figure in the carpet that would make the freaks less freakish. As with *Wise Blood*, reviewers searched for a way to bring O'Connor's strangeness to heel; unlike the case of O'Connor's first work, they now had what they saw as a figurative key to O'Connor's kingdom, an assumption reflected in the very language they used to praise it. For example, writing in the *Charleston (W.V.) Gazette*, W. M. Kirkland urged the collection on those who had been baffled by the likes of Hazel Motes or Mason Tarwater: "Readers who tried unsuccessfully to 'get anything out of' her novels and short stories, but who sensed that she was up to something, might well read these critical essays to see what Flannery O'Connor was really up to. She did, indeed, know what she was doing."[130] The assumption here, that authors have secrets or, in the words of another reviewer, "something like a system"[131]—and that *Mystery and Manners* could be used as a kind of literary enigma machine—appears in many of the book's original reviews. The historian of popular culture M. Thomas Inge praised the collection for reasons identical to Kirkland's: "Anyone who wishes to get at the heart of Miss O'Connor's impressive achievements as a fiction writer can do no better than to read these pieces. With remarkable clarity, they define her stance and explicate her intent in a way that second-hand criticism cannot match."[132] Inge later speaks of the book's "utilitarian value," again emphasizing the view of *Mystery and Manners* as a means to clarify the mysteries mentioned in its title. Other reviewers offered the same notion: a writer for the *Southern Review* called the essays "invaluable in providing abstract formulations of attitudes and values that are dramatized in the fiction."[133] In 1931 Leon Edel argued that James's prefaces were the equivalent of his "placing in the hands of the readers and critics the key to his work," although "very few have ventured to place the key in the lock and open the door."[134] *Mystery and Manners* was similarly seen as an explication of O'Connor's oeuvre or, as one reviewer described it, "a welcome gift, a tiny key to a door or two in a Southern mansion of wondrous beauty."[135]

In her review of *Mystery and Manners* for the *Village Voice*, Jane Mushabac observed, "It is difficult to imagine now, when we have become such gluttons for horror in our fiction, that critics and the public were once irked by all the poverty and violence in Flannery O'Connor's fiction."[136] The critical community's understanding of O'Connor had been accelerated by her early death, her critical stock had risen, and her identity as a Catholic author was established. The response to *Mystery and Manners* also strengthened the connection between O'Connor and her favorite fowl, a connection also fostered by the collection's cover design, which featured, of course, a peacock. In the *Chicago Tribune*, Charles Thomas Samuels drew the comparison: like the peacock, he argued, O'Connor was "partly deformed and partly splendid, symbol of the creator's mingled ludicrousness and glitter."[137] Presumably because of its strangeness, the peacock was described by other reviewers as a "hellish and heavenly"[138] creature and "a bird possibly only Flannery O'Connor could love."[139] A writer for the *Times Literary Supplement* stated that the peacock now seemed "a living allegory of her fiction,"[140] while a critic for *Catholic World* went as far as one could presumably go in making a comparison: "As the peacock stands on a busy road and spreads his tail in disdain of an oncoming truck, so Miss O'Connor scoffs at contemporary philosophies of amorality, anti-mystical approaches to reality, or disbelief in the Devil's existence."[141] The peacock had become a symbol of the author, an outward and visible sign of an inward and invisible talent, a talent that critics and reviewers now almost universally viewed as being present since 1952 and that even death could not stop from growing exponentially.

Chapter 4

Robert Giroux, Sally Fitzgerald, and *The Habit of Being*

A Good Man Found: Robert Giroux and *The Complete Stories*

In the Winter 1970 issue of *Studies in Short Fiction*, Landon C. Burns, a professor of English at Pennsylvania State University, published "A Cross-Referenced Index of Short Fiction and Author-Title Listing," an exhaustive index of over two hundred different short-story anthologies in print at the time. While some of the anthologies were for specialized markets (such as Hill and Wang's *American Negro Short Stories*) and the oldest of them was first published in 1933, almost all the other anthologies were published in the 1950s and 1960s and bore generic names such as Harper & Row's *The World of Short Fiction* or Bantam's *Fifty Great Short Stories*. The index became something of an English professor's industry standard: Burns offered numerous supplements, from the second in 1976 to the twentieth in 1993. His work is useful in generally gauging short-story writers' penetration of the midcentury anthology market and, more specifically, how often O'Connor's work was being assigned to undergraduates in the decade after her death. While readers today might agree with R. Neil Scott of the Georgia College Library that O'Connor's stories are "represented in virtually every introductory literature anthology used in American universities,"[1] such was not always the case, and Burns's index allows us to see O'Connor's literary star rising.

A statistical analysis of Burns's index reveals that European short-story writers (and one Russian) dominated the anthology market and best appealed to what editors and professors understood to be the needs of students in literature courses. O'Connor was represented in 29 percent of the anthologies, just behind Poe (31 percent) and—perhaps surprisingly—ahead of Hawthorne (24 percent).[2] Her most widely anthologized story was "A Good Man Is Hard to Find," appearing in five times as many anthologies as "The Displaced Person," which reviewers had hailed in 1952 as O'Connor's masterpiece.[3] Anthologists apparently found the story of the Misfit to be most representative of O'Connor's art. However, while O'Connor had joined the ranks of the widely anthologized, readers in 1970 still had no complete edition of her short stories, from her earliest works completed for her MFA at the University of Iowa to those she had hidden in her hospital bed.[4] O'Connor had needed an editorial champion and found, to the lasting benefit of her art and reputation, Robert Giroux. From his first editorial encounter with her in 1954 and throughout her career—indeed for many years long after her death—Giroux helped transform her literary identity throughout the English-speaking world from that of "interesting regional writer" to a major figure in American literature.

In his 2008 *New York Times* obituary of Giroux, Christopher Lehman-Haupt described the editor as a behind-the-scenes advocate of literary excellence whose work complemented that of his senior partner: "If the flamboyant Roger Straus presented the public face of Farrar, Straus & Giroux, presiding over the business end, Mr. Giroux made his mark on the inside, as editor-in-chief, shaping the house's book list and establishing himself as the gold standard of literary taste."[5] Speaking in 1981, Bernard Malamud expressed a similar idea: "If Robert Giroux represents good taste, Roger Straus knows what to do with it."[6] Two accomplishments that Giroux took pride in were having brought O'Connor (and *Wise Blood*) to Harcourt, Brace when he worked there as an editor and eventually bringing her full catalog to the firm that included his name. An author's editor, Giroux guided to publication all of O'Connor's work from 1960 onward and capped his efforts with the 1971 publication of O'Connor's *The Complete Stories*, a critical and financial success that confirmed O'Connor as a writer with regional settings but universal themes. In his history of the modern American literary marketplace, James L. W. West III warns, "It is tempting to idealize and even romanticize the relationships between authors and editors,"[7] but Giroux and O'Connor seem to have reached an ideal to which any author and editor might aspire.

Giroux was highly respected by his colleagues and the authors with whom he worked, and a brief look at his editorial style and assumptions exemplifies how and why he became O'Connor's publisher and advocate. He was renowned for his devotion to literature, a devotion sparked in the classroom of Mark Van Doren and in the pages of the *Columbia Review*, where he and the poet John Berryman published the first work of Thomas Merton.[8] According to Isaac Bashevis Singer, Giroux was a man "never misled by politics, by the list of cheap bestsellers, or by the futile machinations of the word-jugglers."[9] His prizing art over commerce was noted by Caroline Gordon, who, upon the publication of *Everything That Rises Must Converge*, wrote to Giroux:

It must be a satisfaction to be able to serve the cause of good letters and, at the same time, promote a kind of theological understanding which has been woefully absent from contemporary literature—until recently. I am astonished when I have time to pause and reflect on some of the changes that have come about since I began writing professionally. You have certainly had your share in bringing them about. Publishing Flannery's stories must have been a real joy.[10]

Long before the 1971 publication of *The Complete Stories* and the introduction he composed for the volume, Giroux was building O'Connor's reputation and affecting the larger literary scene. Giroux felt an almost vocational sense of duty toward the cause of promoting literature: as he stated in 1972, the publisher had to promote sales but also had "another obligation, and that is to keep the middling book in print, or bring new ones out. Because if he doesn't the source of writing and of literature is going to dry up."[11] That a publisher with such an attitude found an author with no pretensions to market dominance or her books rivaling the sales of *Love Story* or *The Godfather* is one of the happiest events in the story of O'Connor's reputation.

In what may be the highest praise that can be lavished on an editor, Giroux was viewed by more than one author as "the professional heir to Maxwell Perkins."[12] Giroux's standard procedure when dealing with writers was to get out of their way—a simple-sounding and Perkinsesque practice that other editors sometimes found difficult. Susan Sontag noted that Giroux and his house perfected "the civilized art of non-interference."[13] Like Perkins, Giroux knew his writers' habits and personalities well enough to know who needed prodding and who needed to be left undisturbed. Perkins's advice to F. Scott Fitzgerald is an apt analogy to Giroux's approach to his authors: "Don't ever defer to my judgment. You won't on any vital point, I know, and I should be ashamed if it were possible to have made you, for a writer of any account must speak solely for himself. I should hate to play . . . the W. D. Howells to your Mark Twain."[14] Giroux was not an editor who advised O'Connor on how best to grapple with her thematic concerns or artistic performance; O'Connor shared ideas about her work with Caroline Gordon much more than she did with Giroux. Rather, Giroux, like Perkins, worked tirelessly to support his authors emotionally and get their works into readers' hands. As a result, and again reminiscent of Perkins, he felt as loyal to his authors as they did to him. Roger Straus noted, "Bob Giroux did not once suggest that authors follow him, but I remember counting that, over the first few years, seventeen authors made their way in our direction. . . . This is a triumphant following that few editors have ever achieved or could achieve again."[15]

Giroux's correspondence proves how seriously he took the responsibility of maintaining O'Connor's reputation and keeping her in the public eye. In 1973, for example, a creator and distributor of educational materials contacted Giroux, asking permission to quote O'Connor in a filmstrip. Giroux wrote to O'Connor's agent, Elizabeth McKee, "Although I dislike the whole approach, I have to admit that it might result in young people becoming interested in Flannery's work who would otherwise never hear of it."[16] This is just one example of dozens of requests that Giroux could have easily denied but over which he paused to consider how they might affect the long-term growth of O'Connor's reputation. (He did grant permission in this instance.) Giroux responded to requests from high school and college students seeking information on O'Connor for their term papers, casual readers who wanted information on O'Connor for their local literary societies, book collectors who sought information about first editions, ordinary readers who spotted typographical errors, and even an Argentine graduate student who asked if she could visit him when she came to New York to get a better sense of O'Connor's work.[17] He also proved instrumental to David Farmer, whose *Flannery O'Connor: A Descriptive Bibliography* (1981) relied on detailed information that Giroux provided concerning when many of O'Connor's stories were first published, and in what order. In one of the more humorous letters Giroux received, a casual reader complained that the hardcover copies of *Wise Blood*, *The Violent Bear It Away*, and *Mystery and Manners* were out of print and had been "bought up by people who (understandably) will not yield up their copies for love or money"; the writer informed Giroux, "If you are not going to publish them again, we will each have to find an owner of an O'Connor book, get in his will, and wait for him to die."[18] Giroux apologized for the books being out of print in hardcover and added, "I'm not surprised to learn that they are rarities in the used-copy market; she's the kind of writer readers don't give up on."[19] Neither did Giroux, as is demonstrated by his efforts in making *The Complete Stories* a reality and increasing O'Connor's readership.

On August 3, 1964, O'Connor's mother telegraphed the news of Flannery's death to Giroux, who wrote to her four days later offering his condolences and suggesting that FS&G's moving forward with plans to publish *Everything That Rises Must Converge* would testify to her daughter's life and work: "Perhaps the greatest memorial we, as publishers, can pay her memory is the publication of her stories which as you know has been in progress since the spring. We would like to go ahead with this."[20] Giroux added that the collection would feature "perhaps a special preface by Robert Fitzgerald if he would be willing to do it" and closed with, "It is an honor to be her publisher, but I also considered myself her friend and yours." Regina's blessing in all matters of her daughter's publication was a requirement, one that would become even more important in the late 1970s as Giroux and Sally Fitzgerald worked to secure copies of O'Connor's letters for *The Habit of Being*. Robert Fitzgerald may have been the literary executor of O'Connor's unpublished work, but Regina's position as executor of the estate and mother of the artist had to be recognized. Giroux first wrote officially to propose *The Complete Stories* to Robert Fitzgerald in 1966, a year after the publication of *Everything That Rises Must Converge*, arguing "there are many good reasons for doing this book" and noting how its publication would further O'Connor's reputation: "Though some of the stories are not at her top level, they are still good and should be available as part of her total body of work.... One of my lesser reasons for advocating the project is to give Flannery another chance at the National Book Award.... Chiefly I think of the book as a document and as a tribute to Flannery's singular contribution to the art of the short story."[21] Giroux thus imagined *The Complete Stories* as a statement or artifact testifying to O'Connor's talent as much as a book to be read and enjoyed. The very existence of the collection would, Giroux hoped, be another leap forward for O'Connor's reputation.

The Complete Stories, however, would not be published until 1971, seven years after her death, partly because of wrangling over reprint permissions for the stories that O'Connor wrote for her MFA at the University of Iowa. There was interest among rival publishers in the years following O'Connor's death to publish selections from O'Connor's thesis, *The Geranium*; Giroux wrote to Regina to express his disapproval of any such publications because he felt they would detract from the impact of *The Complete Stories*.[22] In 1970 the Windhover Press, a publisher of very limited editions of fine books and previously unpublished works by recognized authors based at the University of Iowa, sought permission to publish *The Geranium* on the grounds that O'Connor had developed her style while at the Iowa Writers' Workshop.[23] Giroux again wrote to Regina expressing his disapproval of a rival edition; he also wrote to Robert Fitzgerald, asking him to deny Windhover's request (which Fitzgerald did) and to grant his permission to publish the contents of *The Geranium* as part of *The Complete Stories*. Giroux also worked with Elizabeth McKee, O'Connor's agent and representative of the literary estate, to secure the rights from Harcourt, Brace for the stories originally collected in *A Good Man Is Hard to Find*. He feared that Harcourt, Brace would not "give in easily"[24] and had similar fears regarding Robert Fitzgerald, who was concerned about publishing the stories from *The*

Geranium, since they seemed less than O'Connor's best.[25] Both of these fears, however, proved premature: Harcourt, Brace gave its permission and Fitzgerald gave his, allowing Giroux to move ahead with his project and write to Elizabeth McKee, "I believe I've finally got Robert Fitzgerald housebroken as far as copyright goes."[26]

One request that Fitzgerald denied, however, was to compose an introduction to the proposed volume. In a letter to Giroux, he explained that he had said all he had to say about O'Connor in his introduction to *Everything That Rises Must Converge*: "I couldn't add anything substantial to what I wrote for *Everything*," he stated, "or write anything better."[27] Rather than turn to another of O'Connor's friends or fellow authors, Giroux decided to write the introduction himself. That he sent drafts of it to Regina, Elizabeth McKee, and the Fitzgeralds reflects his determination to portray O'Connor in a way true to her character and in a way that would enhance her status among readers, both those coming to her work for the first time and those revisiting the roads traveled by the Misfit and Manley Pointer. It also reveals his shrewd diplomacy. Like Robert Fitzgerald in his introduction to *Everything That Rises Must Converge*, Giroux presented himself as an insider whose opinions on O'Connor's art and character deserved notice. Also like Fitzgerald's, Giroux's introduction instructed critics how they should respond to the volume.

If the story of the backward-walking chicken is the most often-told biographical anecdote concerning O'Connor, the story of her first meeting with Paul Engle at the Iowa Writers' Workshop runs a close second. The anecdote, which first appeared in Giroux's introduction to *The Complete Stories*, is a test case of how a single incident can be retold and reshaped to suit the teller's aims in the short term and affect the subject's reputation in the long one. In July 1971, the year of *The Complete Stories'* publication, Paul Engle wrote to Robert Giroux in response to Giroux's questions about Engle's first meeting with O'Connor when he was director of the Iowa Writers' Workshop. Noting the difficulty of describing O'Connor "in any way worthy of her,"[28] Engle told of their first meeting, when she entered his office and spoke in a Georgia accent so thick that it sounded like "a secret language" to which Engle was unable to respond: "I asked her to repeat. No comprehension again. A third time. No communication. Embarrassed, suspicious, I asked her to write down what she had just said on a pad. She wrote, 'My name is Flannery O'Connor. I am not a journalist. Can I come to the Writers' Workshop?'" Engle then explained how he and O'Connor came to enjoy a "strange and yet trusting relationship" and how she impressed him with both her stories and work ethic. His letter fosters the image of O'Connor as (in his words) "imaginative, tough, alive" but also, as he describes her stories, "quietly filled with insight." Engle mentioned that O'Connor preferred to have him preserve her anonymity when reading her work aloud during workshops; he also told of a time when he realized that her scene of a young man and woman about to make love rang false because O'Connor was "improvising from innocence." Although O'Connor was uncomfortable with asking Engle's advice on how to make the scene more believable—and did so in the privacy of Engle's car "with the windows rolled up"—she withstood any social unease for the sake of her art: "She was uncomfortable, but the wish to have it right dominated." Distinguishing her from "the exuberant talkers who serenade every writing class with their loudness," Engle portrayed her as a meditative, awkward young woman whose work was unlike anything he had yet encountered at Iowa.

Giroux begins his introduction with the story of this meeting, a story that he knew from Engle's letter and that he quotes extensively. After retelling the scene of O'Connor writing her request on a pad, Giroux quotes Engle's initial assessment:

> At their first meeting in his office in 1946, Mr. Engle recalls, he was unable to understand a word of Flannery's native Georgian tongue ... "I told her to bring examples of her writing and we would consider her, late as it was. Like Keats, who spoke Cockney but wrote the purest sounds in English, Flannery spoke a dialect beyond instant comprehension but on the page her prose was imaginative, tough, alive: just like Flannery herself. The will to be a writer was adamant; nothing could resist it, not even her own sensibility about her own work."[29]

This is not, however, how the seventy-five-year-old Engle retold the story in 1983 to a *Washington Post* reporter, who wrote a long profile of Engle's time at the Iowa Writers' Workshop. In this version, O'Connor's southern roots are heightened (some might say caricatured), and Engle presents a decidedly less polished figure:

> She came out of the red dirt country of Georgia. She walked into my office one day and spoke to me. I understood nothing, not one syllable. As far as I knew, she was saying, "Aaaaraaaraaarah." My God, I thought to myself, this is a retarded young girl. Then I looked at her eyes. They were crossed! Finally, I said, excuse me, my name is Paul Engle. I gave her a pad—believe me, this is true—and said would you please write down what you're telling me. And she wrote, "My name is Flannery O'Connor. I'm from Milledgeville, Georgia. I'm a writer." She didn't

say, "I want to be a writer." She said, "I am a writer." I said do you have any writing
with you. She had one of the most beat-up handbags I'd ever seen. It must have
been put in an old-fashioned water-powered washing machine and churned for
a day. She handed me this paper. I read four lines. You don't need to eat all of an
egg to know if it's good or bad. I looked at her and said to myself, "Christ, this is
it. This is pure talent. What can I do? I can't teach her anything!" I taught her a
little. She had a few problems—with her society, her illness.[30]

Here, the addition of "I am a writer" makes O'Connor seem even more force-
ful and confident, despite her not having yet produced any substantial work;
whether or not anyone's talent can be appraised, even by one as sharp as Engle,
after only "four lines" is debatable. More interesting is that Giroux used the
anecdote as a true account of O'Connor without, perhaps, fully believing it, or
at least not finding that it reflected his experience with her. In a 2007 interview,
he stated that O'Connor's accent "seemed to bother people in New York, but
I never had any trouble understanding her. Never like Paul Engle. And you
know, you'd think she spoke a foreign language or something. I thought she
was very clear. I had no trouble with her."[31] That Giroux did not express any of
these sentiments in his introduction suggests that he, like many reviewers of
The Complete Stories, found the anecdote too perfect a hook on which to hang
his portrait of the artist as an outsider, waiting to be literally and figuratively
understood. As the newspaper editor in John Ford's *The Man Who Shot Liberty
Valance* remarks, "When the legend becomes fact, print the legend."

Reviewers of *The Complete Stories* and later biographers have found in this
anecdotal legend a representative moment for their collective creation of O'Connor's reputation. Soon, O'Connor would be, as she later remarked, shouting
(in her Georgia accent) to the hard of hearing. Paul Elie notes that Giroux's
portrayal of O'Connor as "plainspoken, charming, shy and yet sure of herself,
and with good reason"[32] was one that resonated with many readers of *The Complete Stories*, as it seemed to suit the strange young woman whose fiction would
explore spiritual themes without any ambiguity or hesitation. In his biography,
Brad Gooch refashions the scene to enhance *his* overall portrayal of O'Connor
as socially awkward (and perhaps to soften some of Engle's rough edges as
seen in his 1983 retelling, which Gooch used as a source). In Gooch's version,
O'Connor enters Engle's office after a "gentle knock" on his door, what Engle
in his letter to Giroux called a "shy knock":

After he shouted an invitation to enter, a shy young woman appeared and walked
over to his desk without, at first, saying a word. He could not even tell, as she

stood before him, whether she was looking in his direction, or out the window at the curling Iowa River below. A hulking six foot four inch poet, in his thirties, with wavy dark hair, alert blue eyes, and expressive eyebrows, Engle quickly took the lead. He introduced himself and offered her a seat, as she tightly held onto what he later described as "one of the most beat-up handbags I've ever seen."[33]

Gooch emphasizes Engle's "hulking" physical features as a means of characterizing O'Connor as unafraid and determined to follow her vocation; he changes Engle's original description of O'Connor as "cross-eyed" to her gazing in one of two possible directions. If the scene as Engle, Giroux, or Gooch presents it is not wholly accurate, it is in the spirit of the reputation that Giroux works to fashion in his introduction: that of O'Connor almost as a visitor from that strange country "where silence is never broken except to shout the truth."[34] As with the backward-walking chicken and the iconic peacock, the temptation to not use this anecdote as somehow ultimately reflective of O'Connor's character and art proved too strong for later critics and readers to resist.

At the time of *The Complete Stories*, there were no biographies of O'Connor, but only appreciations such as those collected in *Esprit*. Giroux's introduction, like Robert Fitzgerald's, characterized O'Connor as undeterred by those who could not figuratively understand her. Giroux states that when he first met O'Connor, he "sensed a tremendous strength" and recognized her as "the rarest kind of young writer, one who was prepared to work her utmost and knew exactly what she must do with her talent" (viii). He then proves his own assertions with evidence from O'Connor's correspondence with John Selby, her first editor at Rinehart, who disapproved of the shape that *Wise Blood* was taking. Giroux next quotes O'Connor's then-unpublished letter to her agent, Elizabeth McKee, in which she complains that Selby feared leaving the novel to her "fiendish care" and that he spoke to her in a tone appropriate to "a slightly dimwitted Campfire Girl" (x). Giroux depicts Selby as a self-satisfied *littérateur* who could not recognize the obvious excellence of *Wise Blood*; Paul Elie has it exactly right when he speaks of Giroux "casually assuming her greatness"[35] as he writes of O'Connor's feud with Selby. Readers are invited to see, with the benefit of hindsight, O'Connor as Giroux states he did at their first meeting and to congratulate themselves for doing so.

Like Fitzgerald, Giroux uses the initial reception of *Wise Blood* to suggest O'Connor's literary peculiarity and her initial friction with the critical community. Stating that "I was disappointed with the reviews more than she was; they all recognized her power but missed her point" (xii), Giroux recalls Fitzgerald's assertion in his introduction to *Everything That Rises Must Converge:* "The reviewers, by and large, didn't know what to make of it" (xviii). But Giroux again invites readers to congratulate themselves for *not* "missing her point," noting, "We reissued *Wise Blood* in 1962, on the tenth anniversary of the original publication, and it lives on in both cloth and paperback editions. Didn't some wise man define a classic as a book that does not stay out of print?" (xiii). The fact that readers were holding *The Complete Stories* was proof of their sophistication. Such an assumption would have been unimaginable with a copy of *Wise Blood* nineteen years earlier.

The "wise man" mentioned by Giroux was Mark Van Doren,[36] but the wise man on whom the remainder of Giroux's introduction relies for making its argument about O'Connor's greatness is Thomas Merton. Giroux describes O'Connor's and Merton's mutual admiration: Merton gave Giroux a copy of *A Meditation* to give to O'Connor, and she was very interested in the Abbey of Gesthsemani in Kentucky where Merton then lived. Giroux compares O'Connor to Merton in several important ways: both died (in the by-now familiar phrase of appreciation for O'Connor) "at the height of their powers," both Catholics possessed "deep faith," and both were "as American as one can be" (xiii). Few moments in the story of O'Connor's reputation are as clearly marked as this: all the previous critical commentary about her region seemingly worked toward this moment, where Flannery O'Connor became a fully American—rather than only southern—author. Not once does Giroux mention Caldwell, McCullers, or Faulkner: O'Connor had achieved escape velocity from the South that once seemed to contain and, in some readers' opinions, restrict her art. Giroux argued that O'Connor's work could "only be understood in an American setting" (xiv), an important distinction and one that shows the increasingly widening lens through which O'Connor's fiction was being viewed. Such a lens demanded a comprehensive and definitive version of her stories, which Giroux argues were best arranged (unlike her two previous collections) in chronological order. This desire to publish and preserve a definitive edition of O'Connor's work—from the stories that comprised her master's thesis to "Judgment Day," a reworking of her very first story—was one that Giroux felt himself able to fulfill and for which the critical community and general readers were grateful.

Critics responded to *The Complete Stories* with all the enthusiasm that Giroux, as both friend of the author and partner in the firm publishing her works, could desire. The response to his "fascinating-to-all-O'Connor-fans"[37] introduction reveals his words were seen as a benediction and guide to readers

when approaching O'Connor's fiction. While some critics vaguely compli-
mented Giroux by calling his introduction simply "charming,"[38] "discreet,"[39]
or "useful,"[40] others praised it as "illuminating,"[41] particularly, in the words of
Robert Drake in *Modern Age*, as "perceptive and sympathetic" because Giroux
offered a glimpse of O'Connor's "fortitude and integrity" and "does not do
Miss O'Connor the disservice of indiscriminately praising all the stories."[42]
Such a disservice was seen in other reviews, most notably Martha Duffy's in
Time, in which she seemed eager to atone for her magazine's past dismissals of
O'Connor's art: "This collection brings together for the first time in one book
all of Miss O'Connor's stories. Every one is good enough so that if it were the
only example of her work to survive, it would be evident that the writer possessed high talent and a remarkably unclouded, un-abstract, demanding intelligence."[43] To Drake and like-minded reviewers, that Giroux did not offer this
kind of "indiscriminate praise" of O'Connor made his portrait of her all the
more truthful.

Other reviewers praised Giroux's chronological assemblage of the stories
while also noting the peculiar effects of such an arrangement. Writing in the
Southern Literary Journal, Melvin J. Friedman imagined that "rearranging the
stories might be likened by some critics to the heresy of reordering Joyce's *Dubliners* or Sherwood Anderson's *Winesburg, Ohio*" but also acknowledged that
a chronological arrangement "lets us in on the subtle and gradual maturing
of a remarkable talent."[44] In the *Southern Review*, Frederick P. W. McDowell
noted that Giroux's arrangement "allows us to see her cumulative development
as an artist" and "trace the deepening and maturity of her creativity."[45] Paul
Elie, however, argues that Giroux's ordering "undid the careful selection and
discrimination that O'Connor had brought to her short fiction," since it suggested that her master's thesis and early versions of chapters of her novels were
equally as important as her masterpieces: "'A Good Man Is Hard to Find' was
sandwiched between 'Enoch and the Gorilla' and 'A Late Encounter with the
Enemy,' between an excerpt and a trifle."[46] But Elie's sensible objection is the
exception to the general rule of critics' appreciating Giroux's instinct as an
editor and insight as a reader. Just as Joyce arranged the stories in *Dubliners* to
better convey the theme of paralysis, Giroux arranged those in *The Complete
Stories* to better convey *his* chosen theme: the growth of O'Connor's talent over
time. Whether or not "Greenleaf" and "A View from the Woods" are better
than "The River" or "A Circle in the Fire" can be debated, but this was Giroux's
contention, and he wanted to argue it in the table of contents.

As mentioned earlier, the first reviewers of *The Complete Stories* capitalized on the anecdote about O'Connor's first meeting with Paul Engle to foster the impression of O'Connor as an outsider in terms of both geography and thematic concerns. After retelling the story of Engle's difficulty in understanding his future student, Joel Wells in the *National Catholic Reporter* stated that O'Connor "proved to be one of those very, very few who live up to and surpass the promise-detectors' fondest dreams."[47] But the anecdote of the provincial student with prodigious talent resonated in other ways, even when it was not explicitly mentioned. Writing in the *New York Times*, Thomas Lask praised the stories as "shining examples of what a good many critics look for: regional stories with universal truths."[48] O'Connor's southern foundations were, once again, recognized as a means by which she could explore larger issues—ones even recognizable to readers of the *New York Times*. The formidable Guy Davenport, writing in *National Review*, used the anecdote to emphasize O'Connor's roots and how, for southern writers, the "grand rhythms and terse realities" of the Bible "turn up in their prose as naturally as a shrug rises in a Frenchman's shoulders."[49] Earlier critics pigeonholed her characters as types, outsiders separate from mainstream life belonging to "the genus Southern Neanderthal"[50] and examples of what might today be called "the Other"; with *The Complete Stories*, critics such as Richard Freedman in the *Washington Post* argued that the southern accent pervading O'Connor's work created "an unparalleled picture of the Deep South—at once horrifying and hilarious—as a metaphor for the human condition when the 20th century lurched past its halfway mark."[51] Freedman's review succinctly recast O'Connor's life and death to suit the critical consensus of her as an outsider: "As a Southerner she was cut off from the dominant American culture of the North. As a Catholic she was further cut off from the dominant Protestantism of the South. And as a sufferer for half of her life from the progressive arthritic disease of lupus, she became an invalid who, in 1964, was ultimately cut off from life itself."[52] To Freedman, O'Connor's three-part outsider status "allowed her to see life around her with ultimate objectivity."[53] No longer was O'Connor only a reporter sending dispatches from below the Mason-Dixon line.

One way of gauging whether an author's reputation has taken root in the consciousness of readers is the frequency by which a "typical" character or pattern for that author is spoken of as if its elements are common knowledge. Such is the case when one describes a regime as Orwellian or a bureaucracy as Kafkaesque. While "O'Connoresque" is not part of any lexicon outside of English departments, the critical response to *The Complete Stories* revealed a growing assumption that there was such a thing as a typical O'Connor situa-

tion or a character who could be described as a typical O'Connor type. Chesterton once noted that the force and reach of Dickens's reputation was seen in
people's casually referring to someone as "a perfect Pecksniff";[54] an examination of O'Connor's critics reveals the growing sense that her thematic concerns
and artistic performance had created something unique that would forever
become part of her reputation and of American literature. Reviewing *Everything That Rises Must Converge*, critics spoke of O'Connor types, such as "the
self-righteous who consider themselves saved by good deeds,"[55] the person who
finds him- or herself "doing the right things for the wrong motives,"[56] or "an
anguished human being, trying to control the circle of his existence."[57] Reviewers of *The Complete Stories* continued this trend of noting the O'Connor type
as something like her own brand. For example, writing in the *New York Times
Book Review*, Alfred Kazin stated, "People in her stories are always at the end
of their strength. They are at the synapse between what they are (unknown
to themselves) and what they do,"[58] while a critic for the *Atlanta Journal and
Constitution* later wrote, "Her trademark is the ostensibly good character who
is not, you come to realize, really as nice as the villain of the same story."[59]
Others noted ways in which these types encounter similar ends. In his *Commentary* review of *Everything That Rises Must Converge*, Warren Coffey stated
that O'Connor's "paradigm story" was "a kind of morality play in which Pride of
Intellect (usually Irreligion) has a shattering encounter with the Corrupt Human Heart (the Criminal, the Insane, sometimes the sexually Demonic) and
either sees the light or dies, sometimes both."[60] Reviewing *The Complete Stories*
in *Newsweek* six years later, Walter Clemons distilled O'Connor's stories into
a pattern that echoes Coffey's: "An O'Connor story often begins with a confident figure on a front porch, armed with platitudes, facing down a suspicious-
looking stranger. Before it's over, safety has been violated, pride is stolen, and
the whole house of cards in which a spurious life has been conducted may be
pulled down."[61] The front porch Clemons mentions could take a number of
forms: the literal porch in "The Life You Save May Be Your Own" or a figurative fortress of self-assurance, such as the tarpaper shack in "The Artificial Nigger," Motes's Essex in *Wise Blood*, or Rayber's room at the Cherokee Lodge in
The Violent Bear It Away.

These remarks about O'Connor's types recall the initial perception of her
"limitations" but with a marked change in attitude toward that supposed deficiency. Many reviewers of *Everything That Rises Must Converge* complained of
O'Connor's narrow range and repetitive plotting; such complaints resurfaced in
some reviews of *The Complete Stories*, as when, for example, John Alfred Avant,

in *Library Journal*, stated that O'Connor "reiterated the same themes with too little variety,"[62] or when John Idol, in a review for *Studies in Short Fiction*, stated that her tendency to shock her reader became repetitious to the point where the impact was lessened with each character's death.[63] A survey of the reviews of *The Complete Stories*, however, reveals that while O'Connor's repetitiousness was still acknowledged, it was recast as an example of her persistence in examining a complex subject. Depth was finally beginning to triumph over breadth. For example, Richard Freedman noted that "Miss O'Connor had her obsessive themes and her special provenance, which becomes abundantly clear when her stories are read *in toto*. Yet, the fecundity of her imagination saved her from being merely repetitious, and each story has its peculiar ambience and personality."[64] Robert Drake described the collection as comprised of stories similar in form and content, but not resulting in any repetitiveness or loss of quality:

> One cannot help but think James would have commended her for being so faithful to the writer's sacred office and that Hemingway would also have praised her accordingly—both of them, one remembers, extremely limited writers as well. Miss O'Connor, too, found—or was there found for her?—early in the day what for her was the one thing needful, what her one story was; and she served it well and faithfully all her days.[65]

This critical revision, this transformation of a supposed fault into an argument for her excellence, illuminates how a writer's reputation can be revisited and revised as it is being formed. In a later review of the Faber & Faber imprint of *The Complete Stories* published in the United Kingdom, a critic for *New Statesman and Society* stated, "These deft parables have often been confused with a trick of telling the same story over and over again. Yet the reader is always arrested by the ferocious attention to detail, and O'Connor's forms are no more routine than cut diamonds."[66] In his previously cited review for *Newsweek*, Walter Clemons offered a tongue-in-cheek mea culpa: "It takes some readers (I was one) a while to understand" that O'Connor's work is "more than a superb Punch-and-Judy show."[67] As the watchwords we have previously examined showed their wear—and were still showing it, as when the *New Statesmen* noted that "the term 'Southern Gothic' doesn't do her justice"[68]—so did this past complaint. The old defect had become a new strength and a well-earned claim.

Giroux was grateful for the critical approval of *The Complete Stories* and equally appreciative of the letters he received from his publishing colleagues and readers from across the country and overseas. William Jovanovich, who had become chairman of Harcourt Brace Jovanovich in 1970, wrote a thank-you letter to Giroux, praising him for his work.[69] Jovanovich was not unique in his desire to compliment Giroux for *The Complete Stories*: one reader wrote Giroux to thank him for "bringing Flannery O'Connor's work to us all,"[70] while another wrote to inform him, "Miss O'Connor's fiction always excites the hell out of me," telling Giroux he deserved the highest praise for "the very handsome volume" he had "turned out."[71] Denver Lindley, O'Connor's final editor at Harcourt, Brace before she moved to Farrar, Straus and Giroux, wrote to tell Giroux that he imagined O'Connor would have been thrilled by the peacocks on the dust jacket.[72] One of the more striking pieces of fan mail came from Hajime Noguchi, author of *Criticism of Flannery O'Connor*, the first book written about O'Connor in Japan: Noguchi thanked Giroux for his efforts and praised his introduction.[73] As usual, Giroux personally responded to such letters with humility and grace, noting in one, "I consider it a tragedy that she died so relatively young, and at the height of her power."[74]

In addition to many accolades from a full spectrum of readers, *The Complete Stories* also received the 1972 National Book Award for fiction—the first time that the award was given posthumously. The history of O'Connor and the National Book Awards is one of near-misses with jurors who compared O'Connor to authors who offered works more mainstream than O'Connor's examinations of literal grace under pressure.[75] As Joel Wells noted, the unspoken rule seemed to be that O'Connor "simply couldn't be assimilated into the fine gears of the literary establishment—no Pulitzer or National Book Award."[76] In 1972, however, *The Complete Stories* rose above nine other National Book Award finalists, including Updike's *Rabbit Redux*, Joyce Carol Oates's *Wonderland*, and *Love in the Ruins*, the second novel by fellow southern Catholic Walker Percy. The conferring of a National Book Award is, of course, not necessarily indicative of a winning text's literary quality. However, a work being nominated at all suggests that it has been vetted, if not accepted, by the critical community, since the five judges selected by the National Book Foundation have always been, according to the foundation, "published writers who are known to be doing great work in the genre or field, and in some cases, are past NBA Finalists or Winners."[77]

The 1972 National Book Awards were controversial and closely watched by readers and publishers. The NBF had been working to rebuild some of its own reputation after a decade of insinuations that the awards were merely "an elaborate marketing enterprise of the New York publishing establishment"[78] or, in the words of Anthony West (who served on the 1967 jury), "a farce in the realm of General Foods' Salesman of the Year Awards, a matter of intramural stroking."[79] The previous year's jury, led by William Styron, threatened to resign if the best-seller *Love Story* was listed as a final nominee.[80] In 1972 the NBF introduced a new category, "Contemporary Affairs," into which *The Last Whole Earth Catalogue* fell—a title that prompted Garry Wills, one of the judges, to resign in protest over what he saw as a bending of the rules that allowed a work with an editor, rather than author, to be considered.[81] The awards ceremony was also the site of what the *New York Times* described as "deep worry about the decline of the quality of life in the face of commercialism and technology."[82] But in the midst of all of the critical hand-wringing and debates over the quality of the winners, the jury's revising of the rules so that O'Connor could be given a posthumous award was not met by any controversy; as the *Washington Post* noted, "Few were surprised at the selection,"[83] and, as reported in the *Savannah News-Press*, the decision to recognize *The Complete Stories* "aroused no dispute."[84] This was not the first time that the rules had been bent for O'Connor: in 1966 the NBF explicitly prohibited judges from conferring "special awards or honorable mention,"[85] but the fiction judges (Paul Horgan, Glenway Wescott, and J. F. Powers) flouted the rule by noting the recent death of O'Connor at the awards ceremony and honored her as "a writer lost to American literature" whose work "commands our memory with sensations of life conveyed with an intensity of pity and participation, love, and redemption, rarely encountered."[86] Nor would it be the last, as we shall see in an examination of the National Book Critics Circle Award. Speaking as one of the five fiction judges in 1971, Joseph Heller called O'Connor "among the most distinguished American writers" and added, "her *Complete Stories* contains her best fiction writing."[87] That Heller, like his predecessors in 1966, referred to O'Connor and her art as "American," rather than "southern," affirms the argument of Giroux's introduction and O'Connor's reach extending beyond the South.

Giroux used the occasion of his accepting the award on behalf of O'Connor's mother, Regina, as an opportunity to urge O'Connor's significance upon a world gone wrong. In what the *New York Times* described as "an indictment of literary and moral standards,"[88] Giroux noted, "In an age of mendacity, duplicity, and document shredders, the clear vision of Flannery O'Connor not only burns brighter than ever but it burns through the masks of what she called 'blind wills and low dodges of the heart.'"[89] He offered O'Connor's oft-repeated jest about southern writers still being able to recognize freaks, thus affirming O'Connor's sense of humor as well as her transcendent moral vision. Giroux also took aim at past detractors and used O'Connor's own words against them: "When she was foolishly criticized for writing mainly about one region," he noted, "she said, 'The region is something the writer has to use to suggest what is beyond it.'"[90] Brad Gooch recounts a conversation he had with Giroux in which the publisher described a "contretemps with a celebrated author backstage at the awards ceremony": when the unnamed author asked Giroux, "Do you really think Flannery O'Connor is a great writer? She's such a Roman Catholic," Giroux responded, "You can't pigeonhole her. That's just the point. I'm surprised at you, to misjudge her so completely. If she were here, she'd set you straight. She'd impress you. You'd have a hard time outtalking her."[91] While Gooch does not reveal the identity of the "celebrated author," the person in question seems like one of O'Connor's readers from the 1950s, wrestling with *Wise Blood* and *A Good Man Is Hard to Find* and trying to categorize O'Connor in an attempt to contain her. After he drafted his acceptance speech, Giroux sent a copy of it to Regina, ending his letter with, "I'm greedy and I'm now hoping for the Pulitzer Prize in fiction, to be announced in May,"[92] but Giroux's greed here, as always, was more for readers than revenues, more for another boost to O'Connor's reputation than the increased sales that would accompany the award. (As it happened, *The Complete Stories* was not nominated for the Pulitzer.)

One notable voice raised against the jury's decision was the editorial page of the *New York Times*, which devoted nearly a full column arguing against O'Connor or any deceased author being awarded the NBA. The desire of many critics to avoid erring on the side of conventionality, and in doing so failing to recognize a Melville or Stendhal in their midst, was acknowledged and described as understandable. However, the *Times* argued that bestowing the award on deceased writers, such as O'Connor and Allan Nevins, the winner for history that year, was unjustifiable because of the recipients' present reputations—the very reputations that the award was meant to boost. Nevins had been "widely and deservedly recognized in his lifetime by both his academic peers and the general public as a great historian," and O'Connor had achieved a similar stature: "Miss O'Connor was a brilliant and original writer. The quality of her work is not in dispute. But the work was praised by all serious critics in her own lifetime, and although not a popular writer, she had a devoted following."[93] The *Times* was straightening the road her reputation had traveled and filling in the potholes, assuming its then-present status as a fact: "all serious critics" did not praise her work until after the mid-1960s, and even then, the word "all" is as problematic as the adjective "serious." Arguing that literary prizes spur living authors onto greater works and that such prizes are "robbed of their meaning when living writers have to stand aside for the famous dead," the *Times* articulated the argument that one's reputation could reach a level at which further recognition was superfluous and even unfair to living, working authors. Similar sentiments were expressed a year later, when, in "Confessions of a Book Award Judge," Christopher Lehman-Haupt described his experiences on the 1972 National Book Awards jury. According to Lehman-Haupt, Joseph Heller was the force behind what Lehman-Haupt called "The Tricky Little Question" of bestowing the award on O'Connor. Lehman-Haupt, who felt that his choice, *The Book of Daniel*, would easily take the award, ends his description of the judges' debates with Heller calculatingly suggesting O'Connor's *Complete Stories* and his own reaction to Heller's maneuverings: "It wasn't a bad choice, of course. No one could seriously object. . . . But it wasn't a good choice either. It didn't call attention to a previously uncelebrated novelist. It didn't bestow hitherto withheld recognition. It didn't anoint. It was, come to think of it, a predictable result of mixing politics with art."[94] Such a mixture is what Lehman-Haupt thought he would avoid, but Heller proved to be too able a politician. To the great pleasure of Giroux and his firm, the NBF disagreed with the *Times* and Lehman-Haupt and assumed that the building of one's reputation was not a zero-sum game where the dead could rob the living of their due.

In that same year, 1972, Regina donated her daughter's papers to Georgia College, O'Connor's alma mater, from which she had graduated in 1945 when it was Georgia State College for Women. The papers included over two thousand pages of drafts of *Wise Blood* alone as well as other manuscripts, letters, memorabilia, and ephemera. From our current vantage point, O'Connor's papers being archived at Georgia College seems natural and expected. However, as a Georgian columnist for the *Marion Telegraph* noted at the time, "The generosity of Mrs. Edward F. O'Connor in making this gift is overwhelming, since on the open market, bids for the collection might easily have been in the five-figure category; such universities as Texas, Yale, Harvard, and others with wealthy, generous contributors to their libraries, would probably have bid high for the possession of the materials of the young author whose stature as a writer continues to grow."[95] Not surprisingly, the staff of the Georgia College Library was thrilled by Regina's largess. Gerald Becham, the initial curator of the collection, said, "It is unusual for such a small college library to be given such a valuable manuscript collection. Manuscripts of writers of Miss O'Connor's stature are usually deposited in large research libraries. Through Mrs. O'Connor's generous gift, the collection at the Georgia College Library has been greatly enhanced."[96] Charles E. Beard, director of the library, said that the collection would give the library "preeminence in primary sources for a total picture of Flannery O'Connor, the writer and the person."[97] This "total picture" is one of O'Connor's reputation at this moment, when *The Complete Stories* had been met with overwhelmingly favorable reviews, when its author had been posthumously given the National Book Award, and when O'Connor's personal life began to be viewed as a subject worthy of popular and critical interest.

Soon after Regina decided to donate her daughter's papers to Georgia College, Governor Jimmy Carter declared Sunday, January 16, 1972, as Flannery O'Connor Day. A subsequent proclamation made by Savannah mayor John P. Rousakis proudly echoed Governor Carter's declaration. The official proclamation notes that O'Connor, a "native of Savannah, attained fame in the literary world as an author," and that "her talent as a writer was accorded recognition from many quarters."[98] Rousakis's proclamation lists among her accomplishments "two Kenyon Fellowships, a grant from the National Institute of Arts and Letters, a Ford Foundation grant, the Henry Bellamann Foundation Award, and two O. Henry awards for best short story of the year" and states that "her works are being used in seminaries and other institutions of learning for religious education." The proclamation also, like some of the original southern reviewers of *Wise Blood*, claimed O'Connor as a local hero, universality be damned: "WHEREAS the citizens of Savannah, Miss O'Connor's native city, are indeed proud of her accomplishments and consider such recognition fitting and proper for someone who lived here until she was 14 and received her early education at Sacred Heart School and St. Vincent's Academy," Mayor Rousakis urged the citizens of Savannah to recognize and celebrate Flannery O'Connor Day. He also asked his constituents to "use this occasion to reflect on the valuable contributions to literature made by this talented native daughter, and to pause with a prayer of thanksgiving to Almighty God for her life and good works." O'Connor the writer of fiction was now an occasion for prayer or, as the counterman in "The Life You Save May Be Your Own" calls Lucynell Crater, "an angel of Gawd." Both of these political pronouncements list O'Connor's achievements and insist on a growing interest in her work; they offer, in short, a reputation-by-résumé that reflects, in language part publicity puffery and part commodification, how her native state regarded O'Connor at the time.

In its coverage of the reception at Georgia College Library on Flannery O'Connor Day, the *Milledgeville Union-Recorder* ran a full-page story and extensive photo spread that began by speaking of O'Connor as if she were a kind of magician: "The curtain of mystery which covers the creative process and particularly the creative process of Flannery O'Connor was lifted briefly today at Georgia College during the public showing of the Flannery O'Connor Collection at Georgia College's library."[99] The initial exhibit featured selections from the *Wise Blood* manuscripts and O'Connor's plan for the novel as well as her christening dress, paintings, cartoons, and a report card that urged the young O'Connor to "work on her spelling."[100] The woman was now as interesting as her work. Drawings of the proposed Flannery O'Connor Room (which would be dedicated in 1974) were also displayed, and O'Connor's appearance on the 1955 television interview show *Galley Proof* was screened every half-hour. Over eight hundred people attended the reception in order to view these materials; this once local hero had become a figure worthy of note on a grander scale.[101] The program for the event blazoned critical blurbs from names with a great deal of clout, such as Alfred Kazin, all praising *The Complete Stories*. That the program also featured a chronology of O'Connor's life again shows a growing interest in her biography.[102] More than ever before, readers were fascinated by the person who had written such material, a fascination that would be fed by the publication of *The Habit of Being* in 1979.

A less-publicized yet still-revealing dedication also occurred in 1972, when Regina O'Connor bequeathed something other than manuscripts to a grateful institution. In the week before the reception at Georgia College, Regina donated several of her daughter's peafowl to Stone Mountain Park, a popular site in Georgia that features the eponymous landmark as well as a restored plantation. O'Connor's by-then iconic birds had been left to wander near the enormous bas-relief of Jefferson Davis, Robert E. Lee, and Stonewall Jackson; O'Connor was still very much claimed by her native Georgia. In its coverage of the presentation of the peafowl, the *Union-Recorder* proclaimed that "only Stone Mountain itself is more enduring than the works of Flannery O'Connor."[103] The work belonged to the world, but the woman still, according to many admirers, belonged to the South.

Sally Fitzgerald and *The Habit of Being*: Courting Regina

The story of Sally Fitzgerald's tireless negotiations with Regina to obtain the letters that would be collected in *The Habit of Being* (1979) is one in which those close to O'Connor—her friend, her publisher, and her mother—worked in and out of concert to fashion O'Connor's reputation. Many letters poured into Giroux's office inquiring who was writing O'Connor's authorized biography or, in some cases, offering the writer's services to tackle the job him- or herself. While many unknown and would-be biographers (such as the managing editor of the *Boston Monthly*) sought Giroux's advice and approval, more notable writers also showed interest in such a project. For example, in 1964 the American playwright Leonard Melfi wrote Giroux that he wanted to write a biography of O'Connor and asked his advice on how to proceed; ten years later, Mark Harris, known for his baseball novel *Bang the Drum Slowly*, did the same.[104] As he did to all such requests, Giroux responded by stating that no authorized biographer had yet been chosen. To both Melfi and Harris, however, Giroux added some words concerning the difficulty of such a project, regardless of who was undertaking it: to Melfi, he wrote that a biography of O'Connor would not be "an easy life to do because the most significant aspects of it were all interior and creative,"[105] while he informed Harris, "Flannery's short life was an interior one, characterized by illness and concentration on her work."[106] O'Connor herself had first expressed these ideas in a 1958 letter: "There won't be any biographies of me, because, for only one reason, lives spent between the house and the chicken yard do not make exciting copy."[107] Despite his caution to these would-be biographers, Giroux was soon guiding the hand of another potential biographer—Sally Fitzgerald—in her efforts to bring O'Connor's life to her readers. To Giroux, ever protective of his friend's reputation, only an O'Connor insider would do.

Like Giroux, Elizabeth McKee, O'Connor's agent, had also received many requests by potential biographers. In what would become something resembling a form letter, McKee responded to a professor from the University of Cincinnati by saying that her office had been approached by "a number of scholars who wanted to know personal details" but that they could not be provided: "Because the Estate and her publishers will at some future time probably publish or authorize a book concerning the personal life of Flannery O'Connor and her publishing and agency associations during her lifetime and career, we have adopted a firm rule that we cannot furnish such material to anyone who wants to independently publish a book about Flannery and her works."[108] Such requests prompted McKee to speak with Regina about an authorized biography; Regina was not opposed. McKee reported the conversation to Giroux and added her thoughts about the benefits of choosing an official biographer:

A good biography would stem all the inaccuracies about Flannery which are published these days. And if one could find a good writer for such a project the writer would have the enormous advantage of Regina's cooperation and her introductions to people who knew Flannery intimately. She said hesitatingly that she wished you would write one but she was afraid that you wouldn't have the time. I said that I doubted, too, that you would undertake such a project but that I would tell you. We both agreed that Robert Fitzgerald would not be the proper writer.[109]

If Robert was not the "proper writer" for such a work, McKee, Regina, and Giroux regarded Sally as the natural choice: Giroux wrote of Sally in 1977, "No one could be better equipped to write the biography."[110] In early 1978 Sally applied for a fellowship from Radcliffe to compose a work tentatively entitled, *Flannery and Regina: A Biographical Study of Flannery O'Connor.* In her application for the fellowship, Sally presented her *bona fides* as half of the team that edited and helped bring *Mystery and Manners* to light, as well as her then-current work in preparing the edition of O'Connor's letters that would become *The Habit of Being.* Noting in her application that Regina would have burned O'Connor's letters but for Sally's intervention, Fitzgerald expressed her confidence in getting anything she needed in order to create a compelling biography. She added that there were books "under maternal seal" at Andalusia teeming with O'Connor's annotations but that she believed she could also "gain access to this material."[111] Giroux endorsed Sally's project, writing in his letter of recommendation, "As [O'Connor's] publisher, I am deluged with requests from writers who want to write her life" and that he sent such requests to Regina, who "always turned them down."[112] He observed that Sally, however, had claimed in her application that Regina had "recently asked Sarah H. Fitzgerald to undertake this work, demonstrating her keen awareness" that "Ms. Fitzgerald is uniquely qualified for the job." Radcliffe awarded the fellowship in April 1978, and Sally began working on the project while simultaneously editing the letters. There is significance in all parties' eagerness to confirm Sally as the authorized biographer: O'Connor's mother, her publisher, and her agent all wanted someone to present O'Connor's character to the world in a manner they saw as accurate and that would avoid any potential dents in the armor of her reputation. What none of them could have foreseen was that the title *Flannery and Regina* would come to take on greater significance than any of them realized when they began collecting O'Connor's letters in earnest.

Interest in publishing O'Connor's letters also gained momentum after her death. In 1967 Jean Wylder, one of O'Connor's classmates at the University of Iowa, wrote to John Farrar to propose an edition of O'Connor's letters; Farrar responded that Robert Fitzgerald was already under contract to collect them.[113] Yet no contract between FS&G and a writer was drawn, so Farrar was either mistaken or warding off potential competition: attached to his same letter of refusal was a note from an assistant asking Wylder if she had any letters of her own that they might use. A short time after Wylder's inquiry, Giroux wrote to Regina who had, almost prophetically, suggested a volume of O'Connor's art-work and cartoons much like the one released in 2012; Giroux responded that he did not think it wise to publish the artwork by itself, but mentioned the possibility of including it in "the collection of Flannery's letters" that "one day must be brought out."[114] The plan for publishing O'Connor's letters, however, remained in the background until 1974, when Giroux wrote Robert Fitzger-ald, telling him, "We continue to receive inquiries about an edition of Flan-nery's letters. . . . I wonder if the time has come for us to contract with you and Sally to edit such a book."[115] Noting the rise of O'Connor's reputation, Giroux added, "It's our impression that interest in Flannery's work, and in everything about her, increases every year." However, what stands out from this letter, in hindsight, are Giroux's words about Regina: "I've discussed this with Eliza-beth McKee, who is keen for you both to do it, but she thinks it should be first cleared by Regina—probably by phone. Assuming you agree the time has now come for such an edition, would you undertake to obtain Regina's blessing? If she agrees, as I can't help thinking she will, I'd like to draw up an agreement." Giroux's noting that the project should be "cleared by Regina—probably by phone" as if he knew that Regina had to be handled with care and that Fitz-gerald could be more convincing in conversation than in writing, merits atten-tion. While this blessing was in fact finally obtained, it did not come without a number of difficulties and caveats, all of which related to how Regina sought to steer O'Connor's reputation as a daughter more than as an author. Regina's blessing, as Sally was to learn, was a limited one that initially entailed what Sally viewed as a whitewashing of a reputation but that Regina viewed as the upholding of decorum and good manners.

Robert Fitzgerald responded to Giroux's request with enthusiasm: "Sally and I talked over the possibilities of an edition of Flannery's selected letters and agreed that we were all for it, that it should be done."[116] In the same letter, Fitzgerald added that Sally would do most of the work and expressed his as-surance that "Regina will trust her judgment on the letters," a claim that would latter appear as an overconfident assessment of just how much Regina trusted Sally. Giroux wrote Regina in the autumn of 1974, excited about the project. Sally Fitzgerald wrote to Giroux during the same period to outline her plan: the volume would not present a complete edition of O'Connor's letters but offer enough of them "to sketch for us a recognizable self-portrait of the artist as a remarkable young woman whose lineaments, guessed at from a distance, have often been forbiddingly misdrawn."[117] The ensuing collection, for example, features none of the letters that O'Connor wrote to her mother every day when she lived with the Fitzgeralds in Connecticut for much of 1949 and 1950. Sally Fitzgerald, however, felt confident that she could provide a faithful portrait of O'Connor through the medium of her correspondence.

The next phase of the project predictably entailed a scramble for the letters themselves with Sally making inquiries across the country. Giroux assisted her whenever he could. In September 1973, for example, he wrote to the University of Texas to ask for the letters deposited there; in June 1975 he wrote to the poet and critic G. Roysce Smith, asking for any letters O'Connor had written to him or his fellow poet George Marion O'Donnell. Giroux's requests reveal his desire to help fashion the kind of three-dimensional portrait Sally envisioned: he noted to Smith, "What may seem unimportant by itself perhaps might be a key piece in the total mosaic."[118] His language here recalls that of Charles Beard, the director of the library at Georgia College, who stated that the 1972 donation of O'Connor's papers would allow scholars to form a "total picture" of O'Connor.

A more tangled request illustrates the pains Giroux took to create that "total mosaic." As he assisted Sally in her search, Giroux learned that Duke University had, in 1961, been given a cache of letters by various correspondents, many of them members of the Gossett family.[119] In March 1976 he wrote to Mary Louise Black of Duke University Press to inquire about the letters, complaining that all requests for them addressed to the librarians at Georgia College "have got nowhere." Giroux asked Black to act discreetly on his behalf:

> I wonder if you'll act as my intelligence agent in the matter. Can you find out if anyone—a qualified scholar, for instance—is allowed to see them and under what circumstances? ... Can you look into it quietly without ruffling anyone's bureaucratic feathers? ... I want to get all the facts I can. Did someone, for example, sell the letters to Duke and were considerations of secrecy imposed? ... The circuitous paths in the literary life never cease to amaze me.[120]

Black responded with interesting news about a notice in *American Literary Scholarship*, an annual review by Duke University Press that surveys scholarly work published in the past year. The notice concerned an article by Thomas Gossett in a recent issue of the *Southern Literary Journal* in which Gossett described O'Connor's reactions to contemporary figures such as Isak Dinesen and J. F. Powers (both of whose work she enjoyed). What intrigued Black was Gossett's note that he and his wife possessed "about one hundred and thirty-five letters and postcards from her, most of them written to other people" but that Regina, as executor, "has so far decided not to release them for publication" and prohibited Gossett from directly quoting them.[121] The trickiness of the situation was due to the difference between physical paper and the words printed on it, a difference of which Giroux was fully aware: as he later wrote to Maryat Lee, "The recipients of the letters own the pieces of paper, but the words and their use for publication belong to Flannery's estate. This is an aspect of copyright law that few people are familiar with—understandably, since it is a complicated distinction."[122] Libraries and individuals may have treasured O'Connor's letters as the wonderful artifacts that they were, but Regina held the rights to publishing their contents. Giroux was concerned by Regina's decision, since he had been acting on the assumption that the he and Sally, perhaps because of their closeness to O'Connor, would be granted permission by her mother to print any of the letters that they chose. Still, Giroux was motivated by Gossett's use of the phrase "so far" and wrote to Sally that there was still the potential that they would receive the permission they sought: "The one ray of hope is Regina's saying that she wants more time to think about allowing publication of the very letters you and I have been assuming we can publish."[123] Tactfully, he advised Sally to "drop Regina a line, telling her of your plans."[124] Nine days later, Giroux sent Sally a copy of Gossett's article, which revealed a challenge to their current project: "I don't see how we can bring out a book of her letters without including this large batch of 135 letters which has been deposited (under seal) at Duke University. Since Regina has refused to allow Gossett to quote from the letters, she may well refuse to make copies available for your book. Once again, Regina is the key to the problem.... I hope you can get her to cut the Gordian knot."[125] Unbeknownst to Giroux and the Fitzgeralds, Regina had recently been engaged in other negotiations about her daughter's letters—negotiations that suggested the Gordian knot was still awaiting its Alexander the Great.

Regina had her own ideas about the propriety of publishing her daughter's letters or those of anyone else. Approximately a month before Giroux had written to Sally about their problem, O'Connor's friend and frequent correspondent, the playwright Maryat Lee, had composed an article for the *Flannery O'Connor Bulletin*, which had begun in 1972 under the editorship of Caroline Gordon. Lee's article reminisced about the year in which she had first met O'Connor, and she had wanted to quote from O'Connor's letters to her. Anticipating Regina's sensitivity about this request, Lee sent Giroux a copy of her yet-to-be-sent letter to Regina, asking if she should make any changes for the sake of diplomacy. Giroux thought that Lee had struck the right tone in her request so that, in Lee's words, "O'Connor could speak for herself and not have it filtered."[126] Regina, however, denied Lee's request on the grounds that her daughter was not alive to grant permission or defend herself from any repercussions that might result from such publication: "I couldn't give you or anyone else permission to quote from letters I haven't read," she wrote Lee, adding, "I'm sure you understand how I feel about this."[127] This editorial principle recast as an emotion sparked a heated correspondence between these two women, one who wanted to humanize O'Connor's public persona and one who wanted to guard it. Lee responded by asserting her assumptions about the positive effects from quoting O'Connor's unpublished letters: "It is important right now to encourage publication of her letters to balance the odd fancies and notions some of the literary bigwigs have about her interests. Some of the things you may not think are anybody's business, you know, but since my purpose in this reminiscence is to show how many things interested Flannery, not just a narrow range of things, I think it is useful."[128] Lee mentioned, in the same letter, a rumor she had heard about Sally's work on what would become *The Habit of Being* and stated, "I hope it's true, for I feel her beautiful letters will extend her place in the world of 'letters,' and that we have reached a time when the world is hungry to know more of her and the letters will help enlarge her already considerable influence." Regina, however, persevered, not out of mere stubbornness or a desire for control, but because she was genuinely concerned about her daughter's reputation and betraying her privacy:

> Maryat, about the letters, I can't help but feel Flannery wrote those letters just to you and I wonder if she would like them published. (I'm trying to be honest with you.) I don't know any other way. I appreciate what you said in your letter and it would be nice for people to know another side of her, but people are funny and those who believe that there is no other side, you simply can't change them.[129]

This "other side" of O'Connor was exactly what Fitzgerald and Giroux had sought to convey in their introductions to her books; remember, there was very little biographical work done on O'Connor until decades after these essays. Regina did add, "Please give me a little more time to think about it" before closing—a portent of her eventually relenting. She wrote to Lee again a few days later, saying that Lee could quote the letters directly but only after specific "personal references" were deleted.[130] The grateful Lee responded that same day, thanking Regina for her permission and expressing her confidence that the letters "would correct some misconceptions afloat"[131] about O'Connor, such as that she was a homebody who only cared for her writing and her church. What truly stands out in Lee's response regarding O'Connor's reputation is Lee's assertion that her friend was well aware that her reputation would extend beyond Milledgeville and continually evolve after her death: "I've come to think that Flannery was quite aware that she would or could become a celebrated person—even more than when she was alive." She added that she had "solid reason to believe" that Flannery thought her letters would someday be published. Lee attempted to comfort Regina by telling her that readers would not be looking for private or salacious material; rather, most readers were "people who want to know and take to their hearts not only the literary works, but the person (as seen in letters) who wrote them for the simple reason that such persons give them courage and company." In short, Lee viewed the publication of letters as a means to heightening readers' appreciation of an author's work and life—a view that Regina agreed with, as long as people's feelings were not hurt. To her, a "total picture" or a "total mosaic" was acceptable in theory, but her daughter's privacy trumped literary portraiture.

While Sally was preparing *The Habit of Being*, Lee was interested in producing an annotated edition of letters from O'Connor to her and had already contacted Regina about such a collection. Sally had disliked the way that Lee had portrayed O'Connor in the *Flannery O'Connor Bulletin* piece for which she had sought Regina's permission to quote the letters. She wrote Giroux, "I greatly fear that Maryat's accounts would be subject to the same rules of dramatic rearrangement. She wanted, after all, to be a playwright."[132] Sally here gives the first indication of what would become her editorial principle of not interfering with the voice to be heard in the letters. She wrote Lee and asked for copies of her letters from O'Connor—but never indicated to Lee that the letters would appear in *The Habit of Being*, an omission that Lee rightly resented and which she expressed to Sally in an angry letter.[133] Sally responded by writing Lee that she "planned to give a great deal of importance to Flannery's friendship with you" and that she hoped Lee would help her "put together a good and objective book about our rare friend."[134] The yoking of "good and objective" reflects Sally's assumptions about how to best further O'Connor's reputation: by trusting the letters to speak for themselves, without any critical adornment. Lee fumed to Giroux—who had seen a copy of Sally's letter—that any commentary she offered in her proposed edition of the letters would be honest and faithful to Flannery.[135] Giroux tactfully refereed, writing Lee that he appreciated her intentions but that, legally, Regina—and, by extension, Sally—had the advantage. Lee did not appreciate what she viewed as Giroux's sophistry, and expressed as much in subsequent letters to Regina and Sally. But she did relent in her pursuit of her own collection, and her letters from O'Connor run throughout *The Habit of Being*. Sally's unadorned version of O'Connor had come another step closer to reality.

Lee's skirmish with Regina over these letters for a personal reminiscence in a journal prefigured the longer battle that occurred between Sally and Regina over hundreds of letters for a book. Sally had sent Regina a number of Flannery's letters that she wanted to include in what would become *The Habit of Being* and asked her permission to reprint them. Regina returned them to Sally with enough editorial demands to warrant Sally's responding in a long letter dated May 1, 1977. Many of Regina's requests were matters of what she regarded as good manners, as when she asked that Sally edit the letters in which O'Connor referred to her Uncle Louis by his first name: the thought of Flannery calling him "Louis" in print seemed scandalous to Regina, who feared that this would make her daughter seem like she had not been raised well. Sally noted, "We can't, of course, change Flannery's wording" and urged Regina to view this detail as one that would allow O'Connor to be seen as more three-dimensional:

> I wish you would think over again whether to use the name of the uncle. Flannery always called him Louis—and there wasn't the slightest disrespect in her doing so. She was crazy about him, and admired him very much, as well. But if she is made to call him only "Uncle" then it begins to sound a little unreal. She ought to sound as real as possible. Reality was what Flannery prized, both supernatural reality, and the reality that is part of everyday life.... I hope you will reconsider and let her call him by the name she always used for him and to him. Especially as he is shown to be so very nice in the letters.[136]

Regina eventually relented on this point. In other parts of Sally's letter, she argues for the same practice of letting O'Connor sound like herself, rather than a version her mother thought more proper. For example, Regina expressed her dismay over any association in print between O'Connor and alcohol, which, as one can detect in Sally's reply, Regina assumed made her daughter seem more like F. Scott Fitzgerald than Thomas Merton: "By 'drank with this one and that one,' Flannery obviously meant that she had a glass of sherry at some literary cocktail party. There isn't the slightest suggestion anywhere that she 'drank,' or went out drinking. I'll cut it out if you want me to, but I don't think it is at all misleading, really." Sally's use of "obviously" here reveals a hint of exasperation. Sally was also aware that when O'Connor lived with her and

Robert in Connecticut, she sometimes ended the day with a martini as she and her landlords conducted their literary discussions—a fact that Robert had already mentioned, in print, in his introduction to *Everything That Rises Must Converge*.[137] However, she knew better than to play this card against Regina at this time: if she wanted to foster what she saw as an honest image of O'Connor, she had to cajole her mother.

Sally's response contains other such moments when one can imagine her shaking her head in disbelief yet communicating her ideas in diplomatically strained language. For example, Sally wrote that O'Connor's mentioning Brainard Cheney's past occupation as speechwriter for the governor of Tennessee was no poor reflection on Cheney or the governor, since "All governors, presidents, etc. have speech-writers working for them" because "They really don't have time to write their own speeches." She similarly had to explain that "whiskey priest" was "a very well-known joking term, not made up by Flannery" and certainly not the slur on the priesthood that Regina imagined. Sally, however, became more emphatic when Regina suggested they remove O'Connor's 1954 letter to the Fitzgeralds in which she described Robert Lowell's decision to leave the church: "I really don't think it is too personal. This is Flannery at her best. Very few people had the courage to tell him what they thought. He made a rather public scene about leaving it, and said to many people what she quotes him as saying to her. I think it is better to let her say exactly what *she* said to him in return." Clearly, the two women had different ideas of what constituted "Flannery at her best": Sally prized her friend's honesty while Regina prized unruffled feathers. Sally won this particular battle: the letter was eventually included in *The Habit of Being*. And, in a reminder of the sometimes comic note that these negotiations struck, Sally also informed Regina that O'Connor's mention of Lowell spouting "some other claptrap about Henry Adams being a Catholic anarchist"[138] was no cause for concern: "Henry Adams ... was a Boston writer who died a hundred years ago. No problem about mentioning *him*."[139]

This is not to say that Sally was insensitive to personal issues being put into print: while she told Regina that she did not think Allen Tate would "mind the reference to his getting 'mobbed,'" since O'Connor's term referred to "rowdy students" and not Tate himself, she parenthetically added, "I am of course omitting all references to the domestic struggles and sorrows of the Tates throughout the collection," since "That is the kind of thing that I think has no place in the book." Similarly, in her comments about the term "whiskey priest," Sally states that some of O'Connor's remarks about "the very Irish parish priest in

Milledgeville" could be "toned down" since the person was still alive. Sally's responses throughout her work on *The Habit of Being* generally reveal her desire to tread carefully in the epistolary presence of Regina.

Sally was less constrained in her correspondence with Giroux. The day after she composed the response to Regina, she wrote to inform him, "Regina is sharpening her blade"[140] and enclosed a copy of her May 1 letter concerning O'Connor's uncle Louis and other matters. She also bore worse news about a second batch of letters that Regina had just returned with a new set of demands: "Her objections to letting Flannery *speak* in [the first batch] were as nothing to her objections to the second, far more interesting, batch. Which she tore to pieces. Gutted. I found it yesterday when I got home. I felt sick when I saw what she wants to do, and the shell she is willing to leave." Sally's frustration here reflects her assumption that a reputation is better formed by an author's own words than a "shell" left by others. Sally informed Giroux that she planned to write Regina a letter "on the general principle of allowing Flannery to be herself" and remind her that "if Flannery had written her *stories* to please Milledgeville, or to refrain from displeasing it, nothing whatever would have come of her work." That each woman's point of view was sympathetic only heightened the drama, and Sally even sympathized, to an extent, with Regina and her concerns: "Obviously," she continued in her letter to Giroux, "I don't want her to wound or embarrass living people. . . . Flannery herself was careful not to hurt people deliberately. But Regina's scruples are not of the same kind." Sally promised Giroux that she would send him a copy of her next letter to Regina, one in which she hoped to be "careful and effective." She also asked Giroux not to mention any of these dealings to Elizabeth McKee or to communicate with Regina himself, "lest she feel beleaguered." Courting Regina for the sake of a more genuine portrait of O'Connor would take some tact and political skill. Giroux responded that he found her first letter to Regina "excellent" and that he would not intervene in her plans unless asked; he also offered her his moral support, ending his letter with, "Flannery—of all writers!—should not be falsified."[141]

Sally's next letter to Regina reads as a primer for anyone interested in collecting an author's letters in the interest of furthering a literary reputation. Unlike her previous letter, in which she enumerated her points as they related to specific items in specific letters, this one pleads in eleven paragraphs to let O'Connor speak for herself. Regina had requested, for example, that O'Connor's letters to Fr. James McCown, in which she discussed a number of theological issues, be excised; Sally responded that Fr. McCown had already removed anything he thought too personal when he donated the letters to

Vanderbilt University and that Regina was not seeing the reputation-forest for the trees of social unease: "They are very good examples of the kind of open, frank, joking, but deeply serious and mutually respectful friendship it is possible for a Catholic to have with a priest. You know, most non-Catholics don't know that such a thing is possible. I *do* hope you will consent to have these letters made public. Flannery's loyalty to the church was strongly determined throughout her life, and that fact alone gave her the right to criticize what she felt deserved criticism. Fr. McCown certainly thought nothing she said offensive."[142] Regarding Regina's request that O'Connor's remark about not wanting to bathe at Lourdes ("I am one of those people who could die for his religion easier than taking a bath for it"[143]) be removed on the grounds of near-blasphemy, Sally responded that O'Connor's balking at the act was not "unnatural," that "Many, even most, people would, and wouldn't mind saying so," and, most importantly, that when in a subsequent letter O'Connor "ascribes the unexpected recalcification of her hip bone to Lourdes, she does more to bear witness, and is more humble and truthful, than she would have been if she had held her tongue in the beginning." Sally thus appealed to Regina as both a friend of O'Connor's and a Catholic, implying that by allowing O'Connor to "speak her mind on both scores," Regina would be affecting the reputation of her daughter and her church in a more positive way. Reminding Regina that one reviewer of *Mystery and Manners* praised the work because "there is always audible the sound of her voice speaking; never the sound of a machine clattering," Sally sought to impress upon Regina her editorial principle, much like Giroux's, of non-interference.

Sally also urged Regina to consider ways in which a more open edition of O'Connor's letters would suit her daughter's personality and writing. Statements such as "I do truly believe that her own strong respect for everyday reality and the concrete ought to be honored by letting her speak," and "Let her talk about your life together: she does you proud, and you would do her proud to recognize that and let her speak freely," characterize Sally's tone and overall appeal. Her penultimate paragraph carries her most earnest plea for allowing the voice that spoke so truly about so many issues to surface in her letters—which were, according to Sally, the cause of greater and more meaningful discomfort than O'Connor's mentioning neighbors by name or questioning the decisions of a priest:

> I think that we have to remember that if Flannery had written in her stories only what would please the townspeople, she never would have written everything that has made her one of the most honored of modern American writers. As you

said to me, "she had a message." She observed and made live the world around her, in her stories—and in her letters, as well. So the letters carry the message, too. Ought we to stifle her voice, in that case? She always made people think, even if she didn't always make them comfortable. She will make them think by her letters, too, if we let them speak for her.

Appealing to Regina's pride in her daughter and recasting O'Connor as a minor prophet herself, Sally hoped that her argument would sway Regina from her reluctance to add pieces to the "total mosaic." Ending with "We'll work it out" and typing "With love, as always" above her signature, Sally could only have hoped that Regina would understand the importance of her daughter's honest, unfiltered voice being heard in her uncensored letters.

Her hopes were dashed when she received Regina's response. That this letter was typed, unlike the usually handwritten letters that Regina favored, and copied suggested the seriousness of her response and that Regina was expressing herself in the most formal means possible. While Regina began with a joke—"I guess this letter is special to use this carbon paper"[144]—she twice mentioned that she was at a "disadvantage" by not having all the letters in question at hand, suggesting that this supposedly friendly collaboration was marked by the presence of tough negotiations. Regina quickly got to the point: "I understand that you can't change Flannery's words, but as you say we can leave out certain things or paraphrase her actual words—When we went into this I had no idea you wanted to use all the letters to Betty—Just remember she wrote those to Betty *as her friend* not to the public." Her objections about O'Connor's letters to Betty Hester were followed by others, worded even more emphatically and with spelling and syntax that I have not changed:

> As to the term "whiskey priest," I never thought for a minute Flannery was the originator, but we are not use to priest being referred to in that manner, remember that wasn't for the public but for Betty. The Irish priest is still alive and lives in Atlanta. I want it out. He's a friend of mine.... Cal Lowell, I think it's to personal and I want it left out.... The part about drinking 'with this one and that one' I want it left *out*.

Sally's previous letter describing the benefits of letting an author speak for herself was not as "careful and effective" as she had hoped. Nothing was about to change Regina's set opinions; she was eighty years old and confident of her own opinions regarding the difference between literary property and social propriety.

Sally tried one final time to convince Regina of the need to let Flannery be Flannery. Responding to Regina's questioning Fr. McCown's right to donate his letters to Vanderbilt, Sally informed Regina that this was a common, legitimate practice and that no one could stop scholars from reading the letters or describing their contents in print. "This is precisely the reason," she explained, "why I have wanted to use as much as I have—so that Flannery's own words can be heard, and *not just what somebody said she said*."[145] In the remainder of this three-page letter dated three days after Regina's typed response, Sally conceded to some of Regina's demands, informing her, for example, that she would cut the reference to the "whiskey priest" (although she was unable to resist adding that it was "a joke of course") and telling her that she would remove O'Connor's words about being "irked" because an acquaintance had "failed to mention you when she wrote thanking F. for a weekend." Sally was beginning to show the exhaustion that lay beneath the diplomacy: she reminded Regina that the idea of anyone regarding O'Connor as a drinker was absurd, since it was "abundantly clear from all the letters that Flannery was almost completely abstemious," and sought to correct Regina's impression of Robert Lowell as one to whom religious convictions were a private matter and therefore best excised from the letters: "Cal Lowell has never hesitated to announce that he has left the church, and mention of the fact by Flannery simply suggests that she, too, knew what everybody else had also been told. And that she was grieved by his leaving it." Sally most emphatically argued for the inclusion of O'Connor's letters to her friend Betty Hester, which Regina thought too personal:

> The letters to Betty contain more about Flannery's reading, her literary and theological interests than almost any other of her correspondence. In some ways, they are the most important letters that she wrote. I have chopped them to pieces, to eliminate the things that she said to her in confidence . . . but many of the things she wrote to Betty are of great public interest in setting down her reading interests and her generosity in helping people out with their own writing.

Regina conceded this point, although Hester only allowed the letters to be published after her identity was changed to "A." Sally did admit to Regina that she was at a "disadvantage" (as Regina had earlier called it) in not seeing all the letters, but offered a means of rectifying the situation: "I think perhaps it would be better not to bother you with any more of these packets [of letters] that you have to return. Why don't I simply get the whole manuscript together . . . and when it is entirely finished, as I think it ought to be, I will xerox it and send it off to you, so that you can get a sense of it as a whole, and can ask for any further revisions or cuts you would like to make." Such a solution hinged on Sally's hunch that Regina, upon reading the whole of the collection, would view the letters as integral to the "total picture" of O'Connor or, as she remarked earlier in the letter, that people "are not as easily embarrassed as we might think." Sally tactfully closed the letter by mentioning that she had recently met the cardinal archbishop of Boston and that, when she was introduced to him as the person "working on Flannery's letters," the cardinal "spoke very very highly of Flannery." Mentioning this conversation could not but help her cause.

As we have seen before, Sally found in Giroux a colleague to whom she could vent her frustration. On the same day as her last plea to Regina, she wrote Giroux about her struggles:

> Herewith a copy of my letter to Regina, sent today. I feel like the Laocoön. If you don't want to plow through all three pages, you needn't. This is just for the record. If you do finish it, you will see that I propose to send her just the completed manuscript, rather than throwing myself on the spears every few days. Maybe the whole thing will make her see that Flannery does not come out badly. Her excisions are often fantastic, I fear, and some of them I will restore in the final version, in the hope that she may not notice, or may have ceased to mind, or may have seen the light of reason. She is so afraid of anything personal that she has crossed out references to Henry Adams and Wyndham Lewis. . . . I do not lose hope, however.[146]

In her letter to Regina, Sally offered to send the complete manuscript as a way to atone for any past "disadvantages," while here she remarks that doing so was a way to avoid the "spears" and "fantastic" demands of a mother who would not "see the light of reason." Sally's letter, however, again emphasizes just how important this project would be to O'Connor's reputation: how she would be portrayed ("come out") in the collected letters was a matter of whose principles about the reprinting of private letters would inform the editing.

By all accounts, Regina was always concerned that her daughter was well regarded by their friends and neighbors and wanted her to be the kind of author who produced work that boosted her reputation as an "admirable" author. Regina once asked Giroux, in the presence of O'Connor, "Mister Giroux, can't you get Flannery to write about nice people?"[147] And in one pointed letter to Cecil Dawkins, O'Connor fumed over Regina's desire to have her daughter write a novel more like *Gone with the Wind* and less like *Wise Blood*: "Do you think, she said, that you are really using the talent God gave you when you don't write something that a lot, a LOT, of people like? This always leaves me shaking and speechless, raises my blood pressure 140 degrees, etc. All I can ever say is, if you have to ask, you'll never know."[148] But readers should not regard Regina as benighted or as a philistine; she supported O'Connor in her habit of art throughout her life—a life during which she lived with Regina for all but five of her thirty-nine years. As Jean Cash states, "With limitations of intellect and personality over which she had little control, Regina Cline O'Connor still contributed significantly to the ultimate success of her brilliant daughter."[149] Sally's dedication of the book, "To Regina Cline O'Connor in gratitude for letting readers come to know her daughter better," is an acknowledgment of Regina's power and that she deserved recognition. *The Habit of Being* reminds us that those who affect an author's "ultimate success" and reputation need not be members of the literati.

Like the two other O'Connor insiders who preceded her, Sally used the occasion of an introduction to shape O'Connor's reputation. By the time that *The Habit of Being* was published, readers were less in need of the kind of biographical portrait offered by Robert Fitzgerald in 1965 or Giroux in 1971. However, like her predecessors, Sally assumed that readers did need a further correcting of O'Connor's reputation, this time mostly through the words of the author herself. Sally argues in her introduction that photographs of O'Connor may be empirically accurate but emotionally false and have affected her reputation in an unfortunate, because misleading, way: "The camera was often as unjust as what was written about her."[150] By analogy, Sally argues that O'Connor's letters reveal not an invalid confined to her farm with her mother but a vivacious person whose joie de vivre informed her existence: "These letters reveal her to have been anything but reclusive by inclination: to have been, on the contrary, notably gregarious. She enjoyed company and sought it, sending warm invitations to her old and new friends to come to Andalusia. Once her inviolable three-hour morning stint of writing was done, she looked for, and throve on, companionship. . . . She participated in the lives of her friends, interested herself in their work, their children, their health, and their adventures" (xi).

Sally also explains her choice of title, another means by which she sought to affect O'Connor's reputation. Telling of a time when O'Connor left a copy of Jacques Maritain's *Art and Scholasticism* at the Fitzgeralds' home, Sally explains that, just as Maritain explored the "habit of art" or "attitude or quality of mind" as "essential to the real artist as talent," O'Connor possessed the "habit of being," defined by Sally as "an excellence not only of action but of interior disposition and activity that increasingly related the object, the being, which specified it, and was itself reflected in what she did and said" (xv)—what might be called, in other academic writing, *habitus*. In simpler terms, Sally argued that O'Connor's life was one of her great artistic creations, and she urged readers to study it—through the unadorned letters—as they would O'Connor's fiction. Perhaps her argument explains why the authorized biography was never completed: the life lived was found, as Sally insisted, in the letters and friendships, not in records of travel or other, more routine components of biographies. Such an idea is much like the one that Giroux shared with Leonard Melfi and Mark Harris when each inquired about becoming O'Connor's authorized biographer.

In January 1979, shortly before *The Habit of Being*'s March publication, Giroux wrote to Regina and enclosed a clipping from *Library Journal*: "The first review is excellent. It's an advance notice and couldn't be better."[151] He assured her that anyone to whom she wanted to send a copy had received one, with a card stating, "Compliments of Regina Cline O'Connor." Also, a few days earlier, he assured Regina of the volume's quality: "I think Sally did an excellent job of editing and that the book, in its final form, gives the reader an accurate and attractive picture of Flannery—especially her sense of humor."[152] As other early reviews were published, Giroux kept sending copies to Regina, noting that he was "particularly pleased with Walter Clemons's reference to you in *Newsweek*" and that, at a publication-day luncheon at the Players Club, "we shall all drink a toast to you in absentia."[153] He also sent her a copy of the book to inscribe for his personal collection; Regina replied to this request and many of Giroux's letters with appreciation. Giroux wanted to assure Regina that she had done right by her daughter in allowing Sally to present her letters to the world. With Sally's biography still under construction, Giroux knew that the bridge to Andalusia could not, under any circumstances, be burned. Nor do his papers suggest that he had anything but respect for Regina.

The reviews of *The Habit of Being* were as universally laudatory as Sally, Giroux, or Regina could have wished. Robert Phillips, in *Commonweal*, urged his readers, "Buy this book, for the rare insight into one of our rarest, and in her time least-appreciated artists."[154] If O'Connor was not, as Phillips claimed, given her critical due while alive, critics were now making up for their collective sin of omission. The review in *Library Journal* that Giroux sent to Regina called the collection "one of the most unique achievements in twentieth-century literature."[155] John R. May, writing in *America*, described it as "one of the finest recent instances of a venerable art form and a major contribution to American letters,"[156] while Richard H. Brodhead, in the *Yale Review*, deemed it the "richest volume of correspondence by an American author to have appeared in many years."[157] Across the Atlantic, Graham Greene (no doubt a sympathetic reader) described the book as "a fascinating collection of letters by a fine American novelist much neglected over here in her lifetime."[158] Writing in the *New York Times*, John Leonard stated, "There hasn't been a better collection of letters since the two-volume set of D. H. Lawrence published by Viking in 1962."[159] His colleague at the *Times*, Richard Gilman, noted early in his *Book Review* assessment that "Byron, Keats, Lawrence, Wilde and Joyce come irresistibly to mind"[160] as one reads O'Connor's letters. And Michael True, writing in the *Chronicle of Higher Education*, called *The Habit of Being* "one of the great collections of letters in American literature, equal in range and quality to those of Hawthorne and Melville and comparable, in what they tell us about the craft of fiction and writing, to the prefaces of Henry James and the notebooks of Henry David Thoreau."[161] In the *Southern Literary Journal*, Melvin J. Friedman questioned this level of praise and noted that "O'Connor herself would probably have been amused and slightly embarrassed by this assertion,"[162] but his was the minority report. Several reviewers drew comparisons between *The Habit of Being* and *The Nabokov-Wilson Letters*, also published that same year,[163] while the *New York Times*'s year-end list of best books included *The Habit of Being* alongside the recently published letters of Lewis Carroll, D. H. Lawrence, and Virginia Woolf.[164] Such comparisons marked another rise in O'Connor's critical clout: no longer was she immediately compared to Caldwell, Williams, or Capote but was now being spoken of, quite casually and earnestly, in the same sentences as the names of the masters she admired. One reviewer even called *The Habit of Being* an exercise in "essential insight and self-confrontation," superior to what he saw in Faulkner's *Collected Letters:* "scrupulously arranged tedium."[165] When Carson McCullers was mentioned in these reviews, it was only to illustrate the gulf between her and O'Connor, as when Friedman quoted a letter in which O'Connor described *Clock Without Hands* as "the worst book I have ever read."[166] The seed Giroux had planted in his introduction to *The Complete Stories* about O'Connor transcending the South had germinated.

Many reviewers spoke of how the letters demonstrated praiseworthy aspects of O'Connor's character, a "country humor and shrewd intelligence backed up by a considerable spiritual toughness."[167] Many reviewers also dwelled on O'Connor's courage as she faced death, adding to a mythology about O'Connor and her illness that still exists today. In *Comparative Literature*, Frank E. Moorer and Richard Macksey praised how the letters reveal O'Connor "fighting the energy-sapping advances of her disease but never currying sympathy,"[168] just as Gilman similarly noted that the letters present O'Connor as "heroic" and "a model of valor."[169] Richard H. Brodhead argued that the letters reveal a woman who did not "permit herself emotions like rage and self-pity";[170] Paul Gray, in *Time*, stated, "She had cause to be bitter but never was."[171] Such sentiments about O'Connor as "an exceptionally valiant woman"[172] were epitomized in the headline above Edmund Fuller's review in the *Wall Street Journal*: "A Gallant Life Amidst Profound Insight."[173] The majority of reviewers also mentioned her sense of humor, love of reading, and humility. Only John F. Desmond, in *World Literature Today*, acknowledged that O'Connor was not a saint but a person: he noted that the letters revealed O'Connor's "love of truth" but also "streaks of intolerance and righteous anger, of literary and religious dogmatism, of tactlessness and insensitivity."[174] However, his was a rare voice in a critical crowd that seemed to hold a tacit agreement to not speak ill of the dead.

Amid the collective enthusiasm for the collection, one notes critics using the occasion of their reviews to correct what they saw as misunderstandings of O'Connor's life and works, especially the idea that she was a recluse, confined to her mother's house and living like a southern Emily Dickinson. Writing in *National Review*, J. O. Tate argued that *The Habit of Being* put to rest the notion of O'Connor's hermitage: "Any lingering canards about O'Connor's isolation, which never were true, must henceforth be gone or be damned."[175] A piece in *Kirkus Reviews* offered a similar observation: "The idea of the spinster lady with lupus living cut off from the world in Milledgeville, Georgia ... is dispelled."[176] Miles Orvell, in the *American Scholar*, noted that the letters prove that "we would be much mistaken to assume that Flannery O'Connor led a life which was either provincial or reclusive"[177]; as John Keates, in the London *Spectator*, noted, "Immobility does not necessarily imply isolation."[178] Such an understanding of O'Connor was urged in *New Catholic World*, in which Helen Ruth Vaughn made the similar point that the "small geography of [O'Connor's] physical life ... in no way circumscribed the vast geography of her mind."[179] Perhaps so many critics (among them Mary Gordon, who wrote of O'Connor's "isolation"[180]) described O'Connor's "seclusion"[181] as a way to account for work that was so strange, so southern, and so Catholic. Much had changed for O'Connor's reputation since *Wise Blood*, but the urge to tease out the secret of how she created her work still remained. Some of O'Connor's admirers routinely dismissed such an urge, as when Paul Granahan began his review by saying he was "always dismayed by the prevailing belief that she was a bizarrely morbid Southerner who hated life in general" and expressed relief that the publication of her letters would "do much to dispel the myth that O'Connor was a sour-tempered and unbalanced individual obsessed with death."[182] Isolation could be, they argued, a geographical fact but was irrelevant to the "true picture": as a reviewer for the *South Carolina Review* stated, "She lived on 'Andalusia,' the family farm just outside of Milledgeville, Georgia, but there is no indication in her letters that she felt isolated. . . . Her correspondence helped prevent any feeling of isolation."[183]

Reviewers' praise of O'Connor's character may have been bolstered by the book's cover art, which featured a phoenix rising from its regenerative flames. Here, too, Sally had a hand, discovering this woodcut while working on *The Habit of Being* at Harvard's Houghton Library and sending a card with its likeness to Giroux, suggesting that he consider it for the cover: "A phoenix, not only appropriate by simply being a bird, but doubly so, considering what F. reveals about her struggle with the first blow of her illness in these new letters now, at twelve years' distance from her death."[184] Giroux found the image a perfect representation of what he valued about O'Connor: a month later, he sent a copy of the proposed cover to Sally, calling it "rather unexpected but I think quite good."[185] While critics would never admit to judging books by their covers, the image of the phoenix, linked with O'Connor's name, may have helped to reinforce the image of O'Connor that her editor and publisher hoped to sustain.

Besides their effusive praise of O'Connor the woman and artist as viewed through her letters, reviewers also praised Sally Fitzgerald's skill as an editor and, more importantly in light of the scuffle with Maryat Lee and her negotiations with Regina, her decision to remain in the background and allow O'Connor to speak for herself. In *The Nation*, Robert B. Shaw praised Sally as an "unobtrusive"[186] editor, while Melvin J. Friedman noted that she had "performed a noteworthy service" by avoiding "the elaborate paraphernalia of the scholarly edition,"[187] praise echoed by Eugene Current-Garcia, who, in *Southern Humanities Review*, noted the "sheer artistry" of Sally's editorial decision to provide only a "minimum of commentary."[188] Less became more, and Sally's silencing of her own voice heightened O'Connor's: Josephine Hendin wrote of O'Connor's voice as heard in the letters and praised Sally for "bringing her back to speak to us again,"[189] much as Janet Varner Gunn, in *American Literature*, noted, "What we have here in this remarkable collection is a Flannery O'Connor who speaks for herself by speaking to others."[190] Richard H. Brodhead described the collection as "the record of a remarkable voice."[191] This vindication of Sally's method surfaces throughout the reviews, as when Paul Gray in *Time* described her editorial work as "an act of model scholarship" because, "When factual information is needed, she gives it succinctly and then stands back."[192] Many reviewers singled out O'Connor's letters to "A." as the best in the collection, suggesting that Sally's battle with Regina to include these highly personal letters was worth the cost.[193] Robert Fitzgerald wrote to Giroux to congratulate him on "the book you and Sally made," stating that he found it "very much like the water of life."[194] In *World Literature Today*, John F. Desmond stated that O'Connor's readers usually "only saw what they wanted to see, not the full reality," but that Sally presented O'Connor in all her "complexity"[195]— a reminder of the "total picture" and "total mosaic" that she and Giroux sought to present through the letters.

Other reviews of *The Habit of Being* contain more praise for Sally, and the praise of an editor's work on such a project may be expected. What emerges as a less expected notion is the idea that *The Habit of Being* was, in many ways, the biography that Sally would never complete. In his *National Review* piece, J. O. Tate assessed the collection with language that any biographer would thrill to hear in a review of his or her work, noting that Sally deserved praise for "producing the broadest and deepest of all the accounts of O'Connor's life and mind."[196] In the *Antioch Review*, Nolan Miller stated that the collection may not "tell us all there is to know" about O'Connor, but "it is improbable that any biographer will ever be able to surpass it. Or dare try."[197] *Kirkus* argued, "These hundreds of letters give O'Connor's tough, funny, careful personality to us more distinctly and movingly than any biography probably would,"[198] while John R. May wisely described the collection as one superior even to a hypothetical autobiography, since it "lacks a self-conscious design."[199] May continued, "Together with Robert Fitzgerald's brief biographical introduction to *Everything That Rises Must Converge*, it should satisfy, too, our need for a biography,"[200] while, in the *American Spectator*, Miles Orvell wrote, "We have something better than the single view of any biographer: a collection of O'Connor letters that adds up to a complex self-portrait, a volume that should markedly enrich our understanding of a writer whose reputation has continued to grow since her death in 1964."[201] And, in both *Ms.* and *Maclean's*, reviewers quoted O'Connor's stricture about "lives spent between the house and the chicken yard" not providing compelling biographical material and noted, "Her own letters contradict her,"[202] since the collection could be read as "the biography that O'Connor thought could never be."[203] Many readers of this time knew that Sally was working on the authorized biography, but their praise of her editing argued against the need for a conventional account of O'Connor's formative years and artistic development.

As time passed, Giroux received many inquires about the status of Sally's project. In a 1985 letter, he wrote that Sally's authorized biography was "nearing completion" and he hoped to see it published in 1986.[204] When he was asked in 1990 by the theologian and translator Elmer O'Brien when and if Sally's biography was going to be published, Giroux described Sally as a "perfectionist" but assured O'Brien that she was "hard at work on it" and that "When it is ready, I'm confident it will be a good book."[205] Two years later, Giroux wrote the biographer Deborah Baker that Sally had been working on the book for almost ten years and that "the first draft has been completed."[206] Despite his enthusiasm for the project (and his covering for Sally's delays), Giroux found that Sally had made herself obsolete by doing what she intended: letting O'Connor speak for herself through her letters to the world—a world that did, unlike Dickinson's, write to her.

The Habit of Being was awarded a National Book Critics Circle Award for 1979; as was the case with the National Book Award, a work by O'Connor was honored by a slight bending of the rules. The NBCC Awards, established in 1974, sought to honor work in fiction, nonfiction, poetry, and criticism; the categories have since expanded to include biography and autobiography. At the time of *The Habit of Being*'s release, however, the judges—for the first time—bestowed a Board Award on O'Connor's total work, capped by *The Habit of Being*.[207] Sally accepted the award for O'Connor, noting in her speech the importance of "that indomitable survivor," Regina, and the guidance and enthusiasm of Giroux, who gave O'Connor "the leeway and support she needed while she was writing, and who has continued to serve her well since she had to stop."[208] Her speech crystalized O'Connor's reputation when Sally mentioned O'Connor's character and what she valued:

> In writing all these letters, over the years, Flannery O'Connor didn't mean to tell us what she was like. She didn't think it would matter. Her attention was directed to the given addressee and the subject at hand. What she did think would matter was her fiction, and whether or not *that* was alive, and well thought of. The honor you are showing her today, more than fifteen years after her death, is proof enough that it was, and is. But what she was like turns out to matter, too, as witnessed by what you say of the place her letters hold in the body of work she left us.[209]

O'Connor was concerned not with her reputation, but her work's, a concern that Sally argued was answered by this posthumous recognition and that countered the once-threatening assumptions of Regina. Worth noting here is that all the correspondence, quoted and unquoted here, between Sally and Giroux—like that between anyone connected to this part of O'Connor's posthumous career—never mentions any financial rewards for publishing *The Complete Stories* or *The Habit of Being*. Their editorial work was, of course, motivated by the fact that critical approval would lead to sales, but also the desire to honor their friend by sharing their private understandings of her with the public.

Chapter 5

Adaptation and Reputation

John Huston's *Wise Blood*

In 1968 Robert Giroux wrote Robert Fitzgerald about a request he had received from the actor Tony Randall, who sought to mount a film production of "The Artificial Nigger." Randall was not yet branded as Felix Unger, but his reputation as history teacher Harvey Weskit in *Mr. Peepers* had taken root, causing Giroux to comment, "I think it would be a miracle for *anyone* to make a good movie of 'The Artificial Nigger,' let alone Tony Randall."[1] The project never materialized, but Giroux's response reflects a number of issues regarding the ways in which the adaptation of an author's works can affect his or her reputation. First, Giroux's calling such an adaptation a "miracle" emphasizes his and others' belief that certain texts are simply untranslatable into other media, a belief that may strike one of O'Connor's readers as reasonable: the story climaxes in pages of interior action, where Mr. Head feels the "action of mercy" working on him as he stands as still as the statue upon which he gazes. As Joy Gould Boyum notes in *Double Exposure: Fiction into Film*, "If one were to accept traditional notions of what is possible for the screen, the work of Flannery O'Connor might seem utterly, unequivocally unfilmable."[2] Second, Giroux's dismissive "let alone Tony Randall" comes from the assumption that decisions involving any production will be evaluated according to how well the viewer thinks the adaptation has captured the spirit of the original. Of course, there have been many artists whose adaptations have outshone their sources, Hitchcock being the most notable example. But adaptation, like everything else in the film industry, is a bet against very difficult odds.

Randall was one of many who sought permission to adapt O'Connor's work. Amateurs and professionals alike frequently asked O'Connor's agent, Elizabeth McKee, for her legal blessings. She was asked to grant film rights to "A Good Man Is Hard to Find," "The Life You Save May Be Your Own," and *A Memoir of Mary Ann*, Hungarian television rights for "The Comforts of Home," and theatrical rights to "Good Country People." To all these requests and many others, McKee referred the writers to Regina (who had final say) but often wrote about them to Giroux, who reassured her in counseling Regina to refuse permission.[3] Those in O'Connor's inner circle assumed that her work should remain wholly literary and not become sullied by contact with any amateur screenwriters or more powerful players, such as Robert E. Jiras, a producer who sought to secure the rights to "The River" and sell them to the highest bidder.[4]

However, Giroux, McKee, and Regina did relent, and did so enthusiastically, when a figure from O'Connor's past sought to bring his vision of *Wise Blood* and "O'Connor country" to the big screen. In the early 1970s, Michael Fitzgerald— the oldest son of Robert and Sally—attempted to make a name for himself as a Hollywood producer. Like so many others, however, he eventually found his imagined career an example of the triumph of hope over experience. "It was the usual story in Hollywood," he explained regarding his many false starts and lack of progress.[5] Eventually, he decided that if he were going to expend effort and money making a film, he would make one that he found interesting from start to finish. Fitzgerald wanted to produce a film that would, in his words, give his audience "a jolt" and eventually decided on the source material that could produce such an effect: "Now what do I pick? If I can actually get it made, it'll be so different from anything else that people will be compelled to pay attention to it. And so different from anything else that I will be able to attract talented people to help in the making of it. And suddenly, Flannery sprang back into my memory."[6] O'Connor had babysat Michael Fitzgerald and his brother, Benedict, when she stayed at his parents' Connecticut home and finished *Wise Blood*. But the aspiring producer claimed this neat family tie was secondary in importance to the force of O'Connor's reputation as someone whose work was "so different from anything else" and who could supply the necessary "jolt" to both an audience and Fitzgerald's career. Her reputation had, according to Fitzgerald, prompted him to embark upon his adaptation of *Wise Blood*, an adaptation endorsed by Giroux, McKee, and Regina.

Next on the list of insiders, Fitzgerald determined to midwife O'Connor's work between author and public. But the insider was not alone: others joined him, such as his brother, Benedict, who co-wrote the screenplay, and Sally, who dressed both the actors and the sets. (Benedict would continue to write screen adaptations for television and co-wrote the screenplay for *The Passion of the Christ*.) As with the publication of and introductions to *Everything That Rises Must Converge* and *The Complete Stories*, a member of O'Connor's inner circle attempted to bring her work before a larger audience and shape the ways in which her work would be received. Eight years after *The Complete Stories* and fifteen years after her death, elements of her reputation would resurface and be reinforced as critics responded to a "third edition" of *Wise Blood*, this time with John Huston complicating its reception by virtue of his own artistry and attitude toward O'Connor's concerns.

The continuing reputations of Huston and O'Connor might seem to suggest an insurmountable incompatibility and a doomed partnership. By the time *Wise Blood* went into production in 1979, Huston was well known for a body of work (and personal life) that suggested a dismissal of all that O'Connor, quite literally, held sacred. While filming *The Bible: In the Beginning* in 1966, Huston remarked:

> Every day I'm being asked if I am a believer and I answer I have nothing in common with Cecil B. DeMille. Actually, I find it foolishly impudent to speculate on the existence of any kind of God. We know the world was created and that it continually creates itself. I don't think about those things, I'm only interested in what's under my nose. Also, I believe that whatever man erects, builds and creates has a religious meaning. A painter, when he paints, is religious. The only religion I can believe in is creativity. I'm interested in the Bible as a universal myth, as a prop for numerous legends. It's a collective creation of humanity, destined to solve, provisionally and in the form of fables, a number of mysteries too disquieting to contemplate for a nonscientific era.[7]

However, two aspects of Huston's reputation as a director made him a desirable choice for the brothers Fitzgerald. The first was his long record of skillfully adapting novels into film. Since his first feature—*The Maltese Falcon* in 1941— Huston had consistently demonstrated profound respect for his source material. In a review of *Wise Blood*, Vincent Canby noted, "Movies do many things, but they don't honor the written word,"[8] a rule to which Huston's work often proved the exception. Almost all his films were adaptations of previously published fiction or previously produced plays, and he showed a remarkable ability to translate different genres, such as pulp fiction (*The Maltese Falcon, The Asphalt Jungle*), adventure yarns (*The Treasure of the Sierra Madre, The African Queen*), and moody character studies (*The Night of the Iguana, Reflections in a Golden Eye*) into successful films. Huston also never shied away from more highbrow literary sources, such as *The Red Badge of Courage* and *The Man Who Would Be King*; as David Thomson noted, Huston showed a "Selznick-like urge to cover the respectable literary waterfront."[9] And while *Moby-Dick* and *The Bible* may be his less-impressive adaptations, he had a reputation as a director who never sought to modify or "improve" his source material. As he said of *The Maltese Falcon* in particular and adaptation in general, "You simply take two copies of the book, paste the pages, and cross out what you don't like."[10]

Huston's reputation also made him desirable to the Fitzgeralds for his straightforward shooting style, which one critic aptly described as "unassuming naturalism."[11] Despite his monumental ego and skill at self-promotion, Huston never made himself the unseen star of his films or engaged in the kind of self-reflexive camerawork that reminds viewers that they are in the director's hands. As Benedict Fitzgerald noted, such a style was crucial to an adaptation of *Wise Blood* because it reflected O'Connor's own directness of vision: "We were lucky to have thought of John Huston. There were others that we were considering but they would have been so taken by the allegorical nature of the storytelling—by either what they would have considered the grotesque or by the allegory itself—that it would not have been a story told the way good stories are told: very straightforward. John had never done anything but. He just liked to tell the story the way it was."[12] Huston's invisible—as opposed to heavy—hand was noted by some of the film's original reviewers, as when John Simon noted that Huston had not "indulged himself in directorial liberties"[13] or when Joy Gould Boyum noted that Huston's camera "never underscores, never labors and never exploits."[14] If the Fitzgeralds were going to entrust *Wise Blood* to a director, they would only trust one who would "honor the word" by not attempting to change the manner in which O'Connor presented her chosen issues. Whether he believed in Christ was not as important as whether he believed in O'Connor.

Huston shot *Wise Blood* in Macon, Georgia, and—like everyone else involved in the production—worked for minimum salary.[15] With its budget of less than two million dollars (as opposed to eight million for his previous film, *The Man Who Would Be King*) and use of locals in many supporting roles, *Wise Blood*, like the novel upon which it was based, prompted questions about its marketability and wide appeal. The film premiered at Cannes and was then shown at the New York Film Festival where it received enthusiastic reviews. However, no major distributor offered to market it or manage its broad theatrical release: Archer Winsten (in the *New York Post*) described the film as "an artistic triumph that commercial distributors were slow to grab when it first surfaced at the Film Festival. They wouldn't even grab when heavy crix said 'ooh-la-la' with laurel wreaths."[16] Writing in the *Village Voice*, Andrew Sarris called *Wise Blood* "precisely the kind of property that would have made the late Louis B. Mayer turn over in his grave"[17] and elsewhere predicted, "It's doubtful that this film will find a mass audience."[18] Huston himself acknowledged, "It was hardly the sort of thing to attract investors."[19] Eventually, New Line Cinema—then a fledgling distributor of art-house films—bought the distribution rights, prompting a reporter for *Premiere* to note that even a "front page rave in *Le Monde*" could not woo the Hollywood power brokers; the reporter also quoted Michael Fitzgerald as being "baffled by the response of the majors," saying, "I don't quite understand why . . . but they're terrified of it."[20] Fitzgerald later noted that distributors regarded it as "the least commercial movie ever made."[21]

However, anyone familiar with O'Connor's reputation—as Fitzgerald, despite his presumed perplexity, surely was—could identify the source of that terror: O'Connor's work was financially risky because it was morally so. Taking O'Connor seriously entailed examining, or at least entertaining, her assumptions about the gulf between God and man, a gulf into which theatergoers and Hollywood studios were never eager to peer. Writing in *Time*, Frank Rich noted, "It is not surprising that independent producers, rather than a Hollywood studio, took the considerable risk of financing the project."[22] *Variety* described the film as "downbeat" and one "needing hard sell due to its ambivalent treatment of the kinky religious scene, though it does give some insight into the extension of these loner fanatics into sects."[23] The critic, of course, assumes that Huston was making an exposé about cults, rather than telling the story of a man whose spiritual intuition—his wise blood—leads him to a truth beyond the walls of any church. In a laudatory review, David Ansen described the film as "determinedly uningratiating"[24] to its viewers, a characteristic that, of course, would not prompt distributors to come calling. Similarly, *Box Office* advised its industry readers that the "excellent performances" and the "low-level documentary style photography make this one of the best pictures in Huston's long career—but unfortunately not the most commercial."[25] Rex Reed, however, regarded the film's lack of commercial appeal as a badge of artistic honor, stating, "*Wise Blood* makes no bid for box-office sweepstakes. It looks like it was made by people with no idea of what commercial gimmicks are," calling this "unusually welcome" lack of gimmickry "a strength."[26]

All these remarks about O'Connor's lack of marketability call to mind Rinehart editor John Selby's feud with O'Connor over the first nine chapters of *Wise Blood*, when he sought (in O'Connor's words) to "train it into a conventional novel."[27] As O'Connor wrote of the book to Elizabeth McKee in the summer of 1948, "I cannot really believe they will want the finished thing."[28] O'Connor anticipated the novel's lack of commercial appeal but wanted it to be published by a sympathetic, although not necessarily empathetic, house: "I want mainly to be where they take the book as I write it."[29] The same principle applied to the Fitzgeralds and Huston, who never sought to train the source material into a conventional film. Doing so would have betrayed what drew them to O'Connor and also traduced Huston's method of not placing too many of his fingerprints on his source material.

The press kit provided to the first audiences at the New York Film Festival reflects O'Connor's reputation in 1979 as well as the means by which Fitzgerald and his co-producer (his wife, Kathy) attempted to present an accessible version of O'Connor's work to a moviegoing public. After beginning with the puffery one would predict in a press kit ("This chilling adaptation of Flannery O'Connor's brilliant first novel returns director John Huston to the hardheaded style of *Fat City*"[30]), the Fitzgeralds and their publicity team offered six quotations by O'Connor on a separate page headed, "Author Flannery O'Connor on *Wise Blood* and Life." The first of these, taken from a letter concerning *The Violent Bear It Away*, seems intended to disarm the skeptics who had pigeonholed O'Connor as a "religious fanatic": "I suppose a book like mine attracts all the lunatics."[31] Another reflects the producers' desire to highlight O'Connor's humor, however dark: "In my own experience, everything funny I have written is more terrible than it is funny, or only funny because it is terrible, or only terrible because it is funny."[32] The most important quotation, however, is from a letter to John Hawkes indicating how the producers wanted their viewers to regard Motes's struggle and eventual self-mutilation. It contains what they viewed as the central issue of the film, one that the film's leading man had debated with Huston and that the critics would soon debate with one another: "The religion of the South is a do-it-yourself religion, something which I as a Catholic find painful and touching and grimly comic. It's full of unconscious pride that lands them in all sorts of ridiculous religious predicaments. They have nothing to correct their practical heresies and so they work them out dramatically."[33] O'Connor dramatizes Motes's wise blood as only he can imagine: by "working it out dramatically" and blinding himself. As Michael Fitzgerald stated with some degree of superiority, "If Haze were an educated person, he might have joined a monastery. But he's a hillbilly and he goes all the way as he can.... When he finds the truth in the last way he expects to find it, he goes all the way with what he could do."[34]

The last of the press kit's quotations was taken from the same letter to Hawkes and was included by the producers to imply that Motes's struggle was not born of madness or fanaticism, but a desire to accept as truth what the world seemed to mock: "My gravest concern is always the conflict between an attraction for the Holy and the disbelief in it we breathe with the air of the times."[35] Such conflict was acknowledged by those critics who viewed Motes in a sympathetic light but was wholly disregarded by others, who viewed Motes as

a fool or fanatic for acting on the promptings of his "attraction for the holy"—
his wise blood. The remainder of the press kit offered a biography of Huston in
which *Wise Blood* was described as "steeped in rural mysticism" and the result of
O'Connor's "vivid and baroquely imaginative world." The absence of the adjective "grotesque" is surely no accident; "baroquely imaginative" substitutes for
"grotesque" and sheds, with its tone of admiration, a light of critical favor on
what was once viewed as O'Connor's works' defining characteristic. The Fitzgeralds knew that if Motes repulsed the viewers or was viewed as a caricature
from the Bible Belt, *Wise Blood* would be much less effective and a betrayal of
O'Connor's intentions. It would be a film grounded in mockery instead of the
uneasy empathy that O'Connor sought to evoke.

Many critics responded to the film in ways that the Fitzgeralds and Huston
had hoped. Of all the original reviewers, Vincent Canby, writing in the *New
York Times*, offered the most enthusiastic praise, calling *Wise Blood* "one of John
Huston's most original, most stunning movies" that proved the aging director
to be "in his top form."[36] In a 2008 interview, Michael Fitzgerald noted, "The
reviews from all over the world were extraordinary. I don't think people had
quite seen anything like this. And most people were not familiar with Flannery O'Connor and so the film got a staggering amount of attention at Cannes
and was bought all over the world."[37] Fitzgerald's claims here are reinforced
by Huston's having received a standing ovation after the film's screening at
Cannes,[38] although Huston's age and résumé surely boosted the reception; the
film was frequently praised for its decidedly un-Hollywood subject matter and
the age of its director as much as any specific elements. For example, Frank
Rich called it "the most eccentric American movie in years,"[39] and Jack Kroll,
in *Newsweek*, described it as "Huston's 34th film and one of his best," adding, "to
do such work at 73 is the mark of some kind of a heroic figure."[40] Tim Pulleine
in *Sight and Sound* called it "the work of an old master but scarcely of an old
man,"[41] and David Ansen ended his *Newsweek* review by describing *Wise Blood*
as "further confirmation that Huston is still in his prime."[42] Rob Edelman in
Films in Review labeled it "an eerie, melancholy little film about eerie, melancholy little people,"[43] using "little" as large praise in an era that had seen the
birth of the blockbuster with *Jaws* (1975), *Star Wars* (1977), *Superman* (1978), and
Rocky II (1979). Critical resistance to what seemed a new commercialism—and
confirmation of what Fitzgerald called the distributors' "terror" at optioning
a film such as this—were found in reviews such as Edelman's, in which he
praised Huston as "concerned not with pointlessly splashing millions of dollars
across the screen but with exposing his audience to ideas, emotions, human

beings and human frailties,"[44] or in the headline of a review that read, "'Wise Blood' is a low-budget miracle."[45] The work's lack of mass appeal bestowed other kinds of clout upon it.

Like many of the novel's original readers, some critics found themselves unable to identify just what they had seen or to articulate O'Connor's thematic concerns. Even the sympathetic Roger Angell, in his generally laudatory review for the *New Yorker*, sounded like Polonius as he admitted to being "startled" by his "attachment to a work that may be a broad-scaled holy-picaresque farce, or a Southern-regional historical urban-pastoral, or perhaps a plain metaphysical tragedy."[46] Angell's description recalls the tongue-tied reviewers of the novel, who argued that O'Connor's "farce gets in the way of her satire and will not support the full implications of her allegory"[47] or others who simply called the novel "an obscure piece of writing"[48] and "not a book for casual reading."[49] Some of the film's reviewers were simply inaccurate, resorting to prepackaged phrases and assumptions about the South to help them articulate what had eluded them, as when Archer Winsten, in the *New York Post*, stated, "It's not easy to think that it can be an enjoyable entertainment, unless you dote on religious fanaticism, fools, and religious mania,"[50] recalling the critics who offhandedly (and incorrectly) described the novel as a "satire" of "evangelical preachers with banjo quartets, uniforms, concert soloists, and cheap sensationalism."[51]

The film's reviews reveal the watchword "grotesque" as still current and used to account for (and sometimes belittle) what baffled or disturbed those asked to take Huston's film and O'Connor's characters seriously. Stanley Kauffmann, for example, dismissed the film as too much akin to Huston's *Night of the Iguana* and *Reflections in a Golden Eye*: "Now it's Southern grotesque time again, and again Huston has fumbled."[52] "Grotesque" was, to Kauffmann, a way to easily contain and dismiss O'Connor's art. Philip French, in the London *Observer*, added the runner-up of equally generic labels when he described the film as "a grotesque collection of Southern gothic characters involved in the 'religion business.'"[53] However, by now, almost thirty years after the novel's publication, the watchword was not always pejorative. For example, in *The Nation*, Robert Hatch observed, "The film, like the book, is wildly grotesque" but also called it a "triumph," arguing, "The humor is often grotesque, but we are startled at how often we laugh at this comedy of fanaticism and despair."[54] (Hatch also compared Huston's film to *The Tin Drum*, another adaptation of a work that startled many readers and gave them the kind of "jolt" of which Michael Fitzgerald spoke.) In a glowing review for the *Wall Street Journal*, Joy Gould Boyum described Motes as a "grotesquely comical contradiction" and praised Huston for re-creating "the grotesque imagery and internal logic of O'Connor's phantasmagoric parable."[55] David Ansen used the term as wholly complimentary, stating, "*Wise Blood*, a virulently comic, grotesquely unforgettable adaptation of Flannery O'Connor's celebrated novel of customized redneck religion and redemption, is as strange and original a movie as Huston has ever made."[56] "Grotesque" had evolved along with critics' understanding of O'Connor's art.

Ansen's phrase "redneck religion" raises the issue of how critics responded to O'Connor's southern roots. Despite Giroux's success in making her an "American" author, many critics still viewed O'Connor as something of a regionalist reporter and Huston as a man with a hidden camera, offering dispatches from the Sahara of the Bozart. Writing in *New York* magazine, David Denby resorted to hyperbole while stating that the film was set in "the familiar, Jesus-haunted South, where a ranting prophet, saint, or con man stands on every corner"[57]—a tired formula as laden with assumptions about the South as any to be found in the history of O'Connor's reception. John Simon echoed these assumptions when he, in the same matter-of-fact tone found in many such remarks, stated that the film portrayed "the phenomena that once almost blanketed the South and still lives in many a not-so-isolated pocket."[58] Often critics were so devoted to their assumptions about the South that they told the film what it meant, rather than vice versa. For example, Archer Winsten in the *New York Post* declared that Huston's "amalgam of extreme religiosity, sex, unquestioning belief" presents "a curiously vibrant portrait, one that any student of the South can recognize."[59] But Winsten's desire to mock the hicks interfered with his judgment, for surely Hazel Motes is far from an example of "unquestioning belief." Frank Rich praised Huston for making what he assumed was an exposé: "The film's settings," he wrote, "are glutted with eclectic religious artifacts and the documentary details of the backwater South."[60]

Critics spoke of "the South" (as opposed to the actual South) casually and unquestioningly; indeed, several important critics wrote as if the film's production design, complemented by Huston's straightforward shooting style, made *Wise Blood* more documentary than drama. For example, *New West* praised Huston for taking his viewers "into a world we've rarely seen on film—the seedy South of obsessed religious evangelists and their pathetic prey,"[61] while a blurb regarding the 1986 video release of the film described it as "centered on the gripping power of Bible Belt fundamentalism."[62] Again, preconceptions trumped critical judgment: Motes is far from a "religious evangelist," and the power that grips Motes exhibits the forms, but not the content, of what one would label "fundamentalism." As for "pathetic prey," Motes's and Hawks's troubles arise from their very *lack* of anyone to gull: no one will heed them. The London *Observer* spoke as if Huston had reported on-location from what it called "Billy Graham country" where "religion and guilt pump in the blood"[63]; Robert Asahina in the *New Leader* described Motes's quest as the natural result of his mailing address, stating that the film depicted "the pathetic attempts" of Motes to "find some comfort in the empty universe of the small-town South."[64] *Variety* described the characters as "evangelistic off-shoots" and "overzealous religious preachers from the deep South" (the South mentioned is almost always "deep") who "run the gamut from the dedicated to the false to the almost maniacally obsessed,"[65] an idea reinforced by Howard Kissel's remark that the characters are "all, in the great Southern tradition, obsessed."[66]

Perhaps the clearest example of a critic's assumptions about the South affecting his or her evaluation of the film was found in the *New York Daily News*, where Kathleen Carroll praised Huston for creating a South more like the one she imagined than the one described by O'Connor: "Huston has more than done his part by capturing just right the sleazy Southern atmosphere and recreating the novel's Bible Belt setting. . . . *Wise Blood* presents a scathing vision of the South as a land of lost souls and religious addicts who are quick to latch on to anyone who even looks like a preacher."[67] However, according to O'Connor and her church, the land of lost souls extends far beyond the Mason-Dixon line, and the characters of *Wise Blood* are not so gullible: part of Motes's frustration is that no one is quick to "latch on" to him besides his sole disciple, the idiot Enoch Emery. *Wise Blood*, both on paper and celluloid, is much less a scathing vision of a place than of a spiritual condition. But such larger thematic (and even dramatic) concerns were not as important to some critics as seeing exactly what they wanted to see in the film, as if the screen were a means of reflecting back their assumptions about the South and those who lived there. The critical attitudes here call to mind O'Connor's remark, "Anything that comes out of the South is going to be called grotesque by the northern reader, unless it is grotesque, in which case it is going to be called realistic."[68] In the context of the reception of Huston's film, her words ring prophetic, as critics frequently praised Huston's "realism." That Huston shot the film on location and filled minor roles with local, Macon players surely added to the "realism" for which he was praised, but the general tenor of the remarks about his vision of Taulkingham suggests that critics were eager to praise as "realism" anything that stroked their preconceptions.

Much of the specific praise Huston enjoyed had to do with the degree to which he had successfully appropriated O'Connor's thematic concerns and artistic performance and how, in the words of one reviewer, "the essence of the book blazes from the film."[69] One delightful irony of the language lay in critics' use of religiously charged language when discussing Huston's artistry in bringing the story of a would-be atheist to the screen. Some spoke of Huston as having created "a remarkably faithful"[70] adaptation of the novel, of the "reverent care"[71] of Huston and his "reverent adaptation,"[72] of the novel having been "translated with fidelity"[73] by Benedict Fitzgerald, and of Huston's having been "remarkably faithful"[74] to O'Connor's characters. Kathleen Carroll epitomized this trend of resorting to the language of God to articulate the work of man: "John Huston's film interpretation of Flannery O'Connor's *Wise Blood* must be considered something of a miracle."[75]

But what does it mean to call an adaptation "faithful"—and what was so "miraculous" about Huston's film in terms of how he appropriated O'Connor's art for a moviegoing audience? What led many critics to concur with Rob Baker in the *Soho News*, who called the film so "wonderfully true to the spirit and vision of the writer" that "it should serve as a model for similar literary adaptations in the future"?[76] And, ultimately, how did Huston's film play upon O'Connor's reputation at the time as well as suggest new directions it might take as a wider audience encountered Hazel Motes?

Part of the critical enthusiasm resulted from the generally low expectations that accompanied any attempt to adapt imaginative and original literature (as opposed to genre fiction) into film. In her essay included in the Criterion DVD edition of the film, former PEN American president Francine Prose articulates this general assumption about the broken bridges between the library and the movie-house:

> Novelists learn not to expect too much when their books are made into movies. Obviously, great fiction has been turned into great cinema, but the dents and scrapes that so many classics have sustained on the rocky road from the page to the screen have convinced most writers that the odds of being purely thrilled by the movies made from their books are only slightly better than the odds of winning big in Las Vegas.[77]

Such an assumption helps explain the general enthusiasm for Huston's film, an assumption reflected in the title of Vincent Canby's second review: "Many Try, But *Wise Blood* Succeeds."[78] Specifically, however, the critical praise often had to do with matters relating to Huston's own artistic habit of respecting his source material. In a 1984 interview, he called *Wise Blood* "a wonderful and fascinating book"; when complimented on the striking combination of styles and moods in the film, he replied, "That all comes from Flannery O'Connor. Many writers that we know are sometimes funny, sometimes awful, sometimes strange, but she could be all three at the same time."[79] *Wise Blood* worked on film because, despite their widely divergent views on spiritual matters, Huston and O'Connor both had—artistically—wise blood, and neither was afraid of presenting strange or unlikable characters *in extremis*, a technique that Huston would repeat in his next film, *Under the Volcano*. Huston honored the word of *Wise Blood* by never attempting to train it into a conventional film, unlike John Selby who had wanted to train it into a conventional novel. He could accept O'Connor's work without needing to contain it—although his original ideas about Motes's fate underwent a significant shift. Critics called *Wise Blood* "hardly your typical American movie,"[80] "resembling no other movie that I can recall,"[81] and "not neat by usual movie standards."[82] O'Connor's unconventionality seemed perfectly suited to Huston's own, and this element of her reputation was reflected in a *Film Comment* review by James McCourt, who called Huston's *Wise Blood* "something like a re-creation of the real Flannery O'Connor's famous unnatural two-headed chicken, with one real head and one made out of wax and stuck on with crazy glue."[83] The actual backward-walking chicken resurfaced as a mythical two-headed one and a means to account for both O'Connor's and Huston's unconventionality.

A few critics, however, argued that Huston was not O'Connoresque enough, as when David Sterrit in the *Christian Science Monitor* pointed to the folksy banjo music as an example of how Huston tried to deal in black comedy "but never [got] past light blue."[84] Others faulted what they saw as Huston's short shrift to the character of Enoch Emery, whom Geoffrey Newell-Smith called "little more than a poor simpleton,"[85] while Robert Asahina argued that the compression of Enoch Emery's scenes in the film "unbalances the narrative."[86] Similarly, in *Sight and Sound*, Tim Pulleine argued that "the briefer treatment afforded [Emery] in the movie paradoxically lends his connection to the story a literary overtone."[87] But these complaints were exceptions to the general praise of Huston's fidelity.

What might strike a reader as surprising in a discussion of how well Huston adapted O'Connor's novel was that not every critic viewed fidelity to the written word as an occasion for praise. While critics such as Michael Tarantino in *Film Quarterly* called *Wise Blood* a success because Huston's treatment of the novel met the "unique"[88] demands of the cinema, Stanley Kauffmann expressed his amazement at the Fitzgeralds and Huston's thinking that "honoring the word" would result in a successful adaptation: "They thought that (near) fidelity to the story and the dialogue would in itself recreate the book. It doesn't, of course. What we get are the data of the book: a chamber of horrors and a mass of unexplained behavior."[89] Roger Angell praised Huston for capturing O'Connor's idiom but faulted him for failing to overcome other challenges of adaptation: "I wish the Fitzgeralds had sometimes seen fit to invent more dialogue or some business of their own that would give the members of their extremely capable cast a chance to play together in a more useful, interpretive dramatic form, instead of pursuing their lonely lines of scam or vision in such perfect, cuckoo isolation."[90] But both Kauffmann and Angell seemed to be asking for what the film could not—perhaps should not—give: built-in Cliff's Notes to make the characters' actions more understandable or flesh out their weirdness into more recognizable characteristics. More recently, Jeffrey Meyers, in his 2011 biography, faulted Huston for even trying to bring *Wise Blood* to the screen: "He did a fair amount of work on the script and, ever faithful to the author, preferred to use her dialogue whenever possible and squeeze every word out of the text. But the final script was too unrelentingly faithful. . . . It succeeded in translating the bizarre and disturbing events of the novel into film, but its episodes of black comedy failed to lighten the bleak tone or mitigate the hero's absurd tragedy."[91]

This notion that a director can be too faithful to his source material—too devoted an acolyte—is one that still informs ways we think about issues of film adaptation. As Alan Yuhas recently stated in a *Guardian* piece about Baz Lurhmann's 2013 adaptation of *The Great Gatsby*, "Countless BBC and PBS adaptations of Jane Austen and Charles Dickens have fallen into the trap of fidelity; they're well acted, well produced and constantly remind you that you should be reading the original instead. These are literal translations, made leaden by detail—costumes, accents and affectations—full of footnotes for the scholars and superfans."[92] The director may thus seem damned if he does and damned if he doesn't: including all of Enoch Emery's scenes and actions would satisfy those who found his presence in the film too insubstantial, but doing so would have caused other critics to complain that the scenes detracted from the centrality of Motes's struggles. The critical divide over the film is seen in representative examples: Harold Clurman thought that Huston's film "corresponds to the nature of the writer's work"[93] while Andrew Sarris used the issue of Huston's fidelity to O'Connor to offer what seems, at best, a tempered compliment: "Huston has been remarkably faithful to characters of such emotional, physical, and social grotesqueness that they would have made the old Hollywood moguls choke on their chicken soup and homilies. . . . [But] I am not sure that Flannery O'Connor's vivid gargoyles belong on a movie screen."[94]

Beside the debate over whether Huston's fidelity was a triumph or liability lay the previously examined one about how different audiences responded to O'Connor's work in general. Joy Gould Boyum argues that the director is less of an author than—crucially, for our purposes—a reader: "The simple fact is that an adaptation always includes not only a reference to the literary work on which it's based, but also a reading of it—and a reading which will strike us as persuasive and apt or seem to us reductive, even false. And here, I think, we've come to the only meaningful way to speak of a film's 'fidelity': in relation to the quality of its implicit interpretation of its source."[95] Huston's "implicit interpretation" of O'Connor's novel recalls the previous discussion of her two authorial audiences: the "genuine" readers who accepted the mysteries found in her work and the resistant "ironic" ones whom she imagined refuting the spiritual foundations of her fiction. How Huston read O'Connor and how critics responded to *his* reading of *Wise Blood* reflect the state of O'Connor's reputation at this time as well as the ways in which these two audiences (who had debated the meaning of *The Violent Bear It Away*) were still at odds.

The scene in Huston's film that marks the continuing and representative split between O'Connor's genuine and ironic audiences is the climactic event of Motes's blinding himself with quicklime. The genuine reading of such an event holds that Motes, like Oedipus, punishes himself for his figurative blindness by blinding himself literally and serves a penance for denying the existence of sin (with the prostitute Leora Watts and near-nymphet Sabbath Lily Hawks) by the mortification of his flesh. But the need for such atonement is beyond the grasp of his pragmatic landlady:

> "Mr. Motes," she said that day, when he was in her kitchen eating his dinner, "what do you walk on rocks for?"
> "To pay," he said in a harsh voice.
> "Pay for what?"
> "It don't make any difference for what," he said. "I'm paying."
> "But what have you got to show that you're paying for?" she persisted.
> "Mind your business," he said rudely. "You can't see."[96]

Their conversation about Motes's other form of penance (wrapping barbed wire around his torso) reveals the same opposing attitudes toward the need for redemption:

> "What do you do it for?"
> "I'm not clean," he said.

She stood staring at him, unmindful of the broken dishes at her feet. "I know it," she said after a minute, "you got blood on that night shirt and on the bed. You ought to get you a washwoman . . ."

"That's not the kind of clean," he said.

"There's only one kind of clean, Mr. Motes," she muttered.[97]

These exchanges push the reader toward a genuine reading of Motes's penitential blindness, a reading that O'Connor spoke of in a letter to John Hawkes about how an understanding of the southern "do-it-yourself religion"[98] helped explain why a man like Motes would engage in such shocking behavior:

There are some of us who have to pay for our faith every step of the way and who have to work out dramatically what it would be like without it and if being without it would be ultimately possible or not. I can't allow any of my characters, in a novel anyway, to stop in some halfway position. This doubtless comes from a Catholic education and a Catholic sense of history—everything works toward it or away from it, everything is ultimately saved or lost. Haze is saved by virtue of having wise blood; it's too wise for him to ultimately deny Christ. Wise blood has to be these people's means of grace—they have no sacraments.[99]

O'Connor's art in general reflects this position: characters such as Tarwater, Mrs. Turpin, and the grandmother in "A Good Man Is Hard to Find" experience the action of grace by nonsacramental means and ones equally as unsentimental and shocking as those experienced by Motes. Without sacraments or the Catholic Church, only their own wise blood can move them, however slowly or painfully in their "do-it-yourself" manner, toward salvation.

As members of the genuine authorial audience, many of Huston's critics did read Motes's blindness as an example of his attempt to achieve grace through his own do-it-himself means: Joy Gould Boyum noted in her review that "Haze succumbs to his Christian belief, paying penance for his heresy by committing frightening acts of self-martyrdom,"[100] while David Denby told his readers that Motes "closely works his way to a pitiable but authentic martyrdom."[101] Other critics showed evidence of having consulted O'Connor's works in order to inform their own understanding of the film. Jack Kroll, for example, echoed O'Connor's ideas and phrasing when he stated, "Huston catches the craziness and violence that result when people who lust after grace and redemption have to create their own slapstick sacraments."[102] And David Ansen described Motes as a "Christian *malgré lui*,"[103] the same term used by O'Connor in her note to the 1962 edition of the novel. More directly, Ansen called Motes's self-blinding the "bloody and bizarre atonement" of "a tortured man stumbling ass-backward into salvation."[104] While O'Connor never used such a phrase, one cannot help thinking that she would have agreed.

However, other critics regarded Motes's blindness and suffering ironically, recalling the same split between genuine and ironic audiences for *The Violent Bear It Away*, where some readers assumed, in a genuine authorial spirit, that Tarwater's vocation was as plain as the marks on the page, while others, from an ironic stance, read the novel as an examination of a young man's "brainwashing" by a "religious fanatic." One such ironic reader, Tim Pulleine, in his enthusiastic review for *Sight and Sound*, described Motes as a man who endeavors to "keep alive his godlessness through (anti-) religious acts of purification,"[105] as if Motes had blinded himself to illustrate the meaningless of existence and prove that he was willing to suffer for the sake of his Church Without Christ. (The novel and novelist both imply that he blinds himself for exactly the opposite reason—for decrying the truth of what he had so earnestly mocked, for playing St. Paul before his conversion on the road to Damascus.) In another enthusiastic and ironic British review, Geoffrey Nowell-Smith described Motes's story as a "seemingly purposeless tragedy,"[106] implying that Motes has learned nothing and has not experienced the grace which is so central to O'Connor's art. As was the case with *The Violent Bear It Away*, however, an ironic reviewer could respond to O'Connor's work in a way wholly antithetical to the spirit in which she intended and yet still find it worthy of praise, as many ironic-minded critics did. The same ironic reading appears in the London *Observer*, where Philip French states, "Eventually, in pursuit of total rejection, Motes blinds himself, practices mortification of the flesh with barbed wire, and attains a kind of sainthood."[107]

Motes may attain a kind of sainthood, but not in pursuit of total rejection; his actions are motivated by his total acceptance of what he has spent so much time denying. As with works such as "The River" and *The Violent Bear It Away*, some critics could only approach the fate of the protagonist ironically, jeering at O'Connor's issues and sometimes revealing their inability to imagine that she could take them as seriously and as literally as she did. Late in her *Wall Street Journal* review, Joy Gould Boyum offers what reads like a concession to her ironic colleagues: "In reproducing the book so closely, the film has also reproduced its ambiguities. We cannot be sure just what O'Connor through Huston is telling us here. Is she demonstrating the tenaciousness of belief? Or instead mocking its excesses? How are we to take Haze's martyrdom—as religious distortion, or as embodying the possibility of redemption? As in the book, it's nearly impossible to say."[108] Boyum is sharp about many aspects of O'Connor's work and film adaptation in general, but here, she dances around the meaning of Motes's self-blinding and mortification, describing them as "a grotesque mockery of the excesses of religious faith or as Haze's way to salvation."[109] But it is not "impossible to say" what Motes's blindness means or if his blindness suggests he is slouching toward salvation. If one regards Motes's suffering as an occasion for mockery or self-congratulation for never having fallen prey to such "excesses," one seems to have missed the meaning of the title, that Motes's wise blood triumphs over his foolish mind. And while one could argue here that the title itself is ironic, doing so is akin to arguing that Tarwater's vision at the end of *The Violent Bear It Away* is a psychotic hallucination. It is an interpretation that flatters, rather than challenges, the reader for siding with Rayber rather than with Mason, with Motes's landlady rather than with her tenant. In a 2004 interview, Brad Dourif (who played Motes) stated, "He was insane,"[110] just as some of the novel's first reviewers, such as Isaac Rosenfeld, proposed: "Motes is just plain crazy."[111] But assuming Motes's actions to be the result of insanity rather than grace—and thus approaching *Wise Blood* as an ironic reader—is akin to regarding *Wise Blood* as a work of satire; it is a way to reduce and contain the "terror" that Michael Fitzgerald noted distributors felt when they were asked to release the film. Roger Angell described Motes's blindness as proof that "Jesus has caught him at last,"[112] but to allow for such a reading, one must entertain the possibility that there is a Jesus from which Motes is running in the first place.

Such an allowance may seem obvious to O'Connor or her genuine authorial readers, but it was not so to others, who regarded the film's climactic moment as an ironic, heavy-handed lesson. In a 2013 interview, Daniel Shor, who played Enoch Emery, articulated such an attitude toward the climax: "I see those characters as people who are seeking belonging. They are clinging onto an obvious illusion. *Wise Blood* was really Flannery O'Connor taking a piss out on evangelicalism of all kinds. Not [on] the people themselves but on the preachers. People need something to believe in, and they'll believe in whatever the hell they're told to believe in."[113] Shor is a brilliant actor but a less brilliant literary critic, and his remarks stand as yet another example of the impulse to turn O'Connor into a satirist: if Motes is clinging to an "obvious illusion" at the end for the sake of his own comfort, the viewer is therefore meant to take his potential redemption as a joke and the film as a whole as an elaborate snuff film. The characters themselves certainly do not "believe in whatever the hell they're told to believe in": Motes denies Christ, Hawks is motivated solely by self-interest, and neither of these rival preachers is able to win any converts other than the idiot Enoch Emery, who seeks companionship more than salvation. Shor assumes a secular agenda and satire where neither exists and speaks of *Wise Blood* as if it were akin to *Elmer Gantry*, a work that does attack "evangelicism of all kinds" and the people believing in "whatever the hell they're told to believe in." Like some of the critics who first reviewed O'Connor's fiction, Shor and some film reviewers favored ironic readings of the film that offered some sense of superiority over O'Connor's subject matter.

Huston himself began the project as an ironic reader but then found himself changing sides. In a 2004 interview, Brad Dourif said that Huston wanted to adapt the novel because it complemented the director's own opinions: "He saw it as a nihilistic rebellion. He didn't get that it was really an affirmation of Catholicism, of Christianity. Flannery O'Connor was Catholic as the day is long. . . . John was a devout atheist."[114] Dourif later remarked that Huston "felt it was about how ridiculous Christianity was"[115] and also described a discussion between him and Huston that reflected the director's being firmly encamped in the ironic audience:

> He thought that, in the end, Hazel Motes had some kind of existential revelation. He was a devout atheist. I mean, he didn't like religion. And I remember we were in rehearsal and I finally asked the question. I said, "Well, what do you think happens? Because it seems to me that the script is very clearly saying that Hazel Motes finds God and that's what happened, and he dedicates his life to it." And he said, "No, no, no, no, no."[116]

Benedict Fitzgerald stated that Huston "thought it was a comedy" and that he, his brother, and his mother never attempted to "set right" Huston's "misunderstandings" about the "religious heart" of the story,[117] so pleased were they to have Huston at the helm and so confident that his style of directly presenting the narrative would allow O'Connor's issues to surface. The screenwriter, however, also told the story of Huston's experiencing a form of enlightenment, lesser than the one experienced by Motes, but important nonetheless: "I remember on the last day he put his hands over my shoulders and leaned in and said, 'Ben, I think I've been had.' And I didn't know what he was talking about, but something rang true. . . . And by the end, he realized, 'I've told another story than the one I thought I was telling. I've told Flannery O'Connor's story.'"[118] Huston's begrudging shift from the ironic to the genuine audience, from denying what informs Motes's suffering to acknowledging its presence, is witnessed even more dramatically in Dourif's anecdote about a conversation among the producers and actors: "We're all sitting around the table and Huston kind of looks up at everybody and he looks around and says, 'Jesus wins.'"[119]

Huston was, in some sense, of O'Connor's party without knowing it, an idea reinforced in Lawrence Grobel's biography *The Hustons*, where he recounts the making of the film and comments, "*Wise Blood* was so strange, so offbeat, so insular, that John had his own hard time figuring out what it was about."[120] *Wise Blood* may have first been regarded by Huston and is undoubtedly still regarded by some critics as satirical or a mockery of the very values and truths that O'Connor sought to dramatize. Eventually, however, the director moved closer to the author, who argued in a letter, "What people don't realize is how much religion costs. They think faith is a big electric blanket, when of course it is the cross."[121] Motes's religious awakening does not result in platitudes about loving thy neighbor but in debasement and an acknowledgment of his own pride—a fate similar to the one experienced by Mr. Head in "The Artificial Nigger." In his 2013 book *Hard Sayings: The Rhetoric of Christian Orthodoxy in Late Modern Fiction*, Thomas F. Haddox convincingly argues that Mr. Head's pride is difficult for readers to regard as sinful because we "do not live in a culture in which pride prompts universal fear and loathing."[122] Perhaps this helps explain why some viewers had trouble with the end of Huston's film: Motes admits his own pride as the source of his misery, but others may be slow to do the same.

William Walsh, writing in the *Flannery O'Connor Bulletin*, said that Huston's epiphany of "Jesus wins" was simply the director "capitulating to the obvious,"[123] but Huston, like Motes on a smaller scale, took a circuitous route to his insight. Jeffrey Meyers sneers at the film with remarks such as, "The whole Fitzgerald family genuflected at the altar of Saint Flannery . . . and the movie is a testament to their devotion."[124] But if Huston's *Wise Blood* is a testament to anything, it is to ways in which O'Connor's reputation had grown more complex since 1952 and was still being challenged by readers who regarded her work in very different ways. Much had changed: critics were, on the whole, more amenable to her issues and the ways that she explored them. But the ironic audience and those who could not get past the actors' accents were still affecting how her work was received.

Elsewhere in this study, we have seen ways that publishers and their graphic designers attempted to package O'Connor's books for public consumption. Those working in the New Line publicity department faced a similar challenge: how to market *Wise Blood* to an audience they correctly assumed would regard it as strange and not worth the price of a ticket. Their strategy was to sell *Wise Blood* as a comedy, something less like a work by Flannery O'Connor and more like one by Mark Twain. The film's poster featured the phrase "An American

Masterpiece!" prominently in its top corner, never hinting that the "America" in question here is the South. Indeed, nothing in the poster, except perhaps the small image of Ned Beatty as the guitar-strumming Hoover Shoates, suggests that the film takes place in a fictional Tennessee town. While one blurb calls the film "A brilliant black comedy," the image of the four supporting characters (including Enoch Emery in his gorilla suit) standing on the brim of Motes's hat, combined with blurbs calling the film "An uproarious tale" and "wildly comic," suggest that *Wise Blood* is wacky instead of disturbing, a straightforward comedy rather than one that elicits nervous laughs from a growing sense of unease. The phrase "Based on the novel by Flannery O'Connor" in small type underneath the title reflects New Line's desire to promote the film to a literary audience as well as to a cinematic one. What happened with the covers of *Wise Blood* also happened with the artwork for its cinematic adaptation: a look at the artwork for the original home video release, which used the same graphic as the theatrical poster (fig. 14), and that of the 2009 DVD (fig. 15) reveals the similar shift in advertising O'Connor's themes.

The film's trailer reflected a desire to recast O'Connor as more humorist than moralist. Beginning with Motes saying, "I ain't no preacher" to a cabdriver, the trailer begins with an announcer advising uninitiated viewers about how to regard the issues of the film:

> In a world of sin and seduction, there's a lot of ways of getting saved. Some do it with style. Some have other plans. What Hazel Motes wants is a good car and a fast woman. What he gets is the last thing he wanted. *Wise Blood*. The *New York Times* calls it "an uproarious tale, one of John Huston's most stunning movies." *Wise Blood*. Some got it, some sell it, and some give it away. A new film by John Huston. *Wise Blood*. From the acclaimed novel by Flannery O'Connor.[125]

This voiceover description of the film is intercut with shots and bits of dialogue edited to suggest that *Wise Blood* is more of a lighthearted romp filled with country bumpkins than a disturbing reimagining of the story of St. Paul. The viewer sees Motes nearly hit in the face with the hood of his car, Enoch Emery shaking hands with Gonga the gorilla, the obese Leora Watts cracking, "Mama don't mind if you ain't a preacher—as long as you got four dollars," and the film's one obvious laugh line and certainly the one that led some critics to assume that O'Connor was a satirist:

> MOTES: I started my own church. The Church of Truth Without Christ.
> LANDLADY: Protestant? Or something foreign?
> MOTES: Oh, no, ma'am. It's Protestant.[126]

Figure 14. *Wise Blood*, film ad.

Figure 15. *Wise Blood*, DVD cover.

All these clips are accompanied by jaunty, high-spirited, southern music. The trailer's total effect is greatly different from that of the film, and the viewer who has seen both might be reminded of Robert Ryang's 2006 "trailer" for Stanley Kubrick's *The Shining* that recut scenes from the film and added a new voice-over to make it appear like a family-friendly comedy.[127] In short, the viewer of the trailer for *Wise Blood* is invited to laugh at the characters and feel superior to them, an antithetical effect to O'Connor's practice of shouting to the hard of hearing and drawing large and startling figures. Nothing in the trailer or poster even hints that the film contains a murder, a mock Virgin Mary, or a man who blinds and mutilates himself. These parts of the film had to be downplayed if viewers were to fill theaters; only then would the distributors' "terror" be lessened. The desire to package Huston's adaptation of O'Connor's novel into more palatable and audience-friendly fare was noted by Vincent Canby, who later commented on his initial review by confessing that his enthusiasm colored the way he described it: "It wasn't until I saw the film a second time the other day that I realized that by calling it 'comic,' 'uproarious' and 'rollicking,' among other things, I had probably misled movie audiences for whom those words are more often associated with Mel Brooks than with a tale about the furious soul-searchings of a young redneck Southerner named Hazel Motes."[128]

Of course, such a description was easier for Canby to give than for New Line Cinema. A spiritual dark comedy was not going to sell tickets. One of the reviewers of the novel remarked, "The author calls this 'a comic novel.' It's funny like a case of cancer."[129] New Line Cinema had to sell that case in a package that audiences could easily identify: the misadventures of buffoonish hill-billies, a package with a history that began long before the dawn of Hollywood. A major film that had previously capitalized on the image of southerners as re-gressive and subhuman—John Boorman's *Deliverance* (1972)—had proven, by its commercial and critical success, that such images were taken as fact by broad swaths of moviegoers. "Indisputably the most influential film of the modern era in shaping national perceptions of southern mountaineers,"[130] Boorman's film, while taking place in the wilderness and stylistically far from a dark comedy, could not have been far from viewers' minds as they watched *Wise Blood*.

The reception of Huston's *Wise Blood*, like that of the novel and O'Connor's other work, has proven to enact the previously examined duel between self-congratulating readers who assumed that any work examining religion in the South must be ironic and those whose sympathy for O'Connor's issues—or at least the ability to entertain them—allowed for more genuine readings. The duel continues today. When the film was remastered as part of the Criterion

DVD Collection in 2009, a reviewer for the *Los Angeles Times* accurately described Motes as "a fanatic nonbeliever"—a wholly genuine reading—but also raised the possibility of looking at Motes from an ironic vantage point: "But is he a holy fool or just a pathetically deluded one? The religious inclinations of the viewer will determine whether his eventual fate reads as salvation or as tragedy."[131] The "religious inclinations" of the viewer, however, are not as important as the viewer's ability to entertain the idea that O'Connor saw great meaning in Motes's suffering—as she surely did.

Despite the distributor's efforts and the enthusiasm of several important reviewers, *Wise Blood* was not as big a box-office success as some of Huston's other films.[132] Perhaps O'Connor's characters proved too strange, too possessed, or too "southern" for mass consumption. In his autobiography, Huston acknowledged the film's financial failure but did so in a way that recalls the articles and reviews that fretted over O'Connor's lack of commercial appeal while recasting this lack of appeal as a mark of artistic integrity: "Nothing would make me happier," he wrote, "than to see this picture gain popular acceptance and turn a profit. It would prove something, I'm not sure what ... but something."[133] What it would perhaps prove was that O'Connor was ready to be accepted by the great movie-watching public when translated by a master into a medium that commonly avoided taking spiritual issues as seriously and as earnestly as she did.

O'Connor on the Stage

While *Wise Blood* was certainly the most widely reviewed adaptation of O'Connor's work—and the one that best reflected the complexities of her reputation at the time of its premiere—it was not the only attempt to translate her fiction into another artistic medium. Other adaptations, both before and after Huston's film, reveal similar impulses to bring O'Connor to different audiences and ways in which she was regarded at the time. In 1963 Cecil Dawkins, then a writer of short stories, wrote O'Connor to pitch the idea of using her work as the basis for a play. The two had been regular correspondents since 1957, when Dawkins first wrote to ask her opinions on literature. Regarding the play, O'Connor replied, "I think it's a fine idea if you want to try it,"[134] and expressed more concern over her remuneration than her reputation: "I would not be too squeamish about anything you did to this because I have no interest in the theater for its own sake and all I would care about would be what money, if any, could be got out of it. It's nice to have something you can be completely crass about."[135] However, despite her suggestion that she would keep her hands off Dawkins's work, O'Connor did note one aspect of her own reputation that she hoped Dawkins would keep in mind:

> Did you ever consider *Wise Blood* as a possibility for dramatizing? If the times were different, I would suggest that, but I think it would just be taken for the super-grotesque sub–Carson McCullers sort of thing that I couldn't stand the sound or sight of.... The only thing I would positively object to would be to somebody turning one of my colored idiots into a hero. Don't let any fool director work that on you. I wouldn't trust any of that bunch farther than I could hurl them. I guess I wouldn't want a Yankee doing this, money or no money.[136]

O'Connor knew how she was regarded and feared that a "Yankee" might attempt to refashion her work so it reflected a more northern sensibility, and while a reader today may cringe at her wish for none of her "colored idiots" to be recast as heroes, the larger point remains: O'Connor had read enough reviews of *The Violent Bear It Away* three years earlier to know that many readers who did not share her assumptions were eager to tell her work what it meant, instead of vice versa. But she trusted Dawkins and gave her carte blanche.

Dawkins eventually drafted what would become *The Displaced Person*, a play based on several of O'Connor's stories, and hoped to gain her approval, but O'Connor's death in 1964 led Dawkins to shelve the project. In 1965, however, the artistic director of the American Place Theatre asked Dawkins if she were interested in producing the play. The American Place seemed well suited for Dawkins's work: its first production, Robert Lowell's *The Old Glory* (1964), brilliantly adapted works by Melville and Hawthorne, and the theater was forging its own reputation as a space for (according to its publicity department) "American writers of stature"[137]—a reputation it still has today. The theater did its part in drumming up interest among its 4,500 members, informing them that the play's director, Edward Parone, had recently helmed LeRoi Jones's *Dutchman* and was therefore up to the task of creating a memorable production of a controversial work. Dawkins also wrote a three-column piece that ran in the *New York World Journal Tribune* four days before the play's opening date of December 29, 1966, in which she presented her opinions of O'Connor and addressed the author's current reputation. Dawkins recast O'Connor's southernness—what O'Connor feared would lead directors into creating a "super-grotesque sub–Carson McCullers sort of thing"—as something akin to the net of nationalism over which, in Joyce's novel, the young Stephen Dedalus seeks to fly: "Flannery O'Connor," she wrote, "better than any other Southern writer, escaped regionalism. And she did so by escaping the attitude of the region toward itself. Every region has such an attitude. In the South, it is a certain romanticism toward things Southern. An eye such as Flannery O'Connor's is the eye of a naturalist. Like Audubon, she knew her birds."[138] As Robert Giroux would seek to make O'Connor more American than southern in his 1971 introduction to *The Complete Stories*, Dawkins here and throughout her essay asked readers to forget what they thought they knew about O'Connor as a southern author and instead to appreciate the "clear-sightedness" that allowed her to measure "things-as-they-are against ultimate values."[139] Dawkins also claimed that the "sophistication" of New York audiences presented the "danger" that works of art became occasion for "an intellectual opinion mill," and that in the big city "performers play to severed heads, to eyes and noses in some direct contact with the brain requiring no nervous system, no spinal column, no body, no blood, no heart."[140] She hoped that *The Displaced Person* would invite intellectual New Yorkers to admire the force of O'Connor's unsentimental work and appreciate how she wrestled with the problem of evil.

They did not. Reviewers were unanimous in their complaints about the play's disjointedness, which, they argued, preserved O'Connor's figures and settings but not the emotional weight that Dawkins thought she was urging her New York audiences to accept—the same complaint voiced by Stanley Kauffmann against Huston for offering only the "data" of *Wise Blood*. In *The Village Voice*, Michael Smith stated, "Many of the individual characters are solid and interesting, but the incidents are oddly vague, incomplete, disconnected."[141] In *Newsweek*, Richard Gilman wrote, "The stage is full of fragments" of O'Connor's "unique sensibility, an amalgam of dark humor and unavoidable violence, but there is no dramatic shape or growth to the enterprise."[142] And George Oppenheimer in *Newsday* complained that the actors seemed to be walking "into a series of separate playlets, held together but not firmly enough by a central character."[143] Oppenheimer also called the play "too faithful to Miss O'Connor,"[144] which recalled similar critical complaints about Huston's *Wise Blood*. Dawkins's being an O'Connor insider could not guarantee the success of her adaptation. Even the enthusiastic Robert Giroux wrote to Robert Fitzgerald that both he and Elizabeth Hardwick saw and enjoyed the play, but that "most of the audience thought it was another version of *Tobacco Road*."[145] Perhaps Dawkins's play was caviar to the general, but (as was the case with Huston's film) the general affected how the work was received.

In 2001 Karin Coonrod, who had founded in New York two theatrical companies devoted to reimagining the classics and staging works taken from non-dramatic authors, mounted a production titled *Everything That Rises Must Converge* with the New York Theatre Workshop. The play staged three stories: "A View of the Woods," "Greenleaf," and "Everything That Rises Must Converge," with eight actors playing all the roles. Unlike *The Displaced Person*, however, this adaptation featured every word of each story: actors played not only the characters but the omniscient narrators as well. Coonrod's being granted permission to use the works on the condition that she not alter a single word and ensure every sentence from each story being heard aloud forced her to adapt and present the stories in their entirety,[146] a challenge for an adapter but one that surely allowed Coonrod to "honor the word" with her creative staging. Her director's note to the viewer reinforces O'Connor's reputation for combining horror and humor: "Flannery O'Connor's apocalyptic comedies are peopled with characters whose reality resided in their obstinate wills. They drive themselves at every step deeper and deeper into their own desires, obsessions, disillusionments."[147] Coonrod also mentioned O'Connor's narrative voice, noting its tendency to "mock and celebrate and question the characters, attending their every action with a kind of raucous glee."[148] Such a description stands in contrast to many responses by O'Connor's first readers, who often sought to pigeonhole her at either extreme of mocking or extolling her characters; Coonrod's description suggests a more complex understanding of O'Connor's method of presenting her characters objectively in many different, often contradictory, lights. Finally, Coonrod's description illuminates reasons behind her choice of stories, since all three feature characters who initially are detestable yet become objects of surprising sympathy. In short, Coonrod understood "how O'Connor works" and sought to replicate on stage the experience of reading O'Connor.

Everything That Rises Must Converge fared much better with critics than *The Displaced Person*. It also fared better with audiences, selling out its month-long run.[149] Noting that the production was less "adaptation" than creative staging, Bruce Weber in the *New York Times* called the play a "carefully balanced literary mutation" and—unlike Dawkins's play—"something deftly sewn" together from O'Connor's stories.[150] David Cote, theater editor for *Time Out New York*, similarly noted that Coonrod avoided the "literary-adaptation trap" by simply "not adapting." Cote used the phrase "dark, unsettling magic" to describe how the staging of the title story "makes us actually pity this horrible creature," Julian's mother, who "finds the new South has no place for her genteel condescension,"[151] again attesting to Coonrod's effective approach of jarring the viewer into unexpected sympathy—a technique that O'Connor used throughout her career. In the *Village Voice*, Jessica Winter described the production as an open book whose "pages brim with colorful illustrations." But she also could not resist a tired series of jabs, describing the setting as the "freak-tent medievalist South" and the deaths of the protagonists "swift, near-Falwellian acts of divine justice,"[152] a phrase that both trivializes and misreads the significance of each story's ending. Coonrod's adaptation was revived in 2014–15, when it played at a number of high-profile universities (Emory, Georgetown, Loyola, Yale) and the Cathedral of St. John the Divine. Her efforts suggest that the best way to translate O'Connor for an audience might be to let the author speak for herself—or, in the case of other adapters, sing for herself: a musical of *Wise Blood* premiered in 2011 at the Off Broadway Theater at Yale University, and an opera version was staged at Minneapolis's Soap Factory gallery in 2015. Bryan Beaumont Hayes, a Benedictine monk and former student of Aaron Copland, composed *Parker's Back: An Opera in Two Acts*, but it remains unproduced.

O'Connor and Her Work on Television

O'Connor herself thought very little—in both senses of the phrase—of her works being adapted as a means to reach a wider audience or to examine her chosen themes in different media. Her first and only television appearance was in 1955, when she appeared as a guest on *Galley Proof*, an NBC series designed to appeal to a middlebrow audience and hosted by Harvey Briet, assistant editor of the *New York Times Book Review*. The show combined interviews of authors with dramatizations of their work; its motto, voiced by Briet in the opening minutes, was "Television is a friend, and not an enemy" to books.[153] O'Connor's appearance coincided with the publication of *A Good Man Is Hard to Find*, and Briet used the occasion to ask O'Connor about her status as a southern author:

> BRIET: Do you think . . . that a Northerner, for example, reading [*Wise Blood*] would have as much appreciation of the people in your book, your stories, as a Southerner?
> O'CONNOR: Yes, I think perhaps more, because he at least wouldn't be distracted by the Southern thinking that this was a novel about the South, or a story about the South, which it is not.
> BRIET: You don't feel that it is?
> O'CONNOR: No.[154]

Briet changed tactics immediately after O'Connor's "No," saying, "I don't either," but his line of questioning clearly played upon O'Connor's status as a geographical outsider, and O'Connor resisted his attempts to pigeonhole her.

Later that year, Briet reported, "She doesn't think of herself as a Southern writer,"[155] offering this tidbit as if it were news—which, to Briet and many of his readers, it was. Significantly, her Catholicism was never mentioned, which seems odd in a discussion of *Wise Blood* and which shows that O'Connor's faith was not yet the automatic part of her reputation that modern readers take for granted.

After a few minutes, Briet segued to a dramatization of "The Life You Save May Be Your Own" and, by way of an innocuous question, inadvertently gave O'Connor the opportunity to state one of her core beliefs about her art:

> BRIET: It isn't over. What we're seeing now is only part of the story. Flannery, would you like to tell our audience what happens in that story?
>
> O'CONNOR: No, I certainly would not. I don't think you can paraphrase a story like that. I think there's only one way to tell it and that's the way it is told in the story.[156]

O'Connor found adaptation a losing proposition from the start. All the energy devoted to "fidelity" was never enough; in fact, it was the wrong kind of energy. Even paraphrasing a story or "telling what happens"—itself a kind of adaptation—was futile. As O'Connor remarked elsewhere, "When you can state the theme of a story, when you can separate it from the story itself, then you can be sure the story is not a very good one."[157] The same holds true for a film or other adaptation—but such a line of reasoning was not to be used on Briet, who, as *Galley Proof* continued, spoke more than the ostensible subject of his interview.

O'Connor deprecated her experience on *Galley Proof* in letters to her friends, stating, "I am sure the only people who look at TV at 1:30 p.m. are children who are not financially able to buy *A Good Man Is Hard to Find*"[158] and, "I keep having a mental picture of my glacial glare being sent out over the nation onto millions of children who are waiting impatiently for *The Batman* to come on."[159] She summarized the experience as "mildly ghastly."[160] Two years later, however, O'Connor sold the rights to "The Life You Save May Be Your Own" to Revue Productions for use as an episode of *Schlitz Playhouse*, one of many television dramas that offered adaptations of literary works to its audience. Her motives here were purely financial: in her letters, she said, "It certainly is a painless way to make money"[161] and spoke with enthusiasm of the appliance that selling her story allowed her to buy for herself and her mother: "While they make hash out of my story, she and me will make ice in the new refrigerator."[162] When O'Connor heard that Gene Kelly would be making his television debut as Mr. Shiftlet, she wrote the Fitzgeralds, "The punishment always fits the crime. They must be making a musical out of it."[163] Upon learning (from a New York gossip column) that Kelly would be starring in what the columnist called a "backwoods love story," she wrote Betty Hester, "It will probably be appropriate to smoke a corncob pipe while watching this."[164] O'Connor knew all too well how her story would be repackaged and sold as a small-screen version of *Tobacco Road*.

The episode aired on CBS on March 1, 1957, and also starred Agnes Moorehead as the elder Lucynell Crater and Janice Rule as her deaf daughter. O'Connor's reputation in Milledgeville skyrocketed: she wrote Betty Hester, "The local city fathers think I am a credit now to the community. One old lady said, 'That was a play that really made me think!' I didn't ask her what."[165] Similarly, she wrote Denver Lindley of the "enthusiastic congratulations from the local citizens," who "feel that I have arrived at last."[166] O'Connor detested the adaptation and knew that the ladies of Milledgeville enjoyed it because the ending had been changed to one more formulaic: in the *Schlitz Playhouse* version, Mr. Shiftlet does not abandon his new bride in a roadside diner, but instead drives off with her into the sunset. O'Connor felt that anyone who enjoyed the television play had not read the story and stated, "The best I can say for it is that conceivably it could have been worse. Just conceivably."[167] Kelly described the show as "kind of a hillbilly thing in which I play a guy who befriends a deaf-mute girl in the hills of Kentucky"; when O'Connor shared this description with her friends Brainard and Frances Cheney, she underlined "befriends" to signal her outrage at the adaptation.[168] A short review in the *New York Times* called the episode "an odd little drama" and described it in language that, in hindsight, suits many of O'Connor's works: "The peculiarity of the film, 'The Life You Save,' stemmed from the extremes it reached during the half hour. For considerable periods it was ludicrous, almost like a caricature. At other moments, it was touching."[169] In "Writing Short Stories," O'Connor tells of "The Life You Save May Be Your Own" and says this about the *Schlitz Playhouse*:

> Not long ago that story was adapted for a television play, and the adapter, knowing his business, had the tramp have a change of heart and go back and pick up the idiot daughter and the two of them ride away, grinning madly. My aunt believes that the story is complete at last, but I have other sentiments about it—which are not suitable for public utterance. When you write a story, there will always be people who refuse to read the story you have written.[170]

O'Connor's final sentence here could very well describe so much of the reception of her work from her first publication to Huston's adaptation of *Wise Blood*: some reviewers refused to read how seriously she addressed grace, sin, and redemption, just as Huston had refused—at first—to read *Wise Blood* as something other than a satire.

In April 1965, ten years after the *Galley Proof* episode, *Directions '65* devoted an episode to O'Connor's life and work. *Directions '65* was one of many broadcasts sponsored by the National Council of Catholic Men, whose most notable production was *The Catholic Hour*, Bishop Fulton J. Sheen's radio program that brought Catholic apologetics over the airwaves for twenty years. *Directions '65* consisted of narration and commentary on O'Connor's fiction, intercut with excerpts from her work read by actors. The script and voice-over narration were provided by Richard Gilman, at that time the respected drama critic for *Newsweek* who had a friendly relationship with O'Connor: she valued his favorable review of *A Good Man Is Hard to Find* in *Jubilee* and hosted him at Andalusia in 1960. *Directions '65* sought to popularize an author whose admirers felt he or she deserved a larger audience, and the episode's producer wrote to Elizabeth McKee about his hopes to bring O'Connor's work before a wider audience.[171] Gilman's narration described O'Connor with all the watchwords and convenient categories that now characterized her reputation: "Flannery O'Connor was a splendid writer, but more than that, a woman, a sufferer, a great heart."[172] This tendency to speak of O'Connor in such automatic terms was noted by Gilman himself four years later in his review of *Mystery and Manners*: "Throughout her life," he wrote, "she was caught in the various pressures of our tendency to classify and sociologize art"[173]—pressures that Gilman revealed in his narration here and when later in the episode he stated that "the two most important facts about her" are that she was southern and Catholic. (No one seemed to think that the one most important factor about her was that she was a talented writer.) Gilman told viewers of his visit to Milledgeville and mused that he left her company "infinitely better stocked with knowledge and insight than from a decade of literary cocktail parties."[174] Again, O'Connor's status as an outsider from the northern literary establishment was touted as a virtue, a virtue confirmed by the modest sales figures of her books:

> None of her books ever came close to the best-seller list; indeed, outside of literary circles and a small nucleus of Catholic admirers, you will not hear her talked about at all. Her modesty and illness combined to keep her away from the mainstream of self-advertisement; and her beautiful, stern, and difficult literary vision was not of the kind that makes for popularity. She wrote, lived, knew pain, and died. And now we possess her legacy.[175]

As Huston was praised by some critics for not setting out to create a block-buster with *Wise Blood*, O'Connor was similarly (and paradoxically) praised for not reaching more readers than she did. The fewer the readers, the better the writer.

Horton Foote's "The Displaced Person" more successfully adapted O'Connor to television. In the mid-1970s, Foote—whose own reputation had been greatly bolstered by his adaptation of *To Kill a Mockingbird* in 1962—undertook the adaptation for *The American Short Story*, a PBS series that ran for three seasons. Foote later adapted Faulkner's "Barn Burning" for the same series and wrote about the challenge of adapting works by similarly singular writers: "The plot and the scenes are usually easy to dramatize but it is the style of the writer, which gives life and breath to the whole, that is the most difficult part to capture. In dramatizing both Faulkner and O'Connor, that is the challenge."[176] O'Connor scholar Robert Donahoo states that Foote's adaptation is "for most critics the best translation of O'Connor's work onto the screen,"[177] presumably because Foote—a longtime admirer of O'Connor who frequently mentions her as one of his models—approached her work as an absolutely genuine reader. Like Benedict Fitzgerald with *Wise Blood*, Foote did not alter the plot, although he confessed to some difficulty with rendering its more ethereal elements: "In *The Displaced Person*, the characters intrigued me most and proved wonderfully comic companions in my stay in the O'Connor country. What often eluded me here were the mystic, visionary aspects of the story, qualities that almost defy dramatization."[178] These "mystic" aspects were also a difficulty acknowledged by O'Connor herself. After being approached by a would-be producer, she shared her concerns with Betty Hester:

> Sunday I am to entertain a man who wants to make a movie out of "The River."
> He has never made a movie before but is convinced "The River" is the dish for
> him—"a kind of documentary," he said over the telephone. It is sort of discon-
> certing to think of somebody getting hold of your story and doing something else
> to it and I doubt if I will be able to see my way through him. But we shall see.
> How to document the sacrament of Baptism???????[179]

O'Connor does not mention here that her art rests precisely on this very skill of documenting the most profound moments of grace—of dramatizing what Sophocles called "the encounter of man with more than man." Those who adapted her work attempted, with varying success, to do the same.

Chapter 6

O'Connor and the Common
(Online) Reader

Goodreads and Literary Reputation

Reputations are not only formed in the pages of literary journals, magazines, or the book review sections of notable periodicals. How an author's work is described, recommended, and attacked on social reading sites such as *Goodreads*, *Shelfari*, and *LibraryThing* reveals that author's standing and reputation: both how well—and for what—he or she is known. The cliché and complaint "Everyone's a critic" has become true in a world in which the web has accelerated a process that used to occur only by word-of-mouth and print.

Goodreads, launched in 2007, is described on its site as "a place where you can see what your friends are reading and vice versa" and a site that its founder Otis Chandler claims to be a force for literary democracy: "You can comment on each other's reviews. You can find your next favorite book. And on this journey with your friends you can explore new territory, gather information, and expand your mind. Knowledge is power, and power is best shared among readers."[1] His words are hyperbolic, but the staggering number of readers who use the site attests to the notion that modern readers value *Goodreads* both as a simple recommendation service and, more importantly for our purposes, as a forum in which they can share their elations and frustrations about what they are reading. What makes the reviews on *Goodreads* so valuable is that they are a means to gauge an author's vulgar reputation—"vulgar" here not used pejoratively but in the neutral sense of what the *OED* describes as "commonly current or prevalent, generally or widely disseminated, as a matter of knowledge, assertion, or opinion."[2] Sometimes these reviews make up in passion what they lack in polish, but they generally and compellingly reveal the immediate, articulate, and forthright reactions of millions of people who are interested in discussing what they are reading. Examining both the quantity and quality of reviews on *Goodreads*, with over forty million registered users who have added over one billion books and posted over forty-seven million reviews,[3] is useful for any study of a specific author's reception and (literally) up-to-the-minute reputation.

Lisa Nakamura, professor of American cultures at the University of Michigan, Ann Arbor, has urged that "scholars looking to study reading culture 'in the wild' will be rewarded by a close study of *Goodreads*,"[4] but surprisingly few have taken her advice, perhaps due to snobbery or their disapproval of what they may regard as the corporate takeover of the general reader: *Goodreads*'s acquisition by Amazon in 2013 was met with disapproval in some circles over what was viewed as the corporate takeover of people's reading lives—the dawn of Big Reading, so to speak.[5] However, millions of users still turn to *Goodreads* when they want to find a book or trumpet their opinions about one they have found. Even with the occasional review written by an author's relative or agent, nowhere on the web is there such a collection of readers' opinions of an author. Amazon recognizes that "the business model is moving further towards word of mouth,"[6] especially when that "mouth" is a digital one, and that social reading sites allow word of mouth to work at a rate and volume unimaginable a generation ago; the presence of *Goodreads* on Facebook and Twitter adds to the number of times it is seen and used by millions of readers. In a 2012 examination of online literary communities, Julian Pinder explains quite succinctly the value of such social reading sites to scholars of reputation history: "The ways in which non-expert groups receive, utilize, and explicate texts—and the patterns of reception, utilization, and explication—themselves provide useful information, particularly when that information supplements rather than replaces existing critical and academic exegesis."[7] The "non-expert" critics that post their opinions on *Goodreads* offer a window through which we can see how O'Connor is regarded among everyday readers, a group that includes "professional readers" like professors, authors, and scholars as well as what might be termed the reading laity: those whose careers or working lives are not connected to literature but who nonetheless like to read. Thomas Gray wondered if beneath the stones in a country churchyard lay "some mute, inglorious Milton"; *Goodreads* affords these writers a place where they can offer their opinions. Not all are Miltons, but many are more impressive and perceptive than one may at first suspect.

An investigation of how O'Connor's work fares on *Goodreads* reveals the current state of her reputation and the "patterns of reception" created by the site's users. The fundamental statistic is the actual number of ratings her writings have received; by comparing these total numbers to those of other notable American titles, we can gauge how O'Connor stands in the American literary

Table 1. Some American titles on *Goodreads*
* denotes works by O'Connor

Title	Number of Ratings
To Kill a Mockingbird	2,726,069
The Great Gatsby	2,348,902
The Catcher in the Rye	1,809,151
Adventures of Huckleberry Finn	896,892
Slaughterhouse-Five	764,221
The Scarlet Letter	482,168
Moby-Dick	355,470
The Sun Also Rises	262,501
A Confederacy of Dunces	161,528
Uncle Tom's Cabin	133,570
The Sound and the Fury	117,262
Walden	102,303
The Last of the Mohicans	65,956
The Heart Is a Lonely Hunter	65,132
Native Son	61,661
The Portrait of a Lady	52,713
Infinite Jest	44,932
Rabbit, Run	36,797
O Pioneers	28,803
*The Complete Stories	26,275
*A Good Man Is Hard to Find	25,281
Gravity's Rainbow	24,574
Main Street	18,035
*Wise Blood	17,125
*Everything That Rises Must Converge	13,344
Tobacco Road	10,338
*The Violent Bear It Away	6,477
*Mystery and Manners	2,211
*The Habit of Being	1,384
*A Prayer Journal	1,276

Source: www.goodreads.com, accessed February 22, 2016

pantheon, relative to other well-known figures. Not every rating on *Goodreads* is accompanied by a review: some readers simply rate a book by clicking on the number of stars (out of five) they award a title. Perhaps not surprisingly, O'Connor's *A Good Man Is Hard to Find* (her most frequently rated book) has generated many reviews, but not as many as what are often regarded as other, perhaps more canonical American works. While the statistics on *Goodreads* change daily, a snapshot from the spring of 2016 gives a sense of where O'Connor stands in terms of readers who consult and add content to the site (table 1).

O'Connor's admirers might wish she had even more readers, but they can find satisfaction in the fact that her *Complete Stories* has been rated almost three times more often than *Tobacco Road* (although they may also wince at the fact that *The Heart Is a Lonely Hunter* has been rated more than twice as often). The races between individual titles aside, what these numbers as a whole suggest is that O'Connor has not yet, in these readers' collective opinion, caught up to the major figures in American literature. Why this is so depends on a number of reasons, such as how often works are assigned in high school or college courses or how a film adaptation can boost the number of ratings a book receives. (*The Great Gatsby* appears on more syllabi than *Wise Blood*, and many more moviegoers have seen Leonardo DiCaprio in his white dinner jacket than Brad Dourif in his black preacher's hat.) The number of O'Connor's reviews seems to confirm what many of her admirers suspect: her audience is large but not as large as those of more renowned American authors.

A more specific survey of the thousands of *Goodreads* reviews reveals that some of the watchwords used in print to describe O'Connor have demonstrated remarkable staying power. "Grotesque" and "southern gothic" are ubiquitous, as when a reviewer of *Wise Blood* casually mentions that "O'Connor's grotesque characters are both inexorably tied to and alienated from their Christianity"[8] or when a reviewer of *The Complete Stories* gushes, "What can possibly be said about a woman who defines an entire genre of literature: Southern gothic?"[9] Those who both admire and disparage O'Connor's work rely on the same watchwords to the point where online reviewers can refer to them as critical mainstays, as in, "She has been given many sobriquets, 'Southern Writer,' 'Catholic Writer,' 'Early Feminist,' 'Southern Gothic Writer,' etc. She was all these but much more."[10] New watchwords have taken root in O'Connor's reputation, such as "haunting"[11] and "bleak,"[12] both of which appear in hundreds of online reviews of her work. The most frequently appearing online watchword—"dark"—is found as often on *Goodreads* as "grotesque" in newspapers and magazines. Reviewers of *Wise Blood*, for example, warn readers, "the novel is dark, dark, dark"[13] and describe it as "one of the most astonishingly funny and dark and emotional American novels,"[14] "deliciously dark,"[15] and a depiction of "a dark world"[16] where "dark commingles with beauty"[17] to create "a fascinatingly dark and tremendously profound commentary on original sin."[18] Reviewers also note O'Connor's "dark sense of humor"[19] and describe her tone as "darkly funny."[20] The watchword, useful in its unacademic and general sense, appears in dozens of reviews of O'Connor's other works, and even when it does not literally appear, the same idea surfaces as a critical "given," spoken of as a matter of fact. For example, dozens of online reviewers state that O'Connor is "not for the faint of heart"[21] or speak as if they are warning their readers as they simultaneously urge O'Connor's excellence: "These stories are dark, bitter, angry, and often tragic. But they are a brilliant barometer of the human heart and the depravity of which it is capable when left untouched by divine grace."[22] Many reviewers (such as the author of the mixed metaphor above) use figurative language to suggest the same idea. For example, a reviewer of *A Good Man Is Hard to Find* suggests, "By all means, read this book, but you'll need to clear your palate afterwards,"[23] a reviewer of *The Complete Stories* states, "O'Connor is literary 'shock and awe' in the best sense,"[24] and one reader compares *Wise Blood* to "passing an accident on the highway."[25] A reviewer of *The Violent Bear It Away* notes, "This is a book that will take years off your life; it's like going through a trauma,"[26] and another states, strikingly, "When I read the last three paragraphs, I thought the book might burst into flames in my hand."[27] One reviewer of *Everything That Rises Must Converge* compared herself to "the cliffs along some Scottish beach, constantly pounded by cruel dark waves,"[28] while another employed even more violent language to articulate her reading experience:

> Sometimes Flannery O'Connor feels like a verbally abusive boyfriend that you just keep going back to. You sigh a bit deeper at the end of each tale, feeling a little more defeated by the uglier sides of existence, the weaknesses of human beings, and the general cruelty masked within the humdrum buzzing of life. Her view is grim, you never hope for a Hollywood ending, you sense it building page by page, the inevitable dagger to the gut that will be dealt by the final paragraph, and then that last hit comes at you almost like clockwork. All this, and yet you keep on with her. Why?[29]

All the phrases and longer quotations in this paragraph are taken from enthusiastic and positive reviews where the writers rated the book in question with four or five stars, the highest rating that *Goodreads* allows. One reviewer joked, "Nice Catholic ladies aren't supposed to demolish you like this,"[30] but the online reviews prove that this "demolition" is very much valued by those who appreciate O'Connor. For example, one online reviewer posted this humorous review of *The Complete Stories*:

> "What, you think you're smart? Not as much as you think. You think you're right? You're not. You think you understand racial politics? You don't. You think that old man and his philosophy of life is grotesque? It's not. You think you're charming? Not. You think you're smarter than that child there? Not. You think just 'cause you got a wooden leg you're smart? Not. You think you're smart 'cause you're an atheist? Not. You think you're smart cause you're Saved? Not. You're not smart. You're an idiot. You know NOTHING. Learn to laugh at yourself jackass."—Flannery O'Connor, who can judge anyone she wants 'cause she's smarter than you. Period.[31]

Even those who do not warm to her themes appreciate this aspect of O'Connor's work: "I feel completely judged by the author as a writer, a reader, an American, and a Catholic," one reader of *Mystery and Manners* noted, "But judged so eloquently!"[32] O'Connor's "darkness" and assumptions about the fallen state of man have greatly enhanced her online reputation, in terms of both stature and substance.

All readers do not, however, appreciate the recommendation. Many recognize O'Connor's work as disturbing and unsettling but find this a fault in her artistic performance. Throughout the online reviews, "unlikable" stands as a watchword when readers describe what they find distasteful about O'Connor's characters and, by extension, her work in general. One reviewer of *Everything That Rises Must Converge* stated that she "couldn't find a single redeeming value"[33] in any of the characters, and many others have voiced similar complaints about the characters in each of O'Connor's works. For example, one reader of *The Complete Stories* stated, "Many of the main characters were just plain mean people" and qualified his remark with, "I don't have a problem with reading about the 'dregs of society,' but this seemed too much for me."[34] One reviewer of *The Violent Bear It Away* described the novel as "peopled with mistreated characters who are generally too unlikeable to be properly pitied."[35] Reviews of *Wise Blood* abound with complaints from readers who find Hazel Motes and Enoch Emery simply "too unpleasant"[36] or "delusional and repulsive."[37] As one puzzled reviewer wrote, "I know O'Connor had a purpose in writing about redemption but I cannot understand why she chose to select characters of such low achievement and limited horizons as the context in which she would express herself."[38] Such an assumption—that "low" or "limited" characters make for unpleasant reading—runs through dozens upon dozens of online reviews; many readers find that O'Connor's use of what one reviewer called "Southern troglodytes in the grip of religious mania"[39] keeps them from any consideration of her themes. This assumption that unlikable characters make for unlikable books, wrong as it is, surfaces throughout reviews of O'Connor's work. If a reader complains of being unable to "warm to any of the characters,"[40] he or she is not about to engage O'Connor on the subjects of grace or redemption. While one reader may joke, "I haven't met this many unlikeable characters since *Wuthering Heights*"[41] and another may fume, "Never, in all my reading, have I ever come across an author that despised her characters so deeply,"[42] the implication is the same: O'Connor's unlikable characters damage her reputation among readers who want a less demanding test of their empathy. One reader of *Wise Blood* described the characters as "difficult, if not impossible, to like" and complained, "I couldn't even find myself rooting for any of them to be successful or escape from their unhappy lives."[43] In short, the reader-as-rooter has little use for O'Connor's grotesques.

A second common adjective that appears in hundreds of reviews is "difficult," a word used to describe both the act of reading O'Connor's work and the ability to appreciate her thematic concerns. One reviewer of *A Good Man Is Hard to Find* stated, "This is the kind of book that makes me wish I were reading it in a great college course instead of alone,"[44] a wish shared by many other readers. Likewise, a reviewer of *The Violent Bear It Away* stated, "I wish I were reading this for a class or book club so that I could engage in some discussion,"[45] while another stated of the same novel, "It put my brain in a pretzel."[46] One reviewer of *Wise Blood* called it "definitely not something you can understand in one read,"[47] while another asserted that O'Connor's works "are meant to be discussed" and lamented, "I needed a book club for this one."[48] *Wise Blood* is, for many people, "an English-major type read."[49] One reader of *The Complete Stories* stated that she could "see why English professors read her": although she found the stories "hard to complete," she added that they "spark the need for conversation."[50] But those who acknowledge O'Connor's "difficulty" can still find her work compelling, as when one reviewer of *Wise Blood* described the novel as "a head-scratcher, but a good head-scratcher"[51] or another stated, "So strange it makes me dizzy. But in a good way."[52] Another reviewer of *Wise Blood* articulated ways in which some readers find O'Connor's difficulty invigorating:

What fun this book was! Would I recommend it to most people? No. Its disconnected narrative, strange characters, and focus on the grotesque does not make this read fun ... but, if you love to see someone playing with narrative, playing with how characters can function (none of these characters are likeable, relatable or realistic) as tools in a story, or want to spend hours pondering what the hell any of it means, then this is the book for you. . . . This is a smart lady, versed in the best of Russian literature (there are doubles! Mirrors! Even triples!), some serious Rene Girard (scapegoating! mimesis! violence!) and all sorts of fun theory.[53]

This review reflects the repeated challenge of understanding O'Connor's work, but also the additional challenge of facing the philosophical and spiritual implications of her work—a second kind of "difficulty" noted by many contemporary readers. Thus, one reviewer described *Wise Blood* as "a troubling book so rich in its parts and its effect that I will return to it again and again";[54] another wrote, "So much depth, I'm ready to read it again";[55] and another colorfully opined, "O'Connor delivers a lot to chew on, and no convenient spittoon when you're done."[56] While a novel like *Ulysses* is often regarded as "difficult" in the sense of understanding its narrative and one like *Moby-Dick* "difficult" in the sense of wrestling philosophically with its implications, O'Connor's work is regarded as a combination of difficulties that readers find stimulating, even if they cannot articulate why. One reviewer of *Wise Blood* called it "one of those books I enjoyed without understanding"[57] while another resorted to a near-confessional tone when describing his reaction: "First, I am ashamed it took me 35 years to read one of her novels. I'm sorry. Second, I am ashamed to say that it might take me 35 years to understand it."[58]

Just as online reviewers employ previously established watchwords, they also invoke decades' worth of conventional wisdom concerning other artists to whom O'Connor might be compared. Faulkner remains, for hundreds of reviewers, the fixed point in the southern sky, and many reviewers assume that stating O'Connor "belongs with the ranks of Faulkner"[59] is the highest praise they can bestow. Indeed, she is compared to him so frequently that a reviewer can offhandedly and accurately remark that she is "often spoken of in the same sentence as Faulkner,"[60] and another can brazenly urge his fellow readers, "Put away your Faulkner and start reading O'Connor. The old man should have come and taken lessons from the young woman."[61] Carson McCullers, another author to whom O'Connor was often compared in print, appears throughout the online reviews, as when a reader argues that McCullers's work is "pulsating with more humanity"[62] than O'Connor's. However, Erskine Caldwell, to whom O'Connor was so frequently compared in print, rarely surfaces in *Goodreads* reviews of her work, perhaps because his work has fallen more out of fashion than McCullers's. Some reviewers have compared O'Connor to other authors in an attempt to clarify the public perception of her, as when one reviewer noted, "She has more in common with James Ellroy than Harper Lee,"[63] when another remarked, "She's certainly no Margaret Mitchell, but that's a good thing,"[64] or when another stated, "She has more to do with Poe, Dostoevsky, Aquinas [and] Sophocles than that which is called 'Southern literature.'"[65] Other names surfacing throughout online reviews include Kafka, Shakespeare, Nathanael West, Thomas Hardy, Charles Williams, Cormac McCarthy, and Shirley Jackson, all of which are reasonable and expected.

What the web has allowed and fostered, however, is a far wider array of comparisons than ever appeared in print; with every reader a potential published critic, a multiplicity of tastes has resulted in some striking and unexpected comparisons, all of which help us better appreciate the current state of O'Connor's reputation and how readers are still attempting to describe her "difficult" art. One reviewer, for example, compared *Wise Blood* to a combination of "the murder ballads of Johnny Cash and the paintings of Jon Langford,"[66] while another called O'Connor "a smart woman's Quentin Tarantino."[67] These comparisons epitomize the more striking reviews where O'Connor is compared to nonliterary artists, such as songwriters, painters, or film directors. O'Connor's work has been called "very Springsteen-esque,"[68] "a Brueghel painting of Americana,"[69] and "the literary equivalent of David Lynch."[70] Many reviewers have compared her work to the films of the Coen brothers, "for in them we find violence juxtaposed with humor,"[71] and specific films such as *Taxi Driver*, since "each story works as a morality play or parable."[72] Such remarks—in which O'Connor's work is compared to respected works in other genres—are intended to raise her critical stock among other readers and prod them into picking up her work. However, not every comparison is flattering: one reviewer of *Wise Blood* stated, "Reading this book was akin to watching Jerry Springer,"[73] another wrote, "Before there was Jerry Springer, there was Flannery O'Connor,"[74] and a third reviewer compared reading O'Connor's stories to "watching an episode of the Jerry Springer show minus the chair throwing and fighting."[75] While it is easy for a reader to cringe at such a comparison, the allusion to the worst in daytime television—found in reviews that actually praise O'Connor's work—repeats the same challenge to come to grips with the freaks of O'Connor's fiction that faced her initial reviewers in 1952, heightened by the same paucity of experience and a similar lack of basis for comparison. The difficulty of conveying the sense of reading O'Connor's work explains why so many *Goodreads* reviewers describe it as a literary Mulligan stew: one describes her work as "a mash-up of Catholicism, William Faulkner, and Hieronymus Bosch,"[76] another states that her works read as if "the Grimm brothers and Faulkner got together to rewrite something by F. Scott Fitzgerald,"[77] while another describes her work as what would result if "Kafka did a fusion dance with Cormac McCarthy."[78] Still another jokes, "She makes Sylvia Plath look like A. A. Milne."[79] These struggles with allusion and comparison suggest the degree to which some modern readers find O'Connor's work difficult to describe, just as the original reviewers did in 1952.

As with the print reviews of O'Connor's work, online reviews teem with assumptions—both stated and implied—about the American South. Mencken spoke derisively of the Bible Belt almost eighty years ago; a survey of *Goodreads* reveals a still-strong antisouthern bias and the assumption that the South is populated by *Deliverance*'s "porch-dwelling dueling banjo-players,"[80] with all the accompanying unpleasantness that this stereotype connotes. "I haven't spent much time in the South," one reviewer of *Wise Blood* states, "and O'Connor's description of it makes me want to stay away. Far away. Pennsylvania is bad enough."[81] Similar vows to never travel below the Mason-Dixon line are found in many reviews of *A Good Man Is Hard to Find*, as in one reviewer's quip, "I don't think I will be visiting Georgia any time soon,"[82] in another's remark that the stories will provoke a reader "to make a run for it—probably all the way north, to Canada,"[83] in another's praise of O'Connor's ability to "make the South creepier than it already was,"[84] and in a description of the stories as "really frightening stuff" that "does not make me any more inclined to spend time in the South than I was before."[85] These sentiments can be found in even more vituperative form, as when one reviewer of *A Good Man Is Hard to Find* stated, "This collection of stories basically just reminded me of how much I hate the South and how glad I am to be far, far away from it,"[86] or when another stated that the stories "affirmed how screwed up I know the American South to be," and added, "Sorry, Southern people. You know it's true. After all, here is a whole book about it."[87] These may be the most bald-faced examples, but the assumption that O'Connor's work emphasizes what one reviewer called "the essentially savage nature of the American South"[88] threads throughout the online reviews, regardless of whether the reviewer is praising or attacking O'Connor's performance. Such an assumption has become so widespread that one reviewer noted, "I still have not read a book where [the] South hasn't been portrayed as the devil's pit,"[89] and another imagined that "folks who live in those states like Alabama and Georgia and Mississippi must get a little tired of everyone thinking they're freaks."[90]

One reason why some reviewers respond with such antisouthern sentiments is that they assume themselves to be without sin and so can cast the first stone; assuming the North as normative, they engage in what historian David Gold-field described as feeling "much better about themselves and, consequently, worse about the South," which they regard as "the nation's boobocracy, a receptacle of reprobate preachers, gun-toting toddlers, assorted Bravehearts rampaging against government, education, and the arts; and politicians who raise hogs and lower taxes."[91] Another reason is one we have seen in O'Connor's early reception in print: the assumption that O'Connor is providing reportage or documentary footage rather than artistic creations. That such assumed reportage complements some readers' existing assumptions about the South makes O'Connor's work seem all the more "realistic." Recall that the very first print review of *Wise Blood* stated that it was "about the South,"[92] and note an early print review of *A Good Man Is Hard to Find* that described the difference between O'Connor and Eudora Welty as akin to the difference between dreams and reality: "Miss Welty deals with a South that almost never was. Miss O'Connor deals with a South that is. Miss Welty's regionalism is like trying to evoke the person of Robert E. Lee from the letters of his name on the letterhead of a school of journalism. . . . Miss O'Connor's regionalism is like bumping into the presence of Robert E. Lee were he now the dean of that school of journalism."[93] This notion that O'Connor's work depicts "a South that is" finds its way into many *Goodreads* reviews. One reviewer of *A Good Man Is Hard to Find* asserts, "The writing is factual, dispassionate almost to the point that it reads like a news report,"[94] and other reviews are grounded on a similar assumption, often carried in verbs describing O'Connor's artistic activity. For example, reviewers of *Everything That Rises Must Converge* praise her ability to "capture the darker essence of the South"[95] and state that her collection "captures the South in a very realistic way."[96] Another states O'Connor "places the reader squarely in the midst of the mid-twentieth-century South, a place I appreciate visiting but after seeing it through O'Connor's eyes, am most grateful NOT to be staying."[97]

Such assumptions are also found in reviews of her other works, as when reviewers of *The Complete Stories* state, "If you really want to get a taste of what the deep South is like, read this book,"[98] or promise, "Read her and you will know her dark, demented, brilliant truth of the South."[99] One reviewer of *A Good Man Is Hard to Find* praised O'Connor with, "Nobody does a better job of capturing the realities of life in rural Georgia than Ms. O'Connor,"[100] and another suggested that "Good Country People" could be used "to explain the South to people who don't get it,"[101] as if O'Connor were more like Paul

Theroux than William Faulkner. One reviewer found her life imitating art and stated, "I found a new appreciation for O'Connor when I moved to the South. Before then, I hadn't believed that characters like the ones she wrote could exist. But they can, and they do!"[102] And even when offering more complex views of the South, some reviewers' opinions are still undergirded with the assumption that O'Connor's power as a realistic, regionalist writer was her strongest suit, as in this representative example:

> Published over fifty years ago, [*A Good Man Is Hard to Find*] still rings true to me, someone who lives in the rural South today. Don't get me wrong. Much has changed. But when you get outside the urban areas and the university towns, the themes O'Connor focuses on in these stories (violence, religion, and race) still permeate the culture. Great writing and I highly recommend it.[103]

Such examples confirm the degree to which many readers assume that, in the words of one Canadian reviewer, "the South understands what we call surrealism as a type of hyperreality."[104] And one Brooklyn-based reviewer, who remarked, "The South is a different place,"[105] may not have realized that he was continuing an intellectual trend well documented and described by historian James C. Cobb of regarding the South as "a primitive and exotic land distinctly apart from the rest of America."[106]

That many readers would incorrectly assume O'Connor's writing to be aimed at exposing the "real South" and inviting them to cast the first stone from their own positions of innocence was an aspect of her reception of which she was well aware. For example, in a letter to Robert Giroux after the publication of *The Violent Bear It Away*, O'Connor wrote about the British reception of the book, "The only British review I have seen that you haven't sent me was one by Kingsley Amis in the *Observer*. It was extremely unfavorable but he ended up saying that I had convinced him that this is the way people were in Georgia. (Horrors!)"[107] In her lecture "Some Aspects of the Grotesque in Southern Fiction," O'Connor joked about the same topic: "I am always having it pointed out to me that life in Georgia is not at all the way I picture it, that escaped criminals do not roam the roads exterminating families, nor Bible salesmen prowl about looking for girls with wooden legs."[108] And, of course, there is O'Connor's previously quoted remark from the same lecture concerning what passes for "realism" above and below the Mason-Dixon line.[109] The peculiar brand of "realism" O'Connor pursued was not a matter of mimesis or the phonetic spelling of characters' speech, but a deeper realism of grace and redemption that transcends any region. "When you're a Southerner and in pursuit of reality," she informed Harvey Breit, "the reality you come up with is going to have a southern accent, but that's just an accent; it's not the essence of what you're trying to do."[110] O'Connor thought of the South as Joyce thought of Dublin: "I always write about Dublin," Joyce explained, "because if I can get to the heart of Dublin I can get to the heart of all the cities of the world. In the particular is contained the universal."[111]

This sense of the South as microcosm of the world has been noted by some online readers, such as reviewers of *A Good Man Is Hard to Find* who described the stories as "widely universal,"[112] "universal in depicting the human condition,"[113] and "a reflection of the greater world outside of the South."[114] Similarly, a reviewer of *The Complete Stories* claimed, "The setting is the South of the past, but the bigotry and pettiness characterized within these stories is not an affliction that is confined to a time or place."[115] Such thoughts were exactly what Robert Giroux sought to provoke when he spoke of O'Connor as an "American" author. In "The Life You Save May Be Your Own," Tom T. Shiftlet remarks and later demonstrates, "The world is almost rotten,"[116] and some of O'Connor's readers recognize that O'Connor's thematic concerns transcend specifics of time and space, just as she intended them to do. However, such an approach is found less frequently than ones that disparage the South as a land of freaks. When asked in a 1963 interview if the grotesque elements of her work had anything to do with her being a southerner, O'Connor stated, "We're all grotesque and I don't think the Southerner is any more grotesque than anyone else."[117] Many online reviewers, like their predecessors in print, would disagree.

Some readers find that O'Connor's work fits perfectly their preconceptions of what a southerner might produce; conversely, they find that her work defies what they expect from a writer with an existing reputation as a "Catholic author." Such readers praise O'Connor for not figuratively preaching to the choir. "You'd think," one reviewer noted, "writing that has such heavy religious imagery would be hard to swallow and uninteresting. Not true."[118] Other reviewers concur, as in, "Her masterful understanding of the human condition transcends dogma,"[119] "The stories expose human flaws but do not preach religion,"[120] and, "Catholic? Sure, but they're universal themes no matter what you believe."[121] One reviewer of *The Violent Bear It Away* described, as well as any critic writing in a major journal, O'Connor's method and its effects:

> Flannery O'Connor, with her second novel, again manages to write a story with a strong underpinning of Christian theology without being didactic. This is partly, of course, because her characters are fully imagined and fascinating in their own

right. But another reason is that, paradoxically, she is intent on unequivocally putting forth the Christian view of reality, not as a lesson *per se*, but as a condensed version of an experience which makes that view starkly evident.[122]

Some online reviewers find O'Connor's art an antidote to what they regard as trendy, feel-good works about Christianity, as when one praised her stories as "the complete opposite of Christian bookstore fiction"[123] or another stated that *Mystery and Manners* was "apparently not read by most patrons of the 'Christian' book publishing industry."[124] One reviewer even advised Kirk Cameron, the former child star who now acts in and produces Christian-based films, to read O'Connor on the flaws of Catholic literature and "take O'Connor's criticisms to heart."[125] As some readers value O'Connor's "difficult" vision of humanity, others similarly admire her "difficult" and unsentimental view of Christianity. "I am drawn to Flannery's God," one reviewer of *The Complete Stories* explained, "not as a cosmic Santa Claus, as is often portrayed in American Christianity, but as a God who redeems undeserving souls, even if it means the very moment [they] die."[126]

Other readers, however—perhaps those of "Christian bookstore fiction" mentioned above—find O'Connor's exploration of Catholic issues too hard to take and too far from the tenets of Christianity as they understand or practice it. "I understand that O'Connor was a devout Catholic," one reader posted, "but what I don't understand is why she always leaves out the part about God's love and forgiveness."[127] This reviewer misses the point about the ending of "The Artificial Nigger" and other significant works, but her assertion reflects an assumption about O'Connor's "difficult" Christianity found in many reviews. One reviewer of *A Good Man Is Hard to Find* recalls the previously examined comments about "unlikable" characters when he states, "This was challenging because I knew she was a 'Christian writer' and yet it was so filled with despicable characters, violence, and the seamy side of human nature."[128] Many online reviewers who prefer a more upbeat vision of Christianity express their dislike of O'Connor's: one warns readers of *A Good Man Is Hard to Find*, "There is little redemption in these pages,"[129] while another simply calls O'Connor "un-Christian" and an author who wasted her talent "in the service of hatred and evil."[130] This last judgment is extreme, but it epitomizes ways in which some readers find O'Connor's actual performance at odds with her reputation as a Catholic author: one representative reader gave *The Violent Bear It Away* a three-star rating on the grounds that O'Connor "leaves no room for a quiet, joyful, commonplace Christianity."[131] Some readers use the identical notion of

O'Connor's chief thematic concern to extol or disparage her work: one laudatory reviewer of *The Complete Stories* calls the volume "a must-read if you have
Catholic damage,"[132] while another rails, "I get it, Flannery, you have Catholic
damage. It's engulfed your life, it's all you can think about."[133] Of course, many
readers without any religious convictions can find O'Connor's work inspiring
and moving: one five-star reviewer states, "I can't explain how much I love
these stories. And I'm not even a Christian."[134] The online reviews feature many
such statements from non-Christians, agnostics, and atheists who are drawn
to O'Connor's work. Generally speaking, however, readers who prefer a kinder,
gentler vision of Christianity tend to dismiss O'Connor, while those who prefer what they find to be the bitter truth relish O'Connor's ability to explore it.
Her current reputation as an unsentimental and troubling Catholic author is
found in the opinions of both camps of readers.

One complaint voiced about O'Connor by many online reviewers is the
same one found sometimes in print, especially in the original reviews of *Everything That Rises Must Converge:* the narrowness of her subject matter makes for
a repetitive reading experience. This is especially true in the online reviews of
The Complete Stories, where even the most enthusiastic reviewers express opinions such as, "550 pages is too long for a short-story collection in general, but
in the end O'Connor's subject matter is rather narrow, and becomes repetitive
after a while."[135] One reviewer described how she tried to read the collection
"from cover to cover" but "then stopped, because the themes started to get
repetitive,"[136] just as another reader compared his experience with reading the
entire volume to "watching a *Twilight Zone* marathon."[137] Online reviewers of
Everything That Rises Must Converge have voiced similar complaints, stating
that "each story contains an almost identical emotional footprint"[138] and the
"same pattern."[139] Many of these reviews—very much like the ones that originally appeared in 1965—praise O'Connor's skill while simultaneously dispar-
aging what they regard as her limited subject matter. For example, one review
states, "I thought the writing was fantastic and I was blown away by the first
few stories, although by the end of the book the stories become predictable
since she's always working with the same ideas and themes."[140] In fact, the
charge that "it all gets a bit predictable"[141] is often the reason behind online
readers' middling reviews of O'Connor's collections. The more enthusiastic reviewers offer the suggestion of reading her *Complete Stories* over a long span
of time: because of the "certain sameness" of her characters, plots, and themes,
many reviewers concur that a reading of the collection "should be spread out
over the better part of a year."[142] One reviewer who admires O'Connor but

found *The Complete Stories* "slightly repetitive, especially when read too close together" explained that he "settled for one story per day, over the course of a month."[143] These readers argue that when the stories are read successively over a short period of time, "the characters and themes begin to sound repetitious and drown out the nuances of each vignette";[144] they are therefore best taken in small doses. However, many less enthusiastic readers suggest a different approach: "Variety is not something you will find here. Individually, some of the stories shine. But when taken together, as a collection must be, O'Connor's stories end up repeating themselves to the point that you don't need to read all of them."[145] (Many of the reviewers offering middle to low ratings of the *Complete Stories* suggest reading only some of them, assuming that a handful will do the work of the entire collection.) In short, the issue of O'Connor's artistic limits is treated differently by those who complain that her work features "a few themes, heavily trod, some of which are fairly dated"[146] and those who find the quality of her writing makes such complaints moot: "A good friend's mom once said, 'But it's all the same story!' It's pretty accurate. One good story, though."[147]

The Violent Bear It Online

Goodreads reviewers thus reflect their predecessors in print in a number of ways. However, the most striking similarity between these two sets of critics—professional and amateur—is the way in which they read and misread *The Violent Bear It Away*. The skirmish between the genuine authorial audience (who assume Tarwater's vocation to be undeniable) and ironic audience (who assume Tarwater to be the victim of "brainwashing") in the reception of this work has reappeared in a new generation of readers, who now battle over the meaning of O'Connor's novel just as its characters do over Tarwater's allegiance. The genuine readers state their opinions with clarity and force, often revealing assumptions similar to those held by Mason Tarwater, the protagonist's great-uncle whose death launches Tarwater on his spiritual journey. For example, one reviewer states, "What a ride. O'Connor gives us a scalding and brutally honest critique of American progressive thought and utilitarian morality."[148] Mason is certainly "brutally honest" in his critique of Rayber's secular humanism, with his notions of how "the world was made for the dead"[149] and the need for Rayber's son, Bishop, to be baptized. "I love its unabashed attack on reason," a similarly minded reviewer states. "Reason can never win with O'Connor, because she correctly recognizes the stupidity and finitude of men who try to use it to answer life's existential questions. They come out looking petty and small."[150] Such remarks seem like a more polished version of Mason's invective against his nephew after he is mockingly asked to explain why God formed the mentally retarded Bishop as he did: "Yours not to question the mind of the Lord God Almighty. Yours not to grind the Lord into your head and spit out a number!"[151] Before his death, Mason tells Tarwater that he kidnapped him away from Rayber so that he would be "free" and "not a piece of information inside [Rayber's] head."[152] This struggle between Mason and Rayber, between what one reviewer aptly called "God and the world,"[153] is noted by many readers. One representative review reflects the current genuine reading of the novel:

> Tarwater travels to the city, where he struggles against the need to deny his spiritual inheritance and the call of God. O'Connor paints a macabre picture of Southern life and religious fundamentalism and parodies the blind self-assurances of modern secular thinking. The novel is unsettling because it offers no easy truths; its hero is an unlikable boy who learns that doing God's work entails violence, unreason, even madness. It is not, as might be expected, a parody of religious fanaticism, but a psychological study of the mysterious, frightening, and sometimes offensive nature of the religious calling.[154]

With the phrase "as might be expected," the reviewer calls attention to assumptions that modern readers might bring to a novel about a potential prophet whose kidnapping by his great-uncle in order to raise him in the woods is presented by its author as spiritual rather than criminal.

Such expectations of parody abound in the ironic readings of the novel, where many reviewers, including those who praise it, find the novel exactly what the previous reviewer claimed it is not: a sustained and troubling attack on "religious fanaticism." Print reviewers' descriptions of Mason as a "fanatic" or "insane" had surfaced in the original reviews: their online counterparts rely on the same terms to contain and dismiss Mason's character and mock the issues O'Connor employs him to raise. One online reviewer described the novel as concerning an "orphan raised in the backcountry by a truly insane fundamentalist great-uncle," a relative "so unrelievedly screwed up, so utterly devoid of humanity."[155] Another complained, "Reading about insane evangelicals does my brain no good,"[156] while another offered what he saw as a shorthand version of the novel: "Old Tarwater—a religious fanatic; Young Tarwater, brainwashed by Old, & hence, a very stroppy surly religious fanatic."[157] Another summarized the novel as follows: "A boy raised by a crazy, religiously fanatical uncle wanders out of the woods, finds his 'sane' uncle, faces some difficulties, and becomes a prophet like his crazy uncle."[158] That the reviewer mistakenly takes Mason to be Tarwater's uncle, rather than his great-uncle, is beside the point. What is important here is that the reviewer reflects a common assumption among ironic readers that Mason is insane and Rayber is not, a dichotomy epitomized in a review that mocks O'Connor and her characters for their "screwed-up" assumptions:

> Here it appears that the lunatics and the radicals are portrayed as being "the ones who get it." The insane great-uncle (who repeatedly tries to kidnap relatives to baptize them, who shoots people trying to retrieve their own kin, who seems to be the type from O'Connor's short stories who are the hypocritical and manipulated misled) turns out to be the one who was correct in his ridiculous prophecies.[159]

O'Connor had suspected that many of her readers would side with Rayber and dismiss Mason as a lunatic: "The modern reader will identify himself with the schoolteacher, but it is the old man who speaks for me."[160] Reviews such as these confirm the depth of her insight into the "modern reader's" assumptions and the challenge she faced in writing for an audience that thought God was dead.

One interesting and subtle difference between the novel's initial ironic readers and the online ones is their use of a new magic word. Many original reviewers relied on the term "fanatic" to describe Mason, and while the label is still used, it has been complemented by another: "fundamentalist." Walker Percy once called O'Connor a "Georgia fundamentalist,"[161] and O'Connor herself noted that if she were not Catholic, she would join a Pentecostal Holiness church, a remark that Ralph C. Wood justly interprets as meaning that "belief must be radical or it is not belief at all."[162] To O'Connor, "fundamentalism" included devotion to a mystery that took its shape in attempts to understand that mystery through the five senses; thus, in "A Temple of the Holy Ghost," a hermaphrodite illuminates for the young protagonist the mystery of the Eucharist, and in "Parker's Back," O. E. Parker is much more involved in the mystery of Christ (and sympathetic) than his sanctimonious wife. Many online reviewers, however, use the term pejoratively in a way that Mencken, when he covered the Scopes trial, would have approved. For example, one reviewer—who praised the novel—described it as "perfect" and "chilling for the modern reader who nurses a healthy fear of religious fundamentalism."[163] Another reviewer (a self-described "uneducated atheist") called the novel an "incredible portrait of three generations ruined by religious fundamentalism."[164] These reviews typify the many that urge *The Violent Bear It Away* as a warning against the dangers of fundamentalism, just as, we shall see, others regard O'Connor's stories as parables intended to instruct readers about the horrors of racism. Some argue that, in terms of the battle between Mason and Rayber, O'Connor finds both of them troubling: "For O'Connor, both secularism and fundamentalism are equally heresy, and blind their adherents to God's truth. There is a place for both, just as there is a place for both reason and faith. Each exposes the weaknesses of the other."[165] This seems typical of the reviewer who wants O'Connor to conform to his or her own assumptions, as one who describes the novel as a "tale of both religious and secular fanaticism and the violence they engender."[166] Of course, such claims that both Mason and Rayber are "fanatics" reduce the characters' complexities and oversimplify O'Connor's chief thematic concern, which one reader accurately states as imagining "what it would be like to be a prophet in modern America."[167] And, in a perfect example of a reader unable to believe that O'Connor took her spiritual issues as seriously as she did, one notable reviewer—who gave the novel a five-star review—epitomized O'Connor's ironic reception:

> Children are the ultimate victims of adults who are consumed with self-interest. Young Tarwater's life is essentially stolen by Old Tarwater from the beginning of the book. And then we see Young Tarwater navigate a life after Old Tarwater's death, haunted and weighted with the mission and shame Old Tarwater decided for him. . . . I found this book the perfect example of what happens when a person disappears into religion, essentially "Jesus" erasing the personality and uniqueness of a person. Of Old Tarwater: "He was a one-notion man. Jesus. Jesus this and Jesus that." The boy struggles to differentiate, and a voice within him specifies what his choice in life is: "It ain't Jesus or the devil. It's Jesus or you."[168]

This is the best example I know in the history of O'Connor's reception of what might be called an enthusiastic misreading: what the reviewer has not grasped is that the twice-quoted "voice within" Tarwater is not his conscience or imaginary friend but the devil, who leads Tarwater away from his vocation and is eventually personified by the man in the lavender-colored car who drugs and rapes Tarwater after he simultaneously drowns and baptizes Bishop. That this reader would fall for the devil's line and defend it in the name of children is a perfect example of O'Connor's insight into the workings of the modern mind: there could perhaps be no better example of O'Connor's skill in making evil sound reasonable and "modern." Such reviews that extol O'Connor's novel, while finding in its pages ideas directly opposed to the ones she portrayed in such "large and startling figures,"[169] showcase the accuracy with which O'Connor was able to capture the mind that discounts the existence of evil and is unable to imagine that a twentieth-century novelist could entertain any approach to Christianity other than scorn.

Readers and Race

Key words such as "grotesque," the idea of O'Connor's work as stylistically and thematically "difficult," her unsentimental vision of Catholicism, her artistic "limitations," and her portrayal of the South are all aspects of her reputation that we have traced since the publication of *Wise Blood* in 1952, aspects that resurface in contemporary online reviews, where the general reader has come to many of the same conclusions as the professional readers of a generation or two before them. What sets contemporary online reviewers apart from their predecessors in print, however, is the amount of attention they pay to O'Connor's depiction of race and racial issues, a subject occasionally mentioned in print but found throughout the online reviews. Many reviewers warn prospective readers about race just as they do about the "darkness" of the stories, especially when they are praising O'Connor's work. For example, one laudatory review of *A Good Man Is Hard to Find* begins:

> A word of caution before you read her work. Her stories were written in the forties and early fifties and take place in the Deep South. Language is used to refer to African-Americans that is considered unacceptable today. In my reading, it did not appear that the characters used the word in a derogatory manner, but more like an adjective. As if the word were a substitute for "black." It's the reader's call as to what is offensive and what is not. If you are able to overcome it, you will be rewarded with some entertaining stories and a look into the past.[170]

Another reviewer ended her positive review of *The Complete Stories* with, "I recommend this compilation, but don't expect *Gone with the Wind* sensibilities and niceties. This is the raw South of the late 40s and the 50s. Proceed with caution."[171] Another simply noted, "Not for the easily offended."[172] Online reviewers seem able to find examples of this feature of the "raw South" in virtually every page of O'Connor's work: one warns readers to "Prepare for endless use of the 'n' word,"[173] while another says, "I have never seen so many instances of the N-word in one place."[174] One reviewer (who calls O'Connor one of his "all time favorites") states that some of her stories "are almost entirely composed of an upsetting word,"[175] while another describes this word as "everywhere"[176] in O'Connor's fiction, a remark wholly untrue. Others speak of the "rampant racism"[177] found in O'Connor's work and exaggerate the degree to which O'Connor explored racial issues: one reviewer of *Everything That Rises Must Converge* incorrectly asserts that the stories "focus primarily on racial tensions of the time,"[178] and another erroneously describes her stories as "overwhelmingly concerned with race relations."[179] Such exaggerations of how much O'Connor wrote (or even cared) about racial topics can be found in many online reviews, as well as an almost-palpable nervousness felt by reviewers who wish to suggest the quality of O'Connor's work but find this part of it needing to be declared and explained outright. Hence, the volume of the warnings and caveats that appear in so many positive reviews and the mischaracterization of O'Connor's work as focused on racial themes. While racial topics are found in a small number of stories, they are more examples of the characters' failings than occasions for O'Connor to suggest something about race in America: "The Artificial Nigger" demonstrates Mr. Head's racism to be a symptom of his moral disease and not the whole of his illness, and in "Everything That Rises Must Converge," Julian's mother's nostalgia for the Jim Crow past is used primarily as a means to highlight Julian's own self-congratulatory attitude toward African Americans and to make the story's ending—which has less to do with race than the tearing down of Julian's superiority—so powerful. O'Connor herself stated, "The topical is poison. I got away with it in 'Everything That Rises' but only because I say a plague on everybody's house as far as the race business goes."[180] The "race" O'Connor truly concerned herself with was the human one, but her interest in fallen man as a whole does not always become apparent in the online reviews, where reviewers exaggerate O'Connor's use of racially charged language and interest in racial themes because they seem more glaring to them, a phenomenon that has also occurred with *Adventures of Huckleberry Finn*.[181] Again, her works have not changed but her audiences have.

Online reviewers who discuss O'Connor's treatment of race can be grouped into three broad categories. The first includes readers who assume that O'Connor was a product of her time and that her putting racial slurs in her characters' mouths was simply de rigueur for a southern author in the 1950s. These readers assume that she does so because any writer portraying life in the South would be forced to create racist characters, since the South is presumably filled with them. For example, a reviewer of *Everything That Rises Must Converge* notes, "She is, to some degree, a product of her environment, and her use of certain words can grate on our 21st-century ears,"[182] while another discusses his inability to determine if O'Connor was "racially progressive for her time or merely mired in her context."[183] A reviewer of *A Good Man Is Hard to Find* called it "a good depiction of the South in this era" and, as if what followed was necessary in any such evaluation, gave "fair warning" of the "racist terminology used."[184] A second reviewer of the same collection notes that since the stories "were written in the 1940s (pre–Civil rights), some of the language is a bit hard to take."[185] This reviewer's dating of the stories is as faulty as her assumption about O'Connor as benighted by her times, an assumption shared by other readers, who note that O'Connor's racial themes could be "very shocking and offensive, especially when read out of social context and era"[186] or who complain of O'Connor's "repeated racial overtones" but assume that such overtones— however nebulously identified—were "in the grasp of her every-day"[187] experience. This kind of reviewer, who assumes that O'Connor was a prisoner to generic southern racism, often engages in self-congratulation, as when a reviewer of *A Good Man Is Hard to Find* states that one value of the stories is "to see how wrong our ancestors were, and to see how far we've come, and to think about how far we still have to go"[188] or when a reviewer of *Everything That Rises Must Converge* wonders "if we should blame the era or the miserable characters"[189] for their attitudes about race. One reader employs a common maneuver when he qualifies his mentioning the use of "extremely repulsive" racial slurs with, "In her defense, this was in character for a white southerner of that era."[190] These remarks and others recall the exchange in "The Life You Save May Be Your Own" between Mr. Shiftlet and Lucynell Crater:

> "Why, listen, lady," he said with a grin of delight, "the monks of old slept in their coffins!"
>
> "They wasn't as advanced as we are," the old woman said.[191]

Like the old woman, many modern readers assume a superiority to the very author whom they praise; that the author specialized in cutting down just such superior-minded figures (such as Mrs. Turpin, Julian, and Mr. Head) escapes their notice. As with readers of *The Violent Bear It Away* being of the devil's party without knowing it, we again find readers unknowingly demonstrating how accurately O'Connor captures human flaws and hypocrisies. Not all readers, however, find themselves casting a patronizing eye on O'Connor: one reviewer pointedly remarked that she found it "hard to be self-satisfied and judgmental when reading a book of stories of people who are self-satisfied and judgmental."[192]

The second category of reviewers who address O'Connor's treatment of race assume that she is offering a specific critique or attack, seeking to expose what she found to be a malignant force in southern life. These readers regard O'Connor as more like Swift or Orwell than Faulkner or Welty. For example, one praises O'Connor: "Her criticism of her Southern characters is blatantly open, calling out stupidity and racism."[193] Another states, "There is a ton of racism in many of her characters, but I think O'Connor was trying to point that out to readers, especially in the fifties."[194] One reader values O'Connor's stories as "a snapshot of the appalling state of race relations in this country in the 1950s,"[195] just as another regards them as works in which O'Connor gives "a pointed sizing up of her peers in the segregationist South of the 1950s."[196] As with "the South," so with "the Fifties"—a cultural idea to which many people claim unbiased and absolute insight. Reviewers of *The Complete Stories* praise O'Connor for uncovering what they (like so many others) assume about southern life: one states "Here, hate is exposed as tragic,"[197] while a second states, "O'Connor has a lot to say about how religion and racism shaped the Southern culture in the early twentieth century."[198] That O'Connor was never interested in "exposing" or editorializing ("a lot to say") is a notion that this camp of readers seldom entertains. A subcategory of this group of reviewers includes those who assume that O'Connor used the plots of her stories to instruct her readers, much like a southern Aesop. For example, in a review of *Everything That Rises Must Converge*, one reader describes his unease at her "racial slurs" that "abound" in the collection but ends his review on a note of assurance to those readers who may find his warnings about O'Connor's work too strong: "I couldn't tell you too much about O'Connor's views on Southern racism; I haven't read enough of her personal writings to make a sound call there. I can tell you that the characters who display their investment in social hierarchies, the benefits of slave or underpaid labor, or in their own glory in a general sense are invariably punished."[199] The guarantee of "punishment" is meant to assuage potentially offended readers but also to place O'Connor on the right side of history.

A similar reassurance to potential readers is found in a review of *A Good Man Is Hard to Find*, when the reviewer asks, "Where else can you find prophetic grandmas, artificial leg fiends, and old racist ladies who get their come-uppance?"[200] Like the previous reviewer, this person assumes that O'Connor's works are meant to foil the racism they find so disquieting, but what they fail to grasp is that, for O'Connor, the people "deserving" punishment for their ignorance are of every place and every time. The Misfit's mocking eulogy of the grandmother—"She would have been a good woman if it was someone there to shoot her every minute of her life"[201]—applies to everyone in all times. A good woman is hard to find. As some of her early readers assumed that she was satirizing religion, many online reviewers assume—incorrectly, for O'Connor was neither satirist nor saint—she is doing the same with attitudes about race. Such reviewers exaggerate how often O'Connor's characters employ racist language and simultaneously attempt to defend her use of it on artistic grounds, perhaps prompted by their fear of being called racists themselves for recommending the fiction—a groundless charge against the reviewers, to be sure, but one that they acknowledge in the nervousness of their prose.

Finally, a third broad category of reviewers assumes that O'Connor was simply a racist herself. Such reviews appear less frequently than those which assume O'Connor to be a journalist or writer of fables, but they do surface enough to be noticed, often in negative reviews. For example, one reviewer of *A Good Man Is Hard to Find* stated, "Flannery O'Connor's racism is about as subtle as an atomic bomb,"[202] while another dismissed the collection as "dismal, religious, Southern racist material,"[203] as if O'Connor were writing propaganda for the Klan. Even some reviewers who admire her work assume that O'Connor is guilty as charged: one reader of *A Good Man Is Hard to Find* added in his four-star review, "It seems to me that O'Connor is a racist and a gleeful dogmatist, but those things make her true to her region and time, and they don't detract from the quality of her work."[204] Again, the South and racism are indissolubly linked; again, the idea is that O'Connor simply could not help herself and that her fiction was, in part, written to share her own regressive views with her readers. Such an assumption resulted in the 2000 banning of O'Connor's work from—of all places—a Catholic high school in Louisiana.[205]

The general sense, however, among those who admire and recommend her work is that her racial and even her spiritual themes are less interesting than the force of her prose. Reviews posted on *Goodreads* indicate that O'Connor's value among "common readers" has continued to rise: with more than 105,000 ratings and over 6,600 reviews, enough readers rank her highly enough that her average rating, out of a perfect five, is 4.20.[206] "I couldn't disagree more with her politics," one representative reader states, "but absolutely love her as a writer."[207] But other readers admire her for what they perceive to be a shared set of values (and thus admire themselves for finding such a good spokesperson): one reviewer of *A Good Man Is Hard to Find*, for example, notes that O'Connor's characters "want their heaven a little early, but can't quite understand why their dreams aren't what their God promised them. As in modern society, we have deposed God for not getting with our program."[208] The reviews generally stress character much more than any inventive narrative technique. And just as O'Connor's original print reviewers struggled to describe the content and effects of her fiction, many online reviewers have expressed their inability to articulate their own inexplicable admiration for her work: "Why am I fascinated with Flannery O'Connor's stories?" one reviewer asked. "She was a devout Catholic living in the Southern Bible belt. I'm a lapsed Jewish yankee. Nearly all of her stories have explicit religious themes. I'm an atheist."[209] Another reviewer asked, "Seeing as I have no fear of the wrath of an angry god, why did this book affect me so deeply, leaving me with a stunned expression staring at a blank wall for several minutes after each little story had wrapped up?"[210] Another reviewer stated that she loved *Wise Blood* "even if I may never be able to articulate why."[211] How online readers have read her work and attempted to describe it is epitomized by a five-star review of *A Good Man Is Hard to Find:*

> This stuff is twisted, sparse, clipped, dark, doomy, funny, dramatic, Southern, angry, sexy, super Catholic, death-haunted, maniacal, bizarre, possibly racist, apparently desperate, fatalistic, existential, dreary, ugly, fetid, frenzied, morbid, lax, stern, prepossessing, unforgiving, unrelenting, anti-everything, aged, "retro," haunting, parabolic, anecdotal, moral, redemptive, sublime, reasoned, feverish, dreamlike, unsparing, sparse, I said that one already, seductive, craftsmanlike, worried, extremely well conceived, taut, brooding, polarizing, scary, and powerful.[212]

This playful yet often on-target description reflects the trends, watchwords, and contradictory readings of O'Connor that still inform her reputation. And to conclude this discussion, one might appreciate a one-word review of *The Violent Bear It Away* by a reader in Chile: *cuático*, a word meaning "eccentric," "shocking," or "weird"—a Chilean version of "grotesque."[213]

Conclusion

Her Name Carved in Stone

On November 3, 2014, the Cathedral of Saint John the Divine in upper Manhattan held "A Celebration of Flannery O'Connor," an evening of speakers and performances to commemorate O'Connor's induction into the American Poets Corner, a quiet and dignified niche located off the center aisle. O'Connor had, yet again, "arrived." This unconventional author whose work many readers had once tried to pigeonhole as "southern gothic" was being installed in one of the most august and formal halls of fame, her name literally written in stone and joining the likes of Twain, James, and Faulkner. But the Cathedral of Saint John the Divine is also a very cosmopolitan place: on the night of the celebration, beautiful and enormous steel birds created by the Chinese artist Xu Bing hung from the ceiling, and guests were greeted by the sound of classical guitar as they walked to the altar. New Yorkers—the hippest of the hip—were gathering to reconfirm Giroux's assertion that O'Connor was more American than southern, the scope of her work more universal than local.

As I mounted the steps, I found myself walking next to another person entering the cathedral. I asked her if she were attending the O'Connor celebration. "No," she said. "I just wanted to go in and have a moment." She asked me why I was there and I told her about O'Connor's induction into the American Poets Corner. Her response—"Flannery O'Connor, the author?"—confirmed the writer's name as a household word. Before the event began, I mingled with some of the guests and organizers, one of whom introduced me to Wally Lamb, who told me that he, like so many others, had been introduced to O'Connor by "A Good Man Is Hard to Find" and, like so many of us, became a lifelong admirer. "That was the one that did it for me," he said. I spoke to the poet Alfred Corn, who, as a student at Emory, corresponded with O'Connor about weighty issues two years before she died. He told me, "She was honest with me because she didn't know me or have to put on that 'southern thing,'" an interesting observation; O'Connor was always conscious of her reputation and, at times, played to it. Marilyn Nelson, the cathedral's poet in residence that year, told me that there was, naturally, some debate over who would be installed for 2014, but that the subsequent debate over the quotation carved into the stone under O'Connor's name was much more spirited and protracted, a description later confirmed for me by another of the electors. With a smile, Nelson said, "But we prevailed" in their choice of inscription.

The inscription, carved underneath O'Connor's name and dates, reads: "I can, with one eye squinted, take it all as a blessing" (fig. 16).[1] The statement comes from a 1953 letter to Elizabeth and Robert Lowell in which O'Connor describes her lupus. At first, one might assume that the disease has defined the author and become inexorably linked to her reputation. This much is true, for the quotation reflects, in a perfectly ironic tone, O'Connor's attitude expressed elsewhere that "Sickness before death is a very appropriate thing and I think those who don't have it miss one of God's mercies."[2] To leave out O'Connor's bravery would be to give only part of the picture. But the quotation reflects O'Connor's larger attitude toward life in general and how, in the words of her most famous creation, "Jesus thown everything off balance."[3] What may not seem to be a heavenly gift can be seen as such if one looks at it the right way— and one such way is through the lens of O'Connor's fiction.

By the time the event began, about 150 people were seated at the front of the cathedral, including Louise Florencourt, O'Connor's first cousin. One of the featured speakers, Reverend George Piggford, C.S.C., emphasized O'Connor's devotion to the Eucharist and to the work of Pierre Teilhard de Chardin. According to Piggford, the Jesuit author's reputation mirrored O'Connor's: his work was met by some with "anxiety and confusion," so much so that, in 1962, Rome issued a warning about "doctrinal ambiguities in his work." The Vatican never took such a stance toward O'Connor; indeed, O'Connor complained early in her career of her "silent reception by Catholics."[4] Piggford clearly implied, however, that both visionaries initially upset their readers' assumptions about the foundations of their faith.

Alfred Corn spoke of his correspondence with O'Connor and prefaced his remarks with one of O'Connor's statements about her own celebrity, which she called "a comic distinction shared with Roy Rogers's horse and Miss Watermelon of 1955."[5] While recounting his first meeting O'Connor when she lectured at Emory, Corn addressed the ever-present issue of O'Connor's depictions of the South: "The truth is that reality is often grotesque nor is reality any single region's monopoly. If O'Connor deals with characters whose speech, dress, manner, and stated aims are bizarre, and whose actions are typically outrageous and violent, it is all in the interest of truth on the deepest level as she

Figure 16. O'Connor's stone in Poets Corner.

perceived it." Corn's remarks here recall what O'Connor told the interviewer for *Galley Proof*: "A serious novelist is in pursuit of reality. And of course when you're a Southerner and in pursuit of reality, the reality you come up with is going to have a Southern accent, but that's just an accent; it's not the essence of what you're trying to do."[6] The literary world seemed to have caught up to what O'Connor had been urging about her work all along.

Next came a performance of *Everything That Rises Must Converge* by the Compagnia de Colombari, Karin Coonrod's company that first performed their adaptation in 2001. The audience enjoyed watching Julian's slow burn at his mother's antiquated assumptions about race. Next, Professor James O. Tate, who grew up in Milledgeville, noted the justice of O'Connor's name being placed among others whom she so admired, such as Hawthorne and James. Tate's talk was the most literary of the evening, linking O'Connor to Wyndham Lewis and explaining why O'Connor did not identify Martin Heidegger as the author of the "gibberish" Hulga reads in "Good Country People." The celebration concluded with an address by Marilyn Nelson, who first spoke of Regina and stated that "the world owes her a debt of thanks" for the role she played in her daughter's life. Nelson, an African American, described a time when she visited Milledgeville to give a reading at Georgia College and State University and stayed at the former governor's mansion, a place where she did not feel alone: "I lay awake a long time with the distinct sense that former residents of the mansion were groaning, if not rolling in their graves because of my presence there." She also spoke of Alice Walker's admiration for O'Connor and the pilgrimage Walker made to Andalusia. So much had changed in the life of the South, but the truths that O'Connor sought to convey in her work had remained constant. Nelson spoke of O'Connor as one who, with a "gimlet eye," saw that, as she stated in a 1958 letter, "Human nature is so faulty that it can resist any amount of grace and most of the time it does."[7] The audience chuckled at this quotation, which so perfectly reflects the way that human nature is portrayed in O'Connor's art, as they did with Nelson's subsequent quotations about O'Connor's only diversion during her hospital stays as "disliking the nurses."[8] But Nelson returned to the importance of O'Connor the artist: "She could not stop herself from seeing us as we are, as we truly are," Nelson urged, "yet she could not stop herself from believing that beyond our miserable, warped, shallow, and otherwise limited understanding is a vast and endless divine love." Nelson concluded by reading the end of *The Violent Bear it Away* aloud; the description of Tarwater moving to the city, where the "children of God lay sleeping," silenced everyone there—including the woman I saw as I entered, who had joined the assembly and was, like everyone else, "having a moment" with O'Connor.

A Prayer Journal and the Unconfined O'Connor

Readers continue to have such moments. In 2013 *A Prayer Journal*, a collection that O'Connor wrote while at the University of Iowa, was published by Farrar, Straus and Giroux. Like other volumes of O'Connor's work, the *Prayer Journal* is introduced by an O'Connor insider: in this case, William A. Sessions, one of her friends and correspondents who discovered the collection while working on her authorized biography. Unlike his predecessors, Sessions has little to prove; because of the work of people like Robert Fitzgerald and Robert Giroux, he does not need to assert O'Connor's importance or the value of the text. His introduction is a short, graceful description of the prayers and how they reveal that O'Connor's time in Iowa, a place of "new influences, including intellectual joys," brought "questions and skepticism."[9] Reviewers found this skepticism a surprising corrective to O'Connor's reputation as an oracle whose writing and thinking were, in the words of Ralph C. Wood, "straightforward as a gunshot."[10] For example, Lindsay Gellman, writing in the *Wall Street Journal*, stated that readers "might be caught off-guard at the vulnerability, and at times, despair, that also radiates from these pages."[11] Maryann Ryan, in *Slate*, stated, "Instead of the cocksure writer we've long known—whose confidence is almost a physical force in her mature fiction and essays on religion and art—here we glimpse an unfinished personality, struggling to maintain belief in her talent."[12] Hilton Als, who had previously written about O'Connor in *White Girls*, remarked that the journal was "unintentionally revealing" of a writer whose image to many readers contrasted the one in these pages.[13] Patrick Samway, in the *Flannery O'Connor Review*, praised the volume as an "unpretentious *cri de coeur*,"[14] while a reviewer for the *Michigan Daily* used less refined but equally perceptive language in describing it as "a jewelry box for her artistic anxieties."[15]

But if reviewers were surprised by O'Connor's youthful insecurities and learning that this literary giant and (as the *Atlantic* called her) "turbocharged Catholic"[16] was sometimes beset by common doubts, they were affirmed in their collective estimation of her talent and the notion that talent such as hers would be obvious from a young age. In his introduction, Sessions states that the prayers reveal "a craftswoman of the first order" (viii), and critics concurred, often finding in the *Journal* premonitions of the career to come, as Joyce did in the opening pages of *A Portrait of the Artist as a Young Man*. Writing in the *Georgia Review*, Sarah Gordon observed, "The frequent conjunction of ideas concerning pain and grace certainly forecasts O'Connor's fictional subject matter."[17] Patrick Reardon, in the *Chicago Tribune*, stated that the *Journal* reveals the young O'Connor to be "truly a writer,"[18] while Carlene Bauer, author of *Frances and Bernard*, described the voice of O'Connor's prayers as "utterly her own" and stated that "No one else could have written them."[19] And in a wonderful example of the-last-shall-be-first and the-first-shall-be-last, the *New Yorker*, which had so often dismissed O'Connor's work when first published, offered an enthusiastic review that declared O'Connor's preeminence:

> O'Connor found the same way through cliché to invention in her spirituality and in her writing. How else could the tired old stories of tenant farmers, street prophets, ne'er-do-well teen-agers, agrarian widows, travelling bible salesmen, and murderous misfits become such celebrated works of fiction? Every believer finds a way to speak to God, but O'Connor also found a way to speak to everyone else.[20]

Readers who use *Goodreads* concur: slightly more than two years after its publication, the *Prayer Journal* has a 4.08 out of 5 rating, based on the opinions of over 1,200 reviewers.[21]

To conclude this history of O'Connor's reputation and reception by critics, editors, creative artists, academics, and common readers, we can turn to a moment in one of O'Connor's own works. An early scene in *The Violent Bear It Away* depicts Mason Tarwater's discovery that his nephew, Rayber, had invited him to live in his house under false pretenses: "He had lived for three months in the nephew's house on what he had thought at the time was Charity but what he said he had found out was not Charity or anything like it."[22] Rayber, Mason learns, was actually using his uncle as the unknowing subject of a psychological case study into what O'Connor's critics might term "religious fanaticism." After Rayber hands his uncle a copy of the magazine in which he published his study, Mason sits at his nephew's kitchen table and reads the article until he understands its true subject:

> When the old man looked up, the schoolteacher smiled. It was a very slight smile, the slightest that would do for any occasion. The old man knew from the smile who it was he had been reading about.
>
> For the length of a minute, he could not move. He felt that he was tied hand and foot inside the schoolteacher's head, a space as bare and neat as the cell in the asylum, and was shrinking, drying up to fit it. His eyeballs swerved from side to

side as if he were pinned in a straight jacket again. Jonah, Ezekiel, Daniel, he was at that moment all of them—the swallowed, the lowered, the enclosed. (75–76)

After previous attempts to literally confine Mason in an asylum proved unsuccessful, Rayber has now attempted to place his uncle in another kind of cell. It is a subject against which the old man rails for the rest of his days. "Where he wanted me," he later tells Tarwater, "was inside that schoolteacher magazine. He thought that once he got me in there, I'd be as good as inside his head and be done for and that would be that, that would be the end of it" (20). Mason's insight is perfect: Rayber, the expert on testing at the school where he works, derides the existence of anything he cannot quantify and has dedicated his life, like Hazel Motes, to resisting the urgings of his own wise blood. He can only deride what he is not strong enough to deny. Even the "horrifying love" (113) he feels for his own son must be contained—hence his cold-blooded attempt to drown Bishop.

Many of those involved in the formation of O'Connor's reputation share with Rayber a method of confining what strikes them as strange and powerful—in their case, O'Connor's fiction—to a neat space in which she and her work could be brought to heel. "Southern Gothic," "Grotesque," "Difficult," "Woman Author," "Catholic Novelist," and even "Racist" are some of the cells into which readers have attempted to commit O'Connor. As she remarked, "Even if there are no genuine schools in American letters today, there is always some critic who has just invented one and is ready to put you into it."[23] The desire to categorically confine in order to conquer or dismiss, to do to O'Connor what Rayber tried to do to Mason, has been a feature of her reception by all kinds of readers.

Attempts to master the strangeness of O'Connor's art with confining labels appear throughout the history of her reception, regardless of whether readers admired or detested her work. Such attempts frustrated O'Connor as she sought a wider audience. An examination of how she regarded the phrase "Catholic author" when used to describe her reveals O'Connor's unease with the reductive power of reputation shorthand. In a 1960 letter to Betty Hester, she stated, "I am very much aware of how hard you have to try to escape labels" and described a reporter who interviewed her for *Time* magazine:

He wanted me to characterize myself so he would have something to write down. Are you a Southern writer? What kind of Catholic are you? etc. I asked him what kind of Catholics there were. Liberal or conservative, says he. All I did for an hour was stammer and stutter and all night I was awake answering his questions with the necessary qualifications and reservations.[24]

A year later, she wrote to John Hawkes that "one of the great disadvantages of being known as a Catholic writer is that no one thinks you can lift the pen without trying to show somebody redeemed."[25] The inability of many readers to avoid labels continued to vex her: in a 1962 letter to Cecil Dawkins, she stated, "I must be seen as a writer and not just a Catholic writer, and I wish somebody would do it."[26] And in a 1969 profile for the *New York Review of Books*, Richard Gilman recounted a conversation he had with O'Connor about this very topic: "If she disliked being known as a Southern writer, it wasn't because she thought there was any loss or injury in being one—quite the contrary—but for the same reason she didn't want to be called a Catholic writer: it was reductive, misleading."[27] A later remark from one of her letters concerning *The Violent Bear It Away*—"I suppose my novel too will be called another Southern Gothic. I have an idiot in it"[28]—suggests that such confining labels had retained their power to irk O'Connor throughout her career.

But such labels were not and are not always reductive. One of the reasons why people still read O'Connor today has to do with the very labels she resisted: the *New Yorker*'s statement in its review of the *Prayer Journal*, "It would hardly be an exaggeration to say that she is the most important Catholic author in American letters,"[29] is hardly dismissive or limiting. The same is true for labels used to describe her work: "grotesque" can refer to an artistic method without the word's pejorative sense, and "dark" can be used to illuminate O'Connor's unique vision: in an article about Poets Corner, a *New Yorker* reporter stated, "'Dark' is a word often used to describe O'Connor's fiction. But darkness can have many hues; in twentieth-century literature, it often means emptiness, the horror at nothingness that can't be filled. In O'Connor, the looming darkness isn't a void that threatens to swallow you; it's the shadow of a piano that's about to fall on your head."[30] Even terms like "parochial" and "provincial" can be terms of praise: in a perceptive appreciation of O'Connor that ran in the *New Republic* in 1975, the novelist Ellen Douglas argued that the "novelist's point of view" and "attitude toward one's work grounded in a narrow personal conviction" is a bulwark against what Marshall McLuhan called the "global village," where "every scrap of the human stew is flavored with the same seasoning and pounded to a uniform pastelike consistency."[31] O'Connor's parochialism is to be celebrated as informing her fiction and her provincialism as what allows her to know her chosen settings, her literal province, so well that it passes for real.

Douglas also knew that many readers regard southern writers as purveyors of provincial clichés: "ladies who write novels about hoopskirted heroines dallying in the moonlight with gallant gentlemen; and gentlemen who write novels about good country people with their coon dogs and corn pones."[32] Her allusion to O'Connor's story about Hulga and Hulga's own misunderstanding of that term reminds us just how misleading a description like "southern writer" can be and how O'Connor's reputation is a small part of the larger story of how the South has been regarded by others since before the nation's founding. For example, critics' use of the adjective "southern" often invites their readers to play a game of word association, in which "southern" connotes "anti-modern," "racist," and other undesirable qualities. This game, of course, has a separate and complicated history of its own, detailed in scholarly work such as James C. Cobb's *Away Down South* and David Goldfield's *Still Fighting the Civil War*, neither of which explores O'Connor's work but which illuminate the ways in which her reception was partly a function of how, since the American Revolution, "the dominant vision of the American character emphasized northern sensibilities and perceptions"[33] and how, since Reconstruction, "the South became America's nightmare."[34] The history of O'Connor's reception by urban reviewers proves the truth of these arguments. In *Dreaming of Dixie*, Karen L. Cox concurs with the sociologist John Shelton Reed's contention that those working in cities such as New York and Los Angeles have fostered an image of the South like the one detailed by Cobb and Goldfield; she argues that "films set in the South or ones that featured southern characters were most certainly expressions of the nation's perception of the region and were in line with other forms of popular culture in their construction of various images of the South."[35] While she never mentions Huston's *Wise Blood*, his film can be read as an extension of the story she begins with *The Birth of a Nation* and ends with *Song of the South*.

At the ceremony for O'Connor's induction into the American Poets Corner, the Reverend Canon Julia Whitworth began with remarks about O'Connor's appreciation of both the humorous and the holy. After noting that she herself was "also a southerner," Canon Whitworth stated, "I appreciate in Flannery O'Connor her sense of deep location that helps us to understand something universal about home, about being, about being human, about being a stranger and being familiar all at the same time." This sense of "deep location" has prompted many readers to assume that O'Connor's work is fundamentally "about the South," especially when examined by northern readers who followed the intellectual path laid by their predecessors, a path taken by many of the readers examined throughout this book. But such readers miss the point that original sin is an equal-opportunity employer. In his 1765 *Preface to Shakespeare*, Samuel Johnson argues that the Bard's "adherence to general nature has exposed him to the censure of criticks, who form their judgments upon narrower principles," "narrower" here referring to a verisimilitude that, to Johnson, is wholly irrelevant:

> Dennis is offended, that Menenius, a senator of Rome, should play the buffoon; and Voltaire perhaps thinks decency violated when the Danish usurper is represented as a drunkard. But Shakespeare always makes nature predominate over accident; and if he preserves the essential character, is not very careful of distinctions superinduced and adventitious. His story requires Romans or kings, but he thinks only on men. He knew that Rome, like every other city, had men of all dispositions; and wanting a buffoon, he went into the senate-house for that which the senate-house would certainly have afforded him. He was inclined to show an usurper and a murderer not only odious but despicable, he therefore added drunkenness to his other qualities, knowing that kings love wine like other men, and that wine exerts its natural power upon kings. These are the petty cavils of petty minds; a poet overlooks the casual distinction of country and condition, as a painter, satisfied with the figure, neglects the drapery.[36]

Two hundred years later, in *The Southern Mystique*, Howard Zinn argued that even the "real South" itself—whatever that may be—is less actual than imagined: "Those very qualities long attributed to the South as special possessions are, in truth, *American* qualities," and "the South crystallizes the defects of the nation."[37] Johnson's defense of Shakespeare, Zinn's reimagining of the South, and Whitworth's argument that O'Connor's southern landscape is the setting for "something universal about home, about being human" stand as welcome and necessary correctives to those who have regarded the truths of O'Connor's work as particular rather than universal. For it is ultimately the universality of her themes and her insight into human nature that make her work worth the effort of reading and her reputation as a preeminent American author so well deserved.

Notes

Introduction

1. Bruce Gentry, "Biographical Comments for Unveiling of Flannery O'Connor Stamp," June 14, 2015, http://andalusiafarm.blogspot.com/2015/06/biographical-comments-for-unveiling-of.html.

2. Lawrence Downes, "A Good Stamp Is Hard to Find," *New York Times*, June 5, 2015, A26.

3. Joyce Carol Oates, Twitter post, May 27, 2015, 7:37 a.m., http://twitter.com/JoyceCarolOates.

4. Ralph C. Wood, "Flannery O'Connor: Stamped But Not Cancelled," *First Things*, June 16, 2015, www.firstthings.com/web-exclusives/2015/06/flannery-oconnor-stamped-but-not-cancelled (accessed July 1, 2015).

5. Rodden, *The Politics of Literary Reputation*, 87.

6. Stephen Maine, "*Flannery O'Connor: The Cartoons*," *Art in America*, May 17, 2012, www.artinamericamagazine.com (accessed October 13, 2012).

7. Glen Weldon, "Cartoons of the Artist as a Young Woman," *NPR Books*, July 19, 2012, www.npr.org/2012/07/19/156506520/cartoons-of-the-artist-as-a-young-woman (accessed October 21, 2012).

8. Vanna Le, "Best-Kept Secret: Flannery O'Connor, the Cartoonist," *Forbes*, July 13, 2011, www.forbes.com/sites/booked/2011/07/13/best-kept-secret-flannery-oconnor-the-cartoonist (accessed October 1, 2012).

9. Owen Heitman, "Writer Flannery O'Connor's even shorter career as a cartoonist," *The Australian*, August 18, 2012, www.theaustralian.com.au/arts/review/flannery-oconnors-even-shorter-career/story-fn9n8gph-1226451874246 (accessed September 21, 2012).

10. Casey Burchby, "How Flannery O'Connor's Early Cartoons Influenced Her Later Writing," *Publishers Weekly*, April 9, 2012, www.publishersweekly.com/pw/by-topic/industry-news/comics/article/51455-how-flannery-o-connor-s-early-cartoons-influenced-her-later-writing.html (accessed September 21, 2012).

11. Flannery O'Connor to Thomas Gossett, November 24, 1957, in *The Habit of Being*, 255.

12. Peter Wild, "A fresh look at Flannery O'Connor," *The Guardian Books Blog*, July 5, 2011, www.guardian.co.uk/books/booksblog/2011/jul/05/fresh-look-flannery-o-connor -cartoons (accessed October 11, 2012).

13. Maine, "*Flannery O'Connor*," 2012.

14. Daniel Elkin, review of *Flannery O'Connor: The Cartoons*, by Flannery O'Connor, *Comics Bulletin*, www.comicsbulletin.com/reviews/4479/review-flannery-oconnor-the -cartoons (accessed October 13, 2012).

15. See Peter Messent's examination of this idea in *The Cambridge Introduction to Mark Twain* (Cambridge: Cambridge University Press, 2007), 12–14.

16. Machor, "The American Reception of Melville's Short Fiction in the 1850s," 93.

17. Borges, "Kafka and His Precursors," 200.

18. Gerald, *Flannery O'Connor: The Cartoons*, 99.

19. "By the Book: Bruce Springsteen," *New York Times Book Review*, November 2, 2014, BR8. For others' recommendations in the *Book Review*, see "By the Book: Dean Koontz," July 27, 2014, BR7; "By the Book: Larry McMurtry," July 13, 2014, BR6; and "By the Book: Colson Whitehead," May 18, 2014, BR8.

20. Ohmann, *Politics of Letters*, 66.

21. Tyler, review of *The Complete Stories*, May 8, 2008, Goodreads.com (accessed September 21, 2013).

22. Bloom, *Flannery O'Connor*, 8.

23. Customer review of *Flannery O'Connor: The Complete Stories*, October 21, 1999, Amazon.com (accessed October 13, 2012).

24. O'Connor, *The Violent Bear It Away*, 15.

25. Robert Giroux to G. Roysce Smith, June 17, 1975, Farrar, Straus and Giroux, Inc. records, Manuscripts and Archives Division, New York Public Library, Astor, Lenox, and Tilden Foundations.

26. See, for example, J. Bottum, "Flannery O'Connor Banned," *Crisis* 18 (October 2000): 48–49.

27. Sally Fitzgerald, introduction to *The Habit of Being*, xvi.

28. Terry Eagleton, "Raine's Sterile Thunder," *Prospect*, March 22, 2007, www .prospectmagazine.co.uk/magazine/rainessterilethunder (accessed September 22, 2012).

29. See, for example, Lawrence H. Schwartz, *Creating Faulkner's Reputation: The Politics of Modern Literary Criticism* (Knoxville: University of Tennessee Press, 1988); Scott Donaldson, ed., *The Cambridge Companion to Hemingway* (Cambridge: Cambridge University Press, 1996); Charlotte Templin, *Feminism and the Politics of Literary Reputation: The Example of Erica Jong* (Lawrence: University Press of Kansas, 1995).

30. Friedman, *The Added Dimension*, ix.

31. See, for example, Tison Pugh, *Queer Chivalry: Medievalism and the Myth of White Masculinity in Southern Literature* (Baton Rouge: LSU Press, 2013), Timothy R. Vande Brake, "Thinking Like a Tree: The Land Ethic in O'Connor's 'A View of the Woods,'" *Flannery O'Connor Review* 9 (2011): 19–35, and Claire Raymond, *Witnessing Sadism in*

Texts of the American South: Women, Specularity, and the Poetics of Subjectivity (Burlington, Vt.: Ashgate, 2014) as examples of esoteric O'Connor scholarship.

Chapter 1. The Two Receptions of *Wise Blood*

1. Gooch, *Flannery*, 117.

2. Rabinowitz, *Before Reading*, 46.

3. Gary Saul Morson, *The Boundaries of Genre: Dostoevsky's Diary of a Writer and the Traditions of Literary Utopia* (Austin: University of Texas Press, 1981), 46. Quoted in Rabinowitz, *Before Reading*, 49.

4. Rabinowitz, *Before Reading*, 53.

5. Sylvia Stallings, "Young Writer with a Bizarre Tale to Tell," *New York Herald Tribune Book Review*, May 18, 1952, 3, in Scott and Streight, *The Contemporary Reviews*, 151.

6. "Frustrated Preacher," *Newsweek*, May 19, 1952, 114, in Scott and Streight, *The Contemporary Reviews*, 9.

7. "May 15 Is Publication Date of Novel by Flannery O'Connor, Milledgeville," *Milledgeville Union-Recorder*, April 25, 1952, 1, in Scott and Streight, *The Contemporary Reviews*, 3–4.

8. John W. Simons, "A Case of Possession," *Commonweal* 56 (June 27, 1952): 297.

9. William Goyen, "Unending Vengeance," *New York Times Book Review*, May 18, 1952, 4.

10. "Frustrated Preacher," 9.

11. Martin Greenberg, "Books in Short," *American Mercury* 75 (July 1952): 113, in Scott and Streight, *The Contemporary Reviews*, 15.

12. "Grave and Gay," *Times Literary Supplement*, September 2, 1955, 505, in Scott and Streight, *The Contemporary Reviews*, 25.

13. Mencken, "The Sahara of the Bozart," 491.

14. Edward S. Shapiro, "The Southern Agrarians, H. L. Mencken, and the Quest for Southern Identity," *American Studies* 13, no. 2 (1972): 77.

15. Transcript of the *Galley Proof* television program filmed in May 1955, in Magee, *Conversations with Flannery O'Connor*, 8.

16. O'Connor to Betty Hester, September 1, 1963, in *The Habit of Being*, 537.

17. "May 15 Is Publication Date," in *The Contemporary Reviews*, 3.

18. "Miss O'Connor Adds Luster to Georgia," *Atlanta Journal and Constitution*, May 10, 1952, 4, in Scott and Streight, *The Contemporary Reviews*, 5.

19. Ibid.

20. Martha Smith, "Georgian Pens *Wise Blood*, A First Novel," *Atlanta Journal and Constitution*, May 18, 1952, F 7, in Scott and Streight, *The Contemporary Reviews*, 7.

21. Ibid.

22. "Frustrated Preacher," 114.

23. Greenberg, "Books in Short," 113.

24. Quoted in Elie, *The Life You Save May Be Your Own*, 501.

25. Greenberg, "Books in Short," 113.

26. O'Connor to Betty Hester, September 22, 1956, in *The Habit of Being*, 176.

27. O'Connor to Sally and Robert Fitzgerald, April 1952, in *The Habit of Being*, 33.

28. Gooch, *Flannery*, 207–10.

29. Hazlitt, *Lectures*, 36.

30. Barasch, "Theories of the Grotesque," 84–89.

31. "Wise Blood," *Bulletin from Virginia's Kirkus's Book Shop Service*, May 1, 1952, 285, in Scott and Streight, *The Contemporary Reviews*, 4.

32. "Damnation of Man," *Savannah Morning News*, May 25, 1952, 40, in Scott and Streight, *The Contemporary Reviews*, 11.

33. Sylvia Stallings, "Young Writer with a Bizarre Tale to Tell," *New York Herald Tribune Book Review*, May 18, 1953, 3, in Scott and Streight, *The Contemporary Reviews*, 8.

34. Unsigned review of *Wise Blood*, *United States Quarterly Book Review* 8 (Summer 1952): 256, in Scott and Streight, *The Contemporary Reviews*, 18.

35. Oliver LaFarge, "Manic Gloom," *Saturday Review* 35 (May 24, 1952): 22, in Scott and Streight, *The Contemporary Reviews*, 10.

36. R. W. B. Lewis, "Eccentrics' Pilgrimage," *Hudson Review* 6 (Spring 1953): 148, in Scott and Streight, *The Contemporary Reviews*, 24.

37. Carl Hartman, "Jesus Without Christ," *Western Review* 17 (Autumn 1952): 75–80, in Scott and Streight, *The Contemporary Reviews*, 19. Emphasis in original.

38. Both of the previously cited articles, "Damnation of Man" and John W. Simons, "A Case of Possession," compare O'Connor's work to Dostoevsky's.

39. The unnamed author of "Damnation of Man" notes that *Wise Blood* recalls "the cruelty of Steinbeck."

40. "New Creative Writers," *Library Journal*, February 15, 1952, 354, in Scott and Streight, *The Contemporary Reviews*, 3.

41. "Southern Dissonance," *Time*, June 9, 1952, 110.

42. O'Connor, *Wise Blood*, 228.

43. "New Creative Writers," 3.

44. Milton S. Byam, review of *Wise Blood*, *Library Journal* 77 (May 15, 1952): 894, in Scott and Streight, *The Contemporary Reviews*, 5.

45. O'Connor, "The Fiction Writer and His Country," in *Mystery and Manners*, 34.

46. "Frustrated Preacher," 114.

47. O'Connor to Betty Boyd Love, September 20, 1952, in *The Habit of Being*, 43.

48. Stallings, "Young Writer," 3.

49. Simons, "A Case of Possession," 298.

50. O'Connor, *Wise Blood*, 22.

51. Isaac Rosenfeld, "To Win by Default," *New Republic* 127 (July 7, 1952): 19.

52. LaFarge, "Manic Gloom," 10.

53. Gooch, *Flannery*, 204.

54. Gooch, *Flannery*, 212.

55. Brainard Cheney, review of *Wise Blood, Shenandoah* 3, no. 3 (Autumn 1952): 57.

56. Ibid.

57. Cheney, review of *Wise Blood*, 59. Emphasis in original.

58. O'Connor to Brainard Cheney, February 8, 1953, in Stevens, *The Correspondence of Flannery O'Connor and the Brainard Cheneys*, 3.

59. Ibid., 4.

60. Brainard Cheney to O'Connor, March 22, 1953, in Stevens, *Correspondence*, 4.

61. O'Connor to Cecil Dawkins, July 17, 1961, in *The Habit of Being*, 445.

62. O'Connor to Betty Hester, June 10, 1961, in *The Habit of Being*, 442.

63. O'Connor to Sally and Robert Fitzgerald, May 7, 1962, in *The Habit of Being*, 473.

64. O'Connor, "Author's Note to the Second Edition," *Wise Blood*, 2nd ed., 1962.

65. O'Connor, *The Violent Bear It Away*, 34.

66. Hoke Norris, "A Classic from the Recent Past is Reissued," *Chicago Sun-Times*, September 2, 1962, sec. 3, p. 2, in Scott and Streight, *The Contemporary Reviews*, 190.

67. Paul Levine, review of *Wise Blood, Jubilee* 10 (December 1962): 47.

68. Leonard F. X. Mayhew, review of *Wise Blood, Commonweal* 108 (February 22, 1963): 576.

69. Thomas F. Smith, "Fiction as Prophecy: Novels of Flannery O'Connor Re-Read and Re-Evaluated," *Pittsburgh Catholic*, March 28, 1963, "Fine Arts Supplement," 1, in Scott and Streight, *The Contemporary Reviews*, 194.

70. George Knight, "A Merited O'Connor Revival," *Tampa Tribune*, September 30, 1962, in Scott and Streight, *The Contemporary Reviews*, 191.

71. Charlotte K. Gafford, "Writers and Readers," *The Bulletin*, October 27, 1962, in Scott and Streight, *The Contemporary Reviews*, 192.

72. Dennis Powers, "*Wise Blood* Repays a Second Reading," *Oakland Tribune*, August 24, 1962, in Scott and Streight, *The Contemporary Reviews*, 188.

73. Dean Peerman, "Grotesquerie Plus," *Christian Century* 80 (August 14, 1963): 1008.

74. "Long Day's Preaching," *Times Literary Supplement*, February 1, 1968, 101.

75. Paul Bailey, "Maimed Souls," London *Observer*, February 11, 1968, 27, in Scott and Streight, *The Contemporary Reviews*, 199.

76. Ibid.

77. West, "The Iconic Dust Jacket," 277.

78. Genette, *Paratexts*, 407.

79. O'Connor to Sally and Robert Fitzgerald, April 1952, in *The Habit of Being*, 33.

80. O'Connor to Robert Giroux, October 21, 1955, in *The Habit of Being*, 113.

81. O'Connor to "A.," September 17, 1960, in *The Habit of Being*, 408.

82. Roxanna Bikadoroff, email message to author, October 14, 2012.

83. Brad Leithauser, "A Nasty Dose of Orthodoxy," *New Yorker* 64, no. 38 (November 7, 1988): 154.

84. Amy Hungerford, "The American Novel Since 1945: Lecture 3 Transcript," *Open*

Yale, www.core.org.cn/mirrors/Yale/yale/oyc.yale.edu/english/american-novel-since-1945 /content/transcripts/transcript-3-flannery-oconnor-wise-blood.htm (accessed October 16, 2012).

85. O'Connor to John Selby, February 18, 1949, in *The Habit of Being*, 10.

Chapter 2. The "Discovery" of O'Connor's Catholicism

1. Boswell, *The Life of Samuel Johnson*, 929.

2. O'Connor to Betty Hester, September 6, 1955, in *The Habit of Being*, 100.

3. Rogers, *The Terrible Speed of Mercy*, 105–6.

4. Gooch, *Flannery*, 174.

5. Rabinowitz, *Before Reading*, 21. Emphasis in original.

6. Ibid, 194.

7. Martin A. Sherwood, "Unlimited Prophets," *Montreal Gazette*, June 4, 1960, 39. Sherwood also describes Tarwater's rape as a "rather unfortunate experience with a homosexual" rather than the spiritual trigger that the novel suggests it is. In Scott and Streight, *The Contemporary Reviews*, 145–46.

8. O'Connor to Dr. T. R. Spivey, May 25, 1959, in *The Habit of Being*, 334.

9. O'Connor, quoted in "Recent Southern Fiction: A Panel Discussion," in the *Bulletin of Wesleyan College*, January 1961. Reprinted in Magee, *Conversations with Flannery O'Connor*, 73–74.

10. See Algene Ballif, "A Southern Allegory," *Commentary* 30 (October 1960): 358–62, where Ballif states, "What seems to lie at the heart of all this dualism and image-splitting and spiritual tug-of-war is an elaborate fantasy of what one can call only homosexual incest. The language of the novel is penetrated with images that suggest it." In Scott and Streight, *The Contemporary Reviews*, 151.

11. O'Connor to John Hawkes, November 28, 1961, in *The Habit of Being*, 457.

12. O'Connor to Betty Hester, August 2, 1955, in *The Habit of Being*, 92.

13. O'Connor to Betty Hester, August 28, 1955, in *The Habit of Being*, 97.

14. O'Connor to Betty Hester, November 25, 1955, in *The Habit of Being*, 118.

15. O'Connor to Betty Hester, October 31, 1959, in *The Habit of Being*, 357.

16. O'Connor to Andrew Lytle, February 4, 1960, in *The Habit of Being*, 373.

17. O'Connor to Betty Hester, April 4, 1958, in *The Habit of Being*, 275.

18. Doris Betts, "Total Commitment to Christian Frame," *Houston Post*, March 17, 1960, in Scott and Streight, *The Contemporary Reviews*, 118.

19. O'Connor to Dr. T. R. Spivey, October 19, 1958, in *The Habit of Being*, 299–300.

20. O'Connor to Betty Hester, November 12, 1956, in *The Habit of Being*, 179.

21. O'Connor, "The Nature and Aim of Fiction," in *Mystery and Manners*, 79.

22. O'Connor, "The Church and the Fiction Writer," in *Mystery and Manners*, 145.

23. O'Connor, "The Nature and Aim of Fiction," 78.

24. O'Connor, "The Church and the Fiction Writer," 146.

25. O'Connor to Betty Hester, December 9, 1961, in *The Habit of Being*, 458. Emphasis in original.

26. James Greene, "The Comic and the Sad," *Commonweal* 62 (July 22, 1955): 404, in Scott and Streight, *The Contemporary Reviews*, 43.

27. Granville Hicks, "A Belated Tribute to Short Stories by Eudora Welty and Flannery O'Connor," *New Leader* 38 (August 15, 1955), 17, in Scott and Streight, *The Contemporary Reviews*, 45.

28. Robert Martin Adams, "Fiction Chronicle," *Hudson Review* (Winter 1956): 627, in Scott and Streight, *The Contemporary Reviews*, 66.

29. John Cook Wyllie, "The Unscented South," *Saturday Review*, June 4, 1955, 15, in Scott and Streight, *The Contemporary Reviews*, 33.

30. Unsigned review of *A Good Man Is Hard to Find*, *Grail* 38 (January 1956): 59, in Scott and Streight, *The Contemporary Reviews*, 64.

31. Greene, "The Comic and the Sad," 43.

32. Unsigned review of *A Good Man Is Hard to Find*, *Harper's Bazaar* (July 1955), 72, in Scott and Streight, *The Contemporary Reviews*, 41.

33. Fred Bornhauser, "Book Reviews: Flannery O'Connor's *A Good Man Is Hard to Find* and *The Bride of Innisfallen*," *Shenandoah* 7 (Autumn 1955): 71–81, in Scott and Streight, *The Contemporary Reviews*, 51.

34. Ben W. Griffith Jr., "Stories of Gifted Writer Acquire Stature of Myths," *Savannah Morning News*, June 5, 1955, sec. 6, p. 60, in Scott and Streight, *The Contemporary Reviews*, 34.

35. John A. Lynch, "Isolated World," *Today*, October 11, 1955, 31, in Scott and Streight, *The Contemporary Reviews*, 46–48.

36. Unsigned review of *A Good Man Is Hard to Find*, *U.S. Quarterly Book Review* 11 (December 1955), 472, in Scott and Streight, *The Contemporary Reviews*, 62.

37. In his introduction to *The Complete Stories* (1972), Robert Giroux calls it a "masterpiece of a story"; in *The Life You Save May Be Your Own* (2003), Paul Elie notes that, in 1955, "A Good Man Is Hard to Find" was "being canonized as her greatest story." See Giroux, introduction to *The Complete Stories*, xii, and Elie, *The Life You Save May Be Your Own*, 236.

38. John Cook Wyllie, "The Unscented South," 33.

39. Francis J. Ullrich, review of *A Good Man Is Hard to Find*, *Best Sellers*, June 15, 1955, 59, in Scott and Streight, *The Contemporary Reviews*, 40.

40. Fanny Butcher, "Ten Pokes in the Ribs with a Poisoned Dart," *Chicago Sunday Tribune Magazine of Books*, July 3, 1955, sec. 4, p. 3, in Scott and Streight, *The Contemporary Reviews*, 42.

41. Susan Myrick, "New Stories of Georgia Farm Life: O'Connor Book Rates with the Best," *Macon Telegraph*, May 26, 1955, in Scott and Streight, *The Contemporary Reviews*, 31.

42. "Such Nice People," *Time*, June 6, 1955, 114.

43. O'Connor, "A Good Man Is Hard to Find," in *A Good Man Is Hard to Find*, 22.

44. O'Connor to Ben Griffith, July 9, 1955, in *The Habit of Being*, 89.

45. Sylvia Stallings, "Flannery O'Connor: A New, Shining Talent Among Our Storytellers," *New York Herald Tribune Book Review*, June 5, 1955, 1, in Scott and Streight, *The Contemporary Reviews*, 36.

46. Lynch, "Isolated World," 46.

47. Unsigned review of *A Good Man Is Hard to Find*, *Virginia Quarterly Review* 31 (Autumn 1955): 101, in Scott and Streight, *The Contemporary Reviews*, 59.

48. Louis D. Rubin Jr., "Two Ladies of the South," *Sewanee Review* 63 (Autumn 1955): 680, in Scott and Streight, *The Contemporary Reviews*, 61.

49. Ullrich, review of *A Good Man Is Hard to Find*, 40.

50. Unsigned review of *A Good Man Is Hard to Find*, *Grail* 38 (January 1956): 59, in Scott and Streight, *The Contemporary Reviews*, 64.

51. Butcher, "Ten Pokes in the Ribs," 42.

52. O'Connor, "The Displaced Person," in *A Good Man Is Hard to Find*, 243.

53. Rubin, "Two Ladies of the South," 60.

54. Thomas H. Carter, "Rhetoric and Southern Landscapes," *Accent* 15 (Autumn 1955): 293–97, in Scott and Streight, *The Contemporary Reviews*, 53.

55. Bornhauser, "Book Reviews," 49.

56. Gooch, *Flannery*, 254.

57. O'Connor to Maryat Lee, March 10, 1957, in *The Habit of Being*, 209.

58. See O'Connor to Betty Hester, November 2, 1957: "Anyway, without permission, [the publisher] has changed the title of the collection to *The Artificial Nigger* and on the jacket has featured a big black African, apparently in agony, granite agony; which is supposed to be an artificial nigger." In *The Habit of Being*, 249.

59. Butcher, "Ten Pokes in the Ribs," 42.

60. Hicks, "A Belated Tribute," 45.

61. Celestine Sibley, "Georgia Writer Shuns Escapism," *Atlanta Journal and Constitution*, May 17, 1955, 24, in Scott and Streight, *The Contemporary Reviews*, 29–30.

62. Orville Prescott, "Books of the Times," *New York Times*, June 10, 1955, 23.

63. Ray Dilley, "Flannery O'Connor's Telling of Stories Shockingly Impressive," *Savannah Evening Press*, June 4, 1955, B16, in Scott and Streight, *The Contemporary Reviews*, 32.

64. O'Connor, "A Good Man Is Hard to Find," in *A Good Man Is Hard to Find*, 22.

65. Ullrich, review of *A Good Man Is Hard to Find*, *Best Sellers*, 40.

66. Caroline Gordon, "With a Glitter of Evil," *New York Times Book Review*, June 12, 1955, 5.

67. O'Connor to Betty Hester, July 20, 1955, in *The Habit of Being*, 90.

68. "Briefly Noted: Fiction," *New Yorker*, June 18, 1955, 93.

69. O'Connor to Betty Hester, July 20, 1955, in *The Habit of Being*, 90.

70. Ralph Wood, "Flannery O'Connor," *Religion and Ethics Newsweekly*, PBS, November 20, 2009.

71. Unsigned review of *Wise Blood*, *New Yorker*, March 19, 1960, 179.

72. Joel Wells, "A Genius Who Frustrated Critics," *National Catholic Reporter*, November 19, 1971, 6, in Scott and Streight, *The Contemporary Reviews*, 435.

73. Greene, "The Comic and the Sad," 43.

74. Dale Francis, "Flannery O'Connor," *Commonweal* 62 (August 12, 1955): 471.

75. Martin, *The True Country*, 10. Martin's was one of the first examinations of O'Connor's Catholic themes, and as such, it reveals that these themes needed to be pointed out and elucidated for O'Connor's readers.

76. O'Connor to Frances Neel Cheney, September 7, 1955, in Stevens, *The Correspondence of Flannery O'Connor and the Brainard Cheneys*, 22.

77. O'Connor to Cecil Dawkins, June 8, 1958, in *The Habit of Being*, 287.

78. In Jonathan Rogers's recent biography of O'Connor, for example, he describes the recently baptized Caroline Gordon as possessing "all the zeal of a convert," as if converts were automatically more zealous than those raised in the faith or, as the expression goes, "more Catholic than the Pope." See Rogers, *The Terrible Speed of Mercy*, 51.

79. Orwell, "Inside the Whale," 239.

80. O'Connor to Elizabeth Bishop, April 23, 1960, in *The Habit of Being*, 391.

81. O'Connor to John Hawkes, March 3, 1961, in *The Habit of Being*, 434.

82. O'Connor to Fr. J. H. McCown, May 9, 1956, in *The Habit of Being*, 157.

83. Lynch, "Isolated World," 46.

84. Ibid.

85. Ibid, 47.

86. Ibid.

87. Walter Elder stated, "I suggest that her stories are morally absolute" and that O'Connor "dares to assault the readers." Walter Elder, "That Region," *Kenyon Review* 17 (Autumn 1955): 661–70, in Scott and Streight, *The Contemporary Reviews*, 55–58.

88. "Miss O'Connor is in essence a religious writer. Knowledge of god and evil is at the heart of her stories." See Rubin, "Two Ladies of the South," 61.

89. Hicks, "A Belated Tribute," 45.

90. Unsigned review of *A Good Man Is Hard to Find*, *Commonweal* 66 (February 22, 1957): 541.

91. R. L. Morgan, "Potentiality for Greatness: *The Violent Bear It Away*, Exciting New Fiction Effort," *Arkansas Gazette*, July 24, 1960, in Scott and Streight, *The Contemporary Reviews*, 147.

92. Ben Czaplewski, "Sin and Salvation," *Nexus*, October 1960, 7, in Scott and Streight, *The Contemporary Reviews*, 153.

93. Donald C. Emerson, review of *The Violent Bear It Away*, *Arizona Quarterly* 16 (Autumn 1960): 284, in Scott and Streight, *The Contemporary Reviews*, 156.

94. P. Albert Duhamel, "Flannery O'Connor's *VIOLENT* View of Reality," *Catholic World* 190 (February 1960): 280–85, in Scott and Streight, *The Contemporary Reviews*, 94.

95. C. B. J., "An Exciting New Novel by Young Southerner," *Washington Star*, February 28, 1960, in Scott and Streight, *The Contemporary Reviews*, 86.

96. "New Creative Writers," *Library Journal*, February 15, 1952, 354, in Scott and Streight, *The Contemporary Reviews*, 3.

97. Quoted by Frank Bigley in "Back South with Too Much Despair," *Montreal Daily Star*, April 16, 1960, 34, in Scott and Streight, *The Contemporary Reviews*, 130.

98. Ana C. Hunter, "Micawbre [*sic*] Note Struck by Writer in Powerful Expose of Fanatic," *Savannah Morning News Magazine*, February 21, 1960, 13, in Scott and Streight, *The Contemporary Reviews*, 76.

99. "Hard-Hitting Dixie Belle," *Detroit News*, February 21, 1960, in Scott and Streight, *The Contemporary Reviews*, 74.

100. Deborah Walker, "Flannery O'Connor's Original . . . ," *Providence Journal*, February 28, 1960, in Scott and Streight, *The Contemporary Reviews*, 92.

101. Thomas F. Gossett, "The Religious Quest," *Southwest Review* 46 (Winter 1961): 86–87, in Scott and Streight, *The Contemporary Reviews*, 166.

102. Unsigned review of *The Violent Bear It Away*, *Information: The Catholic Church in American Life* 74 (April 1960): 57–58, in Scott and Streight, *The Contemporary Reviews*, 125.

103. Pat Somers Cronin, "Books," *Ave Maria*, July 2, 1960, 25, in Scott and Streight, *The Contemporary Reviews*, 147.

104. There are dozens of reviews that feature this term. One representative example: "The young Southern novelist Flannery O'Connor inhabits a world as grotesque as anything in contemporary American literature." Harry Mooney Jr., "Dark Allegory," *Pittsburgh Sun-Telegraph*, February 28, 1960, in Scott and Streight, *The Contemporary Reviews*, 87.

105. Louis Dollarhide, "Significant New Work by Flannery O'Connor," *Jackson Clarion-Ledger*, March 27, 1960, D6, in Scott and Streight, *The Contemporary Reviews*, 122.

106. Duhamel, "Flannery O'Connor's *VIOLENT* View of Reality," 97.

107. Butcher, "Ten Pokes in the Ribs," 42.

108. Frank J. Warnke, "A Vision Deep and Narrow," *New Republic* 142 (March 14, 1960): 18–19, in Scott and Streight, *The Contemporary Reviews*, 117.

109. Betts, "Total Commitment to Christian Frame," 117.

110. Emerson, review of *The Violent Bear It Away*, 157.

111. Harold C. Gardiner, "A Tragic Image of Man," *America* 103 (March 5, 1960): 682–83, in Scott and Streight, *The Contemporary Reviews*, 108.

112. Paul Engle, "Insight, Richness, Humor, and Chills," *Chicago Sunday Tribune: Magazine of Books*, March 6, 1960, sec. 4, p. 3, in Scott and Streight, *The Contemporary Reviews*, 112.

113. Gossett, "The Religious Quest," 166.

114. Brainard Cheney, "Bold, Violent, Yet Terribly Funny Tale," *Nashville Banner*, March 4, 1960, in Scott and Streight, *The Contemporary Reviews*, 107.

115. Walter Clemons, "Acts of Grace," *Newsweek*, November 8, 1971, 116.

116. Ibid.

117. O'Connor, *The Violent Bear It Away*, 243.

118. O'Connor to Maryat Lee, July 5, 1959, in *The Habit of Being*, 339.

119. O'Connor to Cecil Dawkins, July 17, 1959, in *The Habit of Being*, 340.

120. O'Connor to Dr. T. R. Spivey, July 18, 1959, in *The Habit of Being*, 341.

121. O'Connor to Sally and Robert Fitzgerald, October 11, 1959, in *The Habit of Being*, 355.

122. O'Connor to Elizabeth Bishop, August 2, 1959, in *The Habit of Being*, 344.

123. O'Connor to Betty Hester, January 30, 1960, in *The Habit of Being*, 372.

124. O'Connor to Betty Hester, July 25, 1959, in *The Habit of Being*, 343.

125. Ibid.

126. O'Connor to John Hawkes, September 13, 1959, in *The Habit of Being*, 350.

127. "A Few to Keep," *America* 103 (May 14, 1960): 245, in Scott and Streight, *The Contemporary Reviews*, 136.

128. Sister Bede Sullivan, "Prophet in the Wilderness," *Today* 15 (March 1960): 36–37, in Scott and Streight, *The Contemporary Reviews*, 122.

129. Sullivan, "Flannery O'Connor and the Dialogue Decade," *Catholic Library World*, May–June 1960, 518, 521, in Scott and Streight, *The Contemporary Reviews*, 143. Ellipses in original.

130. Bud Johnson, "A Literary Gourmet's Delight: Flannery O'Connor's Novel," *Catholic Messenger*, June 2, 1960, 15, in Scott and Streight, *The Contemporary Reviews*, 145.

131. Eileen Hall, review of *The Violent Bear It Away*, *The Bulletin*, March 5, 1950, 5, in Scott and Streight, *The Contemporary Reviews*, 109.

132. Paul Levine, review of *The Violent Bear It Away*, *Jubilee* 8 (May 1960): 52, in Scott and Streight, *The Contemporary Reviews*, 141.

133. Duhamel, "Flannery O'Connor's *VIOLENT* View of Reality," 94.

134. Ibid.

135. Harry Mooney Jr., "Dark Allegory," *Pittsburgh Sun-Telegraph*, February 28, 1960, in Scott and Streight, *The Contemporary Reviews*, 88.

136. Walter Sullivan, "Violence Dominates Fresh Tale," *Nashville Tennessean*, April 24, 1960, in Scott and Streight, *The Contemporary Reviews*, 132.

137. Paul Pickrel, "The New Books: Other Novels," *Harper's Magazine* 220 (April 1960): 114.

138. Cronin, "Books," 147.

139. Gossett, "The Religious Quest," 167.

140. O'Connor to John Hawkes, October 6, 1959, in *The Habit of Being*, 352.

141. O'Connor to Sally and Robert Fitzgerald, April 20, 1959, in *The Habit of Being*, 329.

142. O'Connor to Catherine Carver, April 18, 1959, in *The Habit of Being*, 327.

143. "Fiction," *Kirkus Bulletin*, December 15, 1959, 931, in Scott and Streight, *The Contemporary Reviews*, 71.

144. Charles A. Brady, "A Powerful Novel Turns on Religious Dilemma of Boy, 14,"

Buffalo Evening News, February 20, 1960, B6, in Scott and Streight, *The Contemporary Reviews,* 73.

145. Granville Hicks, "Southern Gothic with a Vengeance," *Saturday Review,* February 27, 1960, 18, in Scott and Streight, *The Contemporary Reviews,* 84.

146. Ruth Wolfe Fuller, "Backwoods Story Is Real Tragedy," *Boston Herald,* February 28, 1960, in Scott and Streight, *The Contemporary Reviews,* 86.

147. Webster Scott, "The Struggle of Ideals Is Reality," *Kansas City Star,* March 5, 1960, 7, in Scott and Streight, *The Contemporary Reviews,* 110.

148. Grady M. Long, "Mad Tennessee Prophet Casts Backwoods Shadow," *Chattanooga Times,* March 6, 1960, in Scott and Streight, *The Contemporary Reviews,* 113.

149. H. B. H., "A Southern Tale by Flannery O'Connor," *Springfield Republican,* March 6, 1960, D5, in Scott and Streight, *The Contemporary Reviews,* 112.

150. Hicks, "Southern Gothic with a Vengeance," 83.

151. Fuller, "Backwoods Story Is Real Tragedy," 86.

152. O'Connor to Cecil Dawkins, November 8, 1958, in *The Habit of Being,* 302–3.

153. H. B. H., "A Southern Tale," 113.

154. William H. Bocklage, review of *The Violent Bear It Away, Cincinnati Enquirer,* n.d., in Scott and Streight, *The Contemporary Reviews,* 106.

155. Prescott, "Books of the Times," 35.

156. T. M., "Violence in Story Evolution Mars New O'Connor Novel," *Houston Chronicle,* March 13, 1960, in Scott and Streight, *The Contemporary Reviews,* 114.

157. B. P., "O'Connor Novel Is Arresting," *Huntington Advertiser,* March 20, 1960, in Scott and Streight, *The Contemporary Reviews,* 120.

158. Frank Bigley, "Back South with Too Much Despair," 130.

159. Mary Elizabeth Reedy, "Conflict of Wills," *Omaha World-Herald,* April 24, 1960, in Scott and Streight, *The Contemporary Reviews,* 132.

160. Francis X. Canfield, review of *The Violent Bear It Away, Critic* 18 (April–May 1960), 45, in Scott and Streight, *The Contemporary Reviews,* 134.

161. G. K. Chesterton, *Orthodoxy* (Hollywood, Fla.: Simon & Brown, 2012), 13.

162. V. G. S., "O'Connor Novel Good," *New Bedford Standard-Times,* March 13, 1960, in Scott and Streight, *The Contemporary Reviews,* 116.

163. Reedy, "Conflict of Wills," 132.

164. Richard Daw, "Georgia Author, Flannery O'Connor, Pens Gripping Story of Backwoods Boy," *Pensacola News Journal,* March 6, 1960, in Scott and Streight, *The Contemporary Reviews,* 111.

165. O'Connor, *The Violent Bear It Away,* 19.

166. "About," *Renascence: Essays on Values in Literature* www.marquette.edu/renascence/about.html (accessed November 30, 2012).

167. Robert O. Bowen, "Hope vs. Despair in the New Gothic Novel," *Renascence* 13 (Spring 1961), 147–52, in Scott and Streight, *The Contemporary Reviews,* 161.

168. Ibid, 164.

169. Ibid, 165.

170. Ibid.

171. Frederick S. Kiley, "In Print: Bargain Book," *Clearing House* 36 (November 1961): 188, in Scott and Streight, *The Contemporary Reviews*, 166.

172. Thomas F. Smith, "Fiction as Prophecy: Novels of Flannery O'Connor Re-Read and Re-Evaluated," *Pittsburgh Catholic*, March 28, 1963, "Fine Arts Supplement," 1, 3, in Scott and Streight, *The Contemporary Reviews*, 170.

173. Hall, review of *The Violent Bear It Away*, 110.

Chapter 3. O'Connor's Posthumous Reputation

1. O'Connor, introduction to *A Memoir of Mary Ann*, 3.

2. John J. Quinn, S.J., review of *A Memoir of Mary Ann*, *Best Sellers* 21 (December 15, 1961), 394, in Scott and Streight, *The Contemporary Reviews*, 178.

3. Celestine Sibley, "Nuns Tell Inspirational Story, Convey 'Mystery' in Child's Life," *Atlanta Journal and Constitution*, November 15, 1961, B7, in Scott and Streight, *The Contemporary Reviews*, 176.

4. Edward F. Callahan, "In and Out of Print: Death of a Holy Innocent," *Boston Pilot*, January 27, 1962, in Scott and Streight, *The Contemporary Reviews*, 181.

5. A. C. H., "Emissary of Love," *Savannah Morning News Magazine*, January 7, 1962, 9, in Scott and Streight, *The Contemporary Reviews*, 180.

6. Obituary of Flannery O'Connor, *The Indiana (Penn.) Gazette*, August 4, 1964, 13.

7. "Deaths Elsewhere: Novelist O'Connor," *Washington Post*, August 4, 1964, B4.

8. "Flannery O'Connor Dead at 39," *New York Times*, August 4, 1964, 29.

9. Ibid.

10. "Milestones," *Time*, August 14, 1964.

11. John J. Quinn, foreword, *Esprit: A Journal of Thought and Opinion* 8 (Winter 1964): 2.

12. John F. Judge, email message to author, February 9, 2013.

13. Quinn, "Flannery O'Connor's Country," *Esprit*, 4.

14. John J. Clarke, "The Achievement of Flannery O'Connor," *Esprit*, 9.

15. Rev. Leonard F. X. Matthew, "Flannery O'Connor—A Tribute," *Esprit*, 34.

16. P. Albert Duhamel, "Flannery O'Connor—A Tribute," *Esprit*, 22.

17. Introduction to "Gracious Greatness," *Esprit*, 50.

18. Saul Bellow, "Flannery O'Connor—A Tribute," *Esprit*, 13.

19. J. F. Powers, "Flannery O'Connor—A Tribute," *Esprit*, 40.

20. Charles Brady, "Flannery O'Connor—A Tribute," *Esprit*, 16.

21. Robert Drake, "Flannery O'Connor—A Tribute," *Esprit*, 19.

22. James F. Farnham, "Flannery O'Connor—A Tribute," *Esprit*, 23.

23. Sr. Mariella Gable, "Flannery O'Connor—A Tribute," *Esprit*, 25.

24. Louis D. Rubin, "Flannery O'Connor—A Tribute," *Esprit*, 44.

25. Nathan A. Scott Jr., "Flannery O'Connor—A Tribute," *Esprit*, 45.

26. Robert Penn Warren, "Flannery O'Connor—A Tribute," *Esprit*, 49.

27. Elizabeth Hardwick, "Flannery O'Connor—A Tribute," *Esprit*, 30.

28. Caroline Gordon, "Flannery O'Connor—A Tribute," *Esprit*, 28. Emphasis in original.

29. Brother Antonius, "Flannery O'Connor—A Tribute," *Esprit*, 13.

30. Elizabeth Hardwick, "Flannery O'Connor—A Tribute," *Esprit*, 28.

31. J. Franklin Murray, S.J., "Flannery O'Connor—A Tribute," *Esprit*, 37.

32. Robie Macauley, "Flannery O'Connor—A Tribute," *Esprit*, 34.

33. Cleanth Brooks, "Flannery O'Connor—A Tribute," *Esprit*, 17.

34. Kay Boyle, "Flannery O'Connor—A Tribute," *Esprit*, 16.

35. Elizabeth Bishop, "Flannery O'Connor—A Tribute," *Esprit*, 16.

36. Warren Coffey, "Flannery O'Connor—A Tribute," *Esprit*, 18.

37. Robert Lowell, "Flannery O'Connor—A Tribute," *Esprit*, 33.

38. Lawrence Perrine, "Flannery O'Connor—A Tribute," *Esprit*, 40.

39. Katherine Anne Porter, "Gracious Greatness," *Esprit*, 50.

40. John Hawkes, "Flannery O'Connor—A Tribute," *Esprit*, 30.

41. Francis L. Kunkel, "Flannery O'Connor—A Tribute," *Esprit*, 33.

42. Bernard A. Yanavich Jr., "The Peacock and the Phoenix," *Esprit*, 82.

43. Charles Poore, "The Wonderful Stories of Flannery O'Connor," *New York Times*, May 27, 1965, 35.

44. Eugenia Thornton, "A Mask of Virtue Hides Wickedness," *Cleveland Plain Dealer*, June 13, 1965, in Scott and Streight, *The Contemporary Reviews*, 252.

45. Rex Barley, "Flannery O'Connor's Legacy of Fiction—Short Stories," *Arizona Republic*, May 23, 1965, in Scott and Streight, *The Contemporary Reviews*, 212.

46. "Grace Through Nature," *Newsweek*, May 31, 1965, 85–86, in Scott and Streight, *The Contemporary Reviews*, 231.

47. R. V. Cassill, "A Superb Final Effort," *Chicago Sun-Times*, June 13, 1965, in Scott and Streight, *The Contemporary Reviews*, 245.

48. "Grace Through Nature," *Newsweek*, 231.

49. Alan Pryce-Jones, "A Poignant Knowledge of the Dark," *New York Herald Tribune*, May 25, 1965, 23, in Scott and Streight, *The Contemporary Reviews*, 217.

50. Riley Hughes, "Books in the Balance," *Columbia* 45 (July 1965): 34, 36, in Scott and Streight, *The Contemporary Reviews*, 274.

51. Unsigned review of *Everything That Rises Must Converge*, *Newsday*, May 29, 1965, in Scott and Streight, *The Contemporary Reviews*, 224.

52. Robert Ostermann, "A World Without Love, as Seen by Miss O'Connor," *National Observer*, June 28, 1965, 19, in Scott and Streight, *The Contemporary Reviews*, 260.

53. Eric Lloyd, "Reading for Pleasure," *Wall Street Journal*, July 9, 1965, 8.

54. Naomi Bliven, "Nothing But the Truth," *New Yorker* 41 (September 11, 1965), 220–21, in Scott and Streight, *The Contemporary Reviews*, 286.

55. Paul J. Hallinan, archbishop of the Diocese of Atlanta, wrote of O'Connor, "She wrote of the South, but her vision was of the world" (*Georgia Bulletin*, August 12, 1965, 8, in Scott and Streight, *The Contemporary Reviews*, 278). An unsigned review in the *St. Louis Post-Dispatch* stated that O'Connor's new stories "are set in the South that their author knew so well, but each of them has a universality that makes all of them true to life anywhere" (*St. Louis Post-Dispatch*, May 16, 1965, in Scott and Streight, *The Contemporary Reviews*, 210). Walter Sullivan stated that "the South as locale and source was quite peripheral" ("Flannery O'Connor, Sin, and Grace: *Everything That Rises Must Converge*," *Hollis Critic* 2 [September 1965]: 1–10, in Scott and Streight, *The Contemporary Reviews*, 295). The most expansive praise of O'Connor's universality may be a remark from *Choice*, the magazine of the American Library Association: "Miss O'Connor's real region may not be the South, but Teilhard's noosphere" (*Choice* 2 [September 1965]: 387, in Scott and Streight, *The Contemporary Reviews*, 294).

56. Marilyn M. Houston, "Potomac Reader," *Georgetowner*, June 24, 1965, in Scott and Streight, *The Contemporary Reviews*, 259.

57. William Kirkland, "Posthumous O'Connor," *Charleston Gazette*, July 19, 1965, in Scott and Streight, *The Contemporary Reviews*, 270.

58. "When I read Flannery I don't think of Hemingway, or Katherine Anne Porter, or Sartre, but rather of someone like Sophocles. What more can be said of a writer? I write her name with honor, for all the truth and all the craft which shows man's fall and his dishonor." Thomas Merton, "Flannery O'Connor: A Prose Elegy," *Jubilee*, November 1964. Reprinted in *A Thomas Merton Reader* (New York: Doubleday, 1989), 257.

59. Unsigned review of *Everything That Rises Must Converge*, *Booklist* 61 (July 1, 1965): 1015, in Scott and Streight, *The Contemporary Reviews*, 264.

60. Ralph Bergamo, "Gallant Georgian's Legacy," *Atlanta Journal and Constitution*, May 23, 1965, B2, in Scott and Streight, *The Contemporary Reviews*, 213.

61. Florence Moran, "Top Newspapers and Magazines Pay Tribute to Flannery O'Connor," *Milledgeville Union-Recorder*, June 10, 1965, in Scott and Streight, *The Contemporary Reviews*, 244.

62. Webster Schott, "Flannery O'Connor: Faith's Stepchild," *The Nation* 201 (September 13, 1965): 142–44, 146, in Scott and Streight, *The Contemporary Reviews*, 290–91.

63. Walter Sullivan, "Flannery O'Connor, Sin, and Grace: *Everything That Rises Must Converge*," *Hollins Critic* 2 (September 1965): 1–10, in Scott and Streight, *The Contemporary Reviews*, 295.

64. Paul Levine, "Flannery O'Connor's Genius," *Jubilee*, October 1965, 52–53, in Scott and Streight, *The Contemporary Reviews*, 301.

65. Sullivan, "Flannery O'Connor, Sin, and Grace," 295.

66. Levine, "Flannery O'Connor's Genius," 301.

67. Warren Coffey, "Flannery O'Connor," *Commentary* 40 (November 1965): 93–99, in Scott and Streight, *The Contemporary Reviews*, 307.

68. Richard Poirier, "If You Know Who You Are You Can Go Anywhere," *New York*

Times Book Review 70 (May 30, 1965): 6, 22, in Scott and Streight, *The Contemporary Reviews*, 226–27.

69. "Memento Mori," *Times Literary Supplement*, March 24, 1966, 242, in Scott and Streight, *The Contemporary Reviews*, 317. Emphasis in original.

70. Ibid, 318.

71. John Coleman, "Small Town Miseries," *London Observer*, March 27, 1966, 27, in Scott and Streight, *The Contemporary Reviews*, 321.

72. Anthony Burgess, "New Fiction," *The Listener* 75 (April 7, 1966): 515, in Scott and Streight, *The Contemporary Reviews*, 324.

73. Irving Howe, "Flannery O'Connor's Stories," *New York Review of Books* 5 (September 30, 1965): 16–17, in Scott and Streight, *The Contemporary Reviews*, 292.

74. Louis D. Rubin Jr., "Southerners and Jews," *Southern Review* 2 (1966): 697–713, in Scott and Streight, *The Contemporary Reviews*, 332.

75. Bloom, *Flannery O'Connor*, 2.

76. John S. Kennedy, "A Sense of Mystery," *Catholic Transcript*, June 3, 1965, 5, in Scott and Streight, *The Contemporary Reviews*, 234.

77. John J. Quinn, S.J., "Short Stories," *Best Sellers* 25 (June 1, 1965): 124–25, in Scott and Streight, *The Contemporary Reviews*, 233.

78. Thomas Hoobler, "Feature Review," *Ave Maria* 102 (July 17, 1965): 18, in Scott and Streight, *The Contemporary Reviews*, 266.

79. Stanley Edgar Hyman, "Flannery O'Connor's Tattooed Christ," *New Leader*, May 10, 1965, 9–10, in Scott and Streight, *The Contemporary Reviews*, 207.

80. Ibid, 209.

81. Ibid.

82. Ibid, 210.

83. Ibid.

84. One representative example from a review of *Wise Blood:* "The style itself, incidentally, is reminiscent of everyone and no one—Erskine Caldwell and Nathanael West, among others, come strongly to mind at various points—but what is here is very much Miss O'Connor's own." Carl Hartman, "Jesus Without Christ," *Western Review* 17 (Autumn 1952): 75–80, in *The Contemporary Reviews*, 21.

85. Ann Hulbert, "A Generation of Wingless Chickens," *Times Literary Supplement*, May 3, 1991, 20, in Scott and Streight, *The Contemporary Reviews*, 466.

86. Gooch, *Flannery*, 9.

87. Elie, *The Life You Save*, 14.

88. O'Connor to Betty Hester, April 20, 1957, in *The Habit of Being*, 216.

89. Unsigned review of *Everything That Rises Must Converge*, *Emporia (Kans.) Gazette*, July 30, 1965, in Scott and Streight, *The Contemporary Reviews*, 272.

90. Roy Newquist, "A Lament for Flannery," *Chicago Heights Star*, May 27, 1965, in Scott and Streight, *The Contemporary Reviews*, 217.

91. Bergamo, "Gallant Georgian's Legacy," 213.

92. Howell Pearre, "Posthumous Collection of Southern Stories," *Nashville Banner,* May 28, 1965, in Scott and Streight, *The Contemporary Reviews,* 221.

93. Poore, "Wonderful Stories," 35.

94. Unsigned review of *Everything That Rises Must Converge, Newsday,* May 29, 1965, in Scott and Streight, *The Contemporary Reviews,* 224.

95. James F. Farnham, "The Essential Flannery O'Connor," *Cross Currents* 15 (Summer 1965): 376–78, in Scott and Streight, *The Contemporary Reviews,* 280.

96. See Gooch, *Flannery,* 365–67, and Sally Fitzgerald, "Chronology," in *Flannery O'Connor: Collected Works* (New York: Library of America, 1988), 1256.

97. O'Connor to Sally Fitzgerald, December 26, 1954, in *The Habit of Being,* 74.

98. Cash, *Flannery O'Connor,* 318.

99. Robert Fitzgerald, introduction to *Everything That Rises Must Converge,* by Flannery O'Connor (New York: Farrar, Straus and Giroux, 1965), x.

100. "A Good Man Is Hard to Find," *Virginia Quarterly Review* 31 (Autumn 1955): ci, in Scott and Streight, *The Contemporary Reviews,* 59.

101. Russell Kirk, "Memoir of Humpty Dumpty," *Flannery O'Connor Bulletin* 8 (1979): 14–16. Quoted in Cash, *Flannery O'Connor,* 214.

102. Whitt, *Understanding Flannery O'Connor,* 114–15.

103. Minnie Hite Moody, "Last, Rare Fruitage of Fine, Brave Talent," *Columbus Dispatch,* June 6, 1965, in Scott and Streight, *The Contemporary Reviews,* 240.

104. Nancy A. J. Porter, "Flannery O'Connor's Last Stories," *Providence Journal,* June 13, 1965, in Scott and Streight, *The Contemporary Reviews,* 251.

105. Hughes, "Books in the Balance," 274.

106. Quinn, "Short Stories," 233.

107. Hoobler, "Feature Review," 268.

108. Patrick Cruttwell, "Fiction Chronicle," *Hudson Review* 18 (Autumn 1965): 442–50, in Scott and Streight, *The Contemporary Reviews,* 308.

109. Elie, *The Life You Save,* 375.

110. Rosenfeld, "To Win by Default," 19–20.

111. Joyce Carol Oates, "Flannery O'Connor's Tragic People," *Detroit Free Press,* August 22, 1965, in Scott and Streight, *The Contemporary Reviews,* 279.

112. "Grace Through Nature," *Newsweek,* 232.

113. William Schemmel, "Southern Comfort," *Travel-Holiday,* June 1988, 72. Quoted in Gooch, *Flannery,* 208.

114. O'Connor to Maryat Lee, March 5, 1960, in *The Habit of Being,* 380.

115. "God-Intoxicated Hillbillies," *Time,* February 29, 1960, 118.

116. V. S. Pritchett, "Satan Comes to Georgia," *New Statesman* 71 (April 1, 1966): 469, 472, in Scott and Streight, *The Contemporary Reviews,* 322.

117. Joseph Nicholson, "Stories Adhere to Grotesque Theme," *Fort Worth Star-Telegram,* June 20, 1965, in Scott and Streight, *The Contemporary Reviews,* 258.

118. Rubin, "Southerners and Jews," 332.

119. Rene Jordan, "A Southern Drawl from Beyond the Grave," *British Association for American Studies Bulletin* 12–13 (1966): 99–101, in Scott and Streight, *The Contemporary Reviews*, 331.

120. "Memento Mori," *TLS*, 318.

121. O'Connor, *The Violent Bear It Away*, 16.

122. In *Book Week*, O'Connor was compared, in her thinking about religious fiction, to Eliot (Beverly Fields, "An Ethically Fearless Voice," *Book Week*, May 18, 1969, in Scott and Streight, *The Contemporary Reviews*, 360); in the *Wichita Falls Times*, she was compared to Keats in terms of her desire to not allow science to "clip an angel's wings" ("Southern Writer Stresses Creativity," *Wichita Falls Times*, May 25, 1969, in Scott and Streight, *The Contemporary Reviews*, 368); in *Catholic World*, her "universal literary theory" was compared favorably to those of Aristotle, Pope, and James (Charles J. Huelsbeck, "Of Fiction, Integrity, and Peacocks," *Catholic World* 210 [December 1969], in Scott and Streight, *The Contemporary Reviews*, 398); in *Sewanee Review*, her ability to depict the workings of the imagination was compared to Thoreau's skill at the same (Miles D. Orvell, "Flannery O'Connor," *Sewanee Review* 78 [1970], in Scott and Streight, *The Contemporary Reviews*, 401); in *Cross Currents*, she was compared to Sidney, Wordsworth, Coleridge, James, Eliot, Dickens, and Hardy in terms of how well she could "write about writing" (James F. Farnham, "Flannery O'Connor and the Incarnation of Mystery," *Cross Currents* 20 [Spring 1970], in Scott and Streight, *The Contemporary Reviews*, 408); and W. A. Sessions compared her to Blake as both artist and critic (W. A. Sessions, *Studies in Short Fiction* 8 [1971], in Scott and Streight, *The Contemporary Reviews*, 419).

123. Unsigned review of *Mystery and Manners*, *New Yorker* 45 (July 19, 1964): 84.

124. John J. Quinn, *Best Sellers* 29 (May 15, 1969): 76, in Scott and Streight, *The Contemporary Reviews*, 358.

125. Unsigned review of *Mystery and Manners*, *Publishers Weekly*, November 10, 1969, 51, in Scott and Streight, *The Contemporary Reviews*, 398.

126. Valarie Edinger, "Articles and Essays by Flannery O'Connor," *Richmond Times-Dispatch*, August 24, 1969, in Scott and Streight, *The Contemporary Reviews*, 397.

127. Maggie Irving, "The Presence of a Gift," *Worcester Telegram & Gazette*, June 22, 1969, in Scott and Streight, *The Contemporary Reviews*, 376.

128. D. Keith Mayo, review of *Mystery and Manners*, *New York Times Book Review*, May 25, 1969, 6–7, 20, in Scott and Streight, *The Contemporary Reviews*, 367.

129. Unsigned review of *Mystery and Manners*, *Kirkus Reviews*, March 1, 1969, 289–90, in Scott and Streight, *The Contemporary Reviews*, 347.

130. W. M. Kirkland, "Flannery O'Connor's Last Essays," *Charleston (W.V.) Gazette*, August 17, 1969, in Scott and Streight, *The Contemporary Reviews*, 391.

131. Saul Maloff, "On Flannery O'Connor," *Commonweal* 90 (August 8, 1969): 490–91, in Scott and Streight, *The Contemporary Reviews*, 388.

132. M. Thomas Inge, "Flannery O'Connor's Works Examined in New Critiques," *Lansing State Journal*, July 27, 1969, E7, in Scott and Streight, *The Contemporary Reviews*, 386.

133. Fredrick P. W. McDowell, "Toward the Luminous and the Numinous: The Art of Flannery O'Connor," *Southern Review* 9 (October 1973): 998–1013, in Scott and Streight, *The Contemporary Reviews*, 426.

134. Edel, *The Prefaces of Henry James*, 15.

135. Joe O'Sullivan, "Mystery and Manners," *Springfield (Mass.) Republican*, July 13, 1969, 68, in Scott and Streight, *The Contemporary Reviews*, 385.

136. Jane Mushabac, review of *Mystery and Manners*, *Village Voice*, July 3, 1969, 7.

137. Charles Thomas Samuels, "Flannery O'Connor: From Theology to Fable," *Chicago Tribune*, May 4, 1969, in Scott and Streight, *The Contemporary Reviews*, 351.

138. Kirkland," O'Connor's Last Essays," 391.

139. John Raymond, "Flannery O'Connor: She Wrote Because She Was Good at It," *Atlanta Journal and Constitution*, May 11, 1969, D10, in Scott and Streight, *The Contemporary Reviews*, 355.

140. "Paradox of the Peacock," *Times Literary Supplement*, February 25, 1972, 213, in Scott and Streight, *The Contemporary Reviews*, 422.

141. Charles J. Huelsbeck, "Of Fiction, Integrity, and Peacocks," *Catholic World* 210 (December 1969), 128–29, in Scott and Streight, *The Contemporary Reviews*, 399.

Chapter 4. Robert Giroux, Sally Fitzgerald, and *The Habit of Being*

1. Scott, "Flannery O'Connor, a Brief Biographical Sketch," in *Flannery O'Connor*, xix.

2. Joyce topped the list of all indexed authors by appearing in 59 percent of the anthologies, followed by Lawrence and Chekhov, each appearing in 54 percent. The leading American authors were Faulkner and James (both at 52 percent), followed by Hemingway (44 percent), Porter (41 percent), Welty (38 percent), Anderson (37 percent), and Crane (36 percent). See Landon C. Burns, "A Cross-Referenced Index of Short Fiction and Author-Title Listing," *Studies in Short Fiction* 7, no. 1 (Winter 1970): 6.

3. "A Good Man Is Hard to Find" appeared in fifteen anthologies; "The Displaced Person" in three.

4. Gooch, *Flannery*, 373.

5. Christopher Lehman-Haupt, "Robert Giroux, Editor, Publisher and Nurturer of Literary Giants, Is Dead," *New York Times*, September 6, 2008, B6.

6. *PEN American Newsletter* 47 (September 1981): 3. The newsletter item concerned Giroux and Roger Straus being awarded the fifth annual PEN Publisher Citation on April 8, 1981.

7. West, *American Literary Marketplace*, 59–70. West uses O'Connor's experience with Rinehart editor John Selby as the exception to the general rule that young authors tend to buckle under the pressure of "high-handed" editors.

8. Donald Hall, "Robert Giroux: Looking for Masterpieces," *New York Times*, January 6, 1980, BR1.

9. *PEN American Newsletter* 47 (September 1981): 3.

10. Caroline Gordon to Giroux, September 12, 1964. Unless otherwise noted, all correspondence quoted in this chapter is located in the Farrar, Straus and Giroux archives at the New York Public Library.

11. Henry Raymont, "Book Publishers See Better Times: But They Differ on Impact of Growth on Authors and Quality of Fiction," *New York Times*, April 10, 1972, 1.

12. *PEN American Newsletter* 47 (September 1981): 4. The comparison was made by Paul Horgan. In his 1980 *New York Times* portrait of Giroux, referenced above, the American poet Donald Hall made the same comparison: "He is the only living editor whose name is bracketed with that of Maxwell Perkins."

13. Ibid.

14. Quoted in Berg, *Maxwell Perkins*, 44–45.

15. *PEN American Newsletter* 47 (September 1981): 5.

16. Giroux to Elizabeth McKee, March 7, 1973.

17. A high school junior from New Orleans who wrote Giroux in 1973 described her term paper—due in six days—and stated, "I am looking for a book that she has written about what she feels about being a writer or writing in particular." Giroux responded that she should read *Mystery and Manners* (Jan Binder to Giroux, October 13, 1973). Another student from what he described as "the small town (pop 2000) of Tunnel Hill, Georgia" wrote on the eve of his senior term paper to ask Giroux six questions about O'Connor, all of which he answered in short phases penciled on the student's original letter: "How much of her work is biographical? None" (Gandi Vaughn to Giroux, April 22, 1988). A member of the Kettering, Ohio, Literary Club wrote to ask his advice about giving a talk on "O'Connor's heroines"; a book collector wrote to describe his copy of *Everything That Rises Must Converge* to see if it was a first edition; a couple interested in starting a foundation to raise money to cure lupus solicited his advice. The range and number of requests that Giroux answered is impressive; the Farrar, Straus and Giroux Archives at the New York Public Library house these and many similar requests.

18. Gary B. Brockman to Giroux, November 19, 1973.

19. Giroux to Gary B. Brockman, November 27, 1973.

20. Giroux to Regina O'Connor, August 7, 1964.

21. Giroux to Robert Fitzgerald, December 29, 1966.

22. Giroux to Regina O'Connor, September 16, 1966.

23. K. K. Merker to Giroux, June 12, 1970.

24. Giroux to Elizabeth McKee, December 29, 1966.

25. Robert Fitzgerald to Elizabeth McKee, August 14, 1967.

26. Giroux to Elizabeth McKee, September 14, 1967.

27. Robert Fitzgerald to Giroux, September 20, 1969.

28. Paul Engle to Giroux, July 13, 1971. All subsequent quotations in this paragraph are from this letter.

29. Robert Giroux, introduction to O'Connor, *The Complete Stories*, vii.

30. Colman McCarthy, "The Servant of Literature in the Heart of Iowa: Paul Engle's Years of Bringing People Who Write to a Place Where People Farm," *Washington Post*, March 27, 1983, G1.

31. Frances Florencourt, interview of Robert Giroux, January 24, 2007, in *At Home with Flannery O'Connor*, 84.

32. Elie, *The Life You Save*, 145.

33. Gooch, *Flannery*, 117.

34. O'Connor, *The Violent Bear It Away*, 242.

35. Elie, *The Life You Save*, 432.

36. Robert Giroux, "Thomas Merton's Durable Mountain," *New York Times*, October 11, 1998.

37. Joel Wells, "A Genius Who Frustrated Critics," *National Catholic Reporter*, November 19, 1971, 16, in Scott and Streight, *The Contemporary Reviews*, 435.

38. J. J. Quinn, review of *The Complete Stories*, by Flannery O'Connor, *America* 125 (December 11, 1971): 519, in Scott and Streight, *The Contemporary Reviews*, 442.

39. Melvin J. Friedman, "Flannery O'Connor: The Canon Completed, the Commentary Continuing," *Southern Literary Journal* 5 (Spring 1973): 116–23, in Scott and Streight, *The Contemporary Reviews*, 457.

40. George Core, "Unflinching Honesty, Rare Perception—That's O'Connor," *Nashville Tennessean*, February 27, 1972, C10, in Scott and Streight, *The Contemporary Reviews*, 449.

41. Jim Vollmar, "Flannery O'Connor: An Authentic Voice of the American South," *The Month* 24 (September–October 1991): 443–47, in Scott and Streight, *The Contemporary Reviews*, 472.

42. Robert Drake, "Her Sacred Office," *Modern Age* 16, no. 3 (Summer 1972): 322–24, in Scott and Streight, *The Contemporary Reviews*, 452.

43. Martha Duffy, "At Gunpoint," *Time*, November 21, 1971, 88.

44. Friedman, "Flannery O'Connor," 458.

45. Frederick P. W. McDowell, "Toward the Luminous and the Numinous: The Art of Flannery O'Connor," *Southern Review* (New Series) 9, no. 4 (1973): 998–1013, in Scott and Streight, *The Contemporary Reviews*, 458, 463.

46. Elie, *The Life You Save*, 432.

47. Wells, "A Genius Who Frustrated Critics," 435.

48. Thomas Lask, "Death Never Takes a Holiday," *New York Times*, December 3, 1971, 37.

49. Guy Davenport, "Even as the Heathen Rage," *National Review* 123 (December 31, 1971): 1473–74, in Scott and Streight, *The Contemporary Reviews*, 444.

50. Webster Schott, "Flannery O'Connor: Faith's Stepchild," *The Nation* 201 (September 13, 1965): 142–46, in Scott and Streight, *The Contemporary Reviews*, 288.

51. Richard Freedman, "The Pride of the Peacock Is the Glory of God," *Washington Post*, January 30, 1972, 11, in Scott and Streight, *The Contemporary Reviews*, 447.

52. Ibid, 448.

53. Ibid.

54. Chesterton, *Chesterton on Dickens*, 96.

55. Edward M. Hood, "Rural Georgia and the Starry Universe," *Shenandoah* 16 (Summer 1965): 109–14, in Scott and Streight, *The Contemporary Reviews*, 284.

56. Richard A. Duprey, "New Books," *Catholic World* 202 (October 1965): 54, in Scott and Streight, *The Contemporary Reviews*, 299.

57. James F. Farnham, "The Essential Flannery O'Connor," *Cross Currents* 15 (Summer 1965): 376–78, in Scott and Streight, *The Contemporary Reviews*, 282.

58. Alfred Kazin, review of *The Complete Stories*, by Flannery O'Connor, *New York Times Book Review*, November 28, 1971, 1.

59. Donovan Young, "3 New Books Cull Stories, Letters of Flannery O'Connor," *Atlanta Journal and Constitution*, April 8, 1984, H9, in Scott and Streight, *The Contemporary Reviews*, 464.

60. Warren Coffey, review of *The Complete Stories*, by Flannery O'Connor, *Commentary* 40, no. 5 (November 1965): 97.

61. Walter Clemons, "Acts of Grace," *Newsweek*, November 8, 1971, 116–17, in Scott and Streight, *The Contemporary Reviews*, 431.

62. John Alfred Avant, review of *The Complete Stories*, by Flannery O'Connor, *Library Journal* 97 (January 1, 1972): 85, in Scott and Streight, *The Contemporary Reviews*, 445.

63. John Idol, review of *The Complete Stories*, by Flannery O'Connor, *Studies in Short Fiction* 10 (1973): 103–5, in Scott and Streight, *The Contemporary Reviews*, 454.

64. Freedman, "The Pride of the Peacock," 447.

65. Drake, "Her Sacred Office," 452.

66. Chris Savage King, review of *Wise Blood*, in *New Statesmen and Society* 4 (February 8, 1991): 37–38, in Scott and Streight, *The Contemporary Reviews*, 465.

67. Clemons, "Acts of Grace," 431.

68. King, review of *Wise Blood*, 465.

69. William Jovanovich to Giroux, October 13, 1971.

70. Mildred V. Cabrera to Giroux, October 2, 1979.

71. Michael Hefner to Giroux, July 2, 1971.

72. Denver Lindley to Giroux, October 26, 1971.

73. Hajime Noguchi to Giroux, January 27, 1988.

74. Giroux to Michael Hefner, November 4, 1971.

75. *Wise Blood* was not nominated, but *A Good Man Is Hard to Find* was in 1956; it lost to John O'Hara's *Ten North Frederick*, a novel about a decidedly un–Mr. Smith figure who goes to Washington. In 1961 *The Violent Bear It Away* was nominated, along with *Rabbit, Run, A Separate Peace,* and *To Kill a Mockingbird* but lost to Conrad Richter's *The Waters of Kronos. Everything That Rises Must Converge* was nominated in 1966 but lost to *The Collected Stories of Katherine Anne Porter*.

76. Wells, "A Genius Who Frustrated Critics," 435.

77. "How the National Book Awards Work," *National Book Foundation*, www.national book.org/nba_process (accessed April 2, 2013).

78. Trimmer, *The National Book Awards for Fiction*, xiv.

79. Quoted in Trimmer, *National Book Awards*, xvi.

80. Trimmer, *National Book Awards*, xvii.

81. *The Last Whole Earth Catalogue* eventually won the award: see "Judge Resigns in Dispute: 'Whole Earth Catalogue' Gets Award," *Daytona Morning Beach Journal*, April 12, 1972, 10.

82. Henry Raymont, "Notes of Concern Mark Book Awards Ceremony," *New York Times*, April 14, 1972, 21.

83. William McPherson, "The National Book Awards," *Washington Post*, April 12, 1972, C1.

84. Larry Powell, "O'Connor Book Honored," *Savannah News-Press*, April 23, 1972, F 5, in Scott and Streight, *The Contemporary Reviews*, 450.

85. Farrar, Straus and Giroux press release, March 15, 1966.

86. Harry Gilroy, "Book Awards Go to 4 U.S. Writers," *New York Times*, March 16, 1966, 42.

87. Ibid.

88. Raymont, "Notes of Concern."

89. Ibid.

90. Robert Giroux, copy of acceptance speech for National Book Award, 1972, Farrar, Straus and Giroux Archives, New York Public Library.

91. Quoted in Gooch, *Flannery*, 372.

92. Giroux to Regina O'Connor, April 13, 1972.

93. "Author! Author!" *New York Times*, April 15, 1972, 30.

94. Christopher Lehman-Haupt, "Confessions of a Book Award Judge," *Saturday Review of the Arts* 1, no. 4 (April 1973): 35.

95. Susan Myrick, "Flannery O'Connor," *Marion Telegraph*, January 27, 1972.

96. Sally Foster, "O'Connor Reception at Georgia College Library," *Milledgeville Union-Recorder*, January 20, 1972.

97. "Flannery O'Connor Papers to Be Presented Sunday," *Milledgeville Union-Recorder*, January 13, 1972.

98. Mayor John P. Rousakis, proclamation, "Flannery O'Connor Day," January 13, 1972.

99. Foster, "O'Connor Reception."

100. Ibid.

101. The statistic about eight hundred visitors is found in the *Georgia College Bulletin* 57, no. 7 (March 1972), as well as a letter of February 23, 1972, from Dorrie P. Neligan, director of Alumni Affairs, to Robert Giroux.

102. Program for O'Connor reception at Georgia College Library, Farrar, Straus and Giroux Archives, NYPL.

103. Sally Foster, "O'Connor Peacocks Presented to the Stone Mountain Plantation," *Milledgeville Union-Recorder*, January 13, 1972.

104. Leonard Melfi to Giroux, September 28, 1964; Mark Harris to Giroux, September 17, 1974.

105. Giroux to Leonard Melfi, September 30, 1964.

106. Giroux to Mark Harris, September 25, 1974.

107. O'Connor to Betty Hester, July 5, 1958, in *The Habit of Being*, 290.

108. Elizabeth McKee to Mary Stephen, April 9, 1970.

109. Elizabeth McKee to Giroux, April 28, 1972.

110. Giroux to Gerald Beecham, April 18, 1977.

111. Sally Fitzgerald, proposal for Research Apprentice Program at Radcliffe College, January 1978. Farrar, Straus and Giroux Archives, NYPL.

112. Robert Giroux, letter of recommendation for Sally Fitzgerald's application for the Research Apprentice Program at Radcliffe College, January 15, 1978. Farrar, Straus and Giroux Archives, NYPL.

113. John Farrar to Jean Wylder, January 6, 1967.

114. Giroux to Regina O'Connor, December 11, 1968.

115. Giroux to Robert Fitzgerald, July 24, 1974.

116. Robert Fitzgerald to Giroux, September 12, 1974.

117. Sally Fitzgerald to Giroux, undated memorandum. Farrar, Straus and Giroux Archives, NYPL.

118. Giroux to G. Roysce Smith, June 17, 1975.

119. Email message to author from David Pavelich, head of Research Services, David M. Rubenstein Rare Book and Manuscript Library, Duke University, April 16, 2013.

120. Giroux to Mary Louise Black, March 26, 1976.

121. Thomas F. Gossett, "Flannery O'Connor's Opinions of Other Writers: Some Unpublished Comments," *Southern Literary Journal* 6, no. 2 (Spring 1974): 82.

122. Giroux to Maryat Lee, April 20, 1977.

123. Giroux to Sally Fitzgerald, June 7, 1976.

124. Ibid.

125. Giroux to Sally Fitzgerald, June 16, 1976.

126. Maryat Lee to Giroux, April 25, 1976.

127. Regina O'Connor to Maryat Lee, May 9, 1976.

128. Maryat Lee to Regina O'Connor, May 18, 1976.

129. Regina O'Connor to Maryat Lee, May 30, 1976.

130. Regina O'Connor to Maryat Lee, June 4, 1976.

131. Maryat Lee to Regina O'Connor, June 4, 1976.

132. Sally Fitzgerald to Giroux, February 14, 1977.

133. Maryat Lee to Sally Fitzgerald, February 12, 1977.

134. Sally Fitzgerald to Maryat Lee, February 21, 1977.

135. Maryat Lee to Giroux, March 7, 1977.

136. Sally Fitzgerald to Regina O'Connor, May 1, 1977. Emphasis in subsequently quoted passages in original.

137. Robert Fitzgerald, introduction to *Everything That Rises Must Converge*, xiv. Also see Gooch, *Flannery*, 181.

138. O'Connor to Sally and Robert Fitzgerald, April 26, 1954, in *The Habit of Being*, 71.

139. Sally Fitzgerald to Regina O'Connor, May 1, 1977. Emphasis in original.

140. Sally Fitzgerald to Giroux, May 2, 1977. All emphases in subsequent quotations are in the original.

141. Giroux to Sally Fitzgerald, May 6, 1977.

142. Sally Fitzgerald to Regina O'Connor, May 4, 1977. Emphasis in original.

143. O'Connor to Betty Hester, December 14, 1957, in *The Habit of Being*, 258.

144. Regina O'Connor to Sally Fitzgerald, May 15, 1977. All emphases in subsequent quotations are in the original.

145. Sally Fitzgerald to Regina O'Connor, May 18, 1977. Emphasis in original.

146. Sally Fitzgerald to Giroux, May 18, 1977.

147. Gooch, *Flannery*, 317.

148. O'Connor to Cecil Dawkins, April 3, 1959, in *The Habit of Being*, 326.

149. Cash, *Flannery O'Connor*, 173.

150. Sally Fitzgerald, introduction to *The Habit of Being*, ix.

151. Giroux to Regina O'Connor, January 8, 1979.

152. Giroux to Regina O'Connor, February 5, 1979.

153. Giroux to Regina O'Connor, March 12, 1979.

154. Robert Phillips, "On Being Flannery O'Connor," *Commonweal* 106 (April 13, 1979): 220.

155. Quentin Vest, "An Intensity of Intelligent Purpose," *Library Journal* 104 (January 15, 1979): 194.

156. John R. May, "Seekers and Finders," *America* 140 (June 16, 1979): 499.

157. Richard H. Brodhead, "A Life of Letters," *Yale Review* 69, no. 3 (Spring 1980): 451.

158. Graham Greene, review of *The Habit of Being*, by Flannery O'Connor, *The Observer* (December 7, 1980), 27.

159. John Leonard, "Impatient with Freudian's Down-Home Humor," *New York Times*, March 9, 1979, C23.

160. Richard Gilman, "A Life of Letters," *New York Times Book Review*, March 18, 1979, 1.

161. Michael True, "The Luminous Letters of a Writer of Genius," *Chronicle of Higher Education*, (April 16, 1979, R7.

162. Melvin J. Friedman, "'The Human Comes Before Art': Flannery O'Connor Viewed Through Her Letters and Her Critics," *Southern Literary Journal* 12, no. 2 (1980): 115.

163. See, for example, Janet Groth's reflection on the power of epistolary collections

in *Commonweal*, December 1, 1979. Other reviewers drew similar comparisons between Nabokov and O'Connor as letter-writers.

164. "A Selection of the Best Books of 1979," *New York Times*, November 25, 1979, BR4.

165. Douglas Hill, "As She Lay Dying," *Books in Canada* 8, no. 5 (May 1979): 17.

166. Quoted in Friedman, "'The Human Comes Before Art,'" 119.

167. Brodhead, "A Life of Letters," 452.

168. Frank E. Moorer and Richard Macksey, review of *The Habit of Being*, by Flannery O'Connor, *Modern Language Notes*, 94, no. 5 (December 1979): 1274.

169. Gilman, "A Life of Letters," 32.

170. Brodhead, "A Life of Letters," 452.

171. Paul Gray, review of *The Habit of Being*, by Flannery O'Connor, *Time* 113, no. 10 (March 5, 1979): 87.

172. Unsigned review of *The Habit of Being*, by Flannery O'Connor, *Publishers Weekly* 216, no. 3 (January 15, 1979): 120.

173. Edmund Fuller, "A Gallant Life Amidst Profound Insight," *Wall Street Journal* 193 (March 12, 1979): 18.

174. John F. Desmond, review of *The Habit of Being*, by Flannery O'Connor, *World Literature Today* 54, no. 2 (Spring 1980): 289.

175. J. O. Tate, "The Village Theist," *National Review* 31, no. 11 (March 16, 1979): 364.

176. Unsigned review of *The Habit of Being*, by Flannery O'Connor, *Kirkus Reviews* 47 (January 15, 1979): 109.

177. Miles Orvell, "Blessed in Deprivation," *American Scholar* 48, no. 4 (Autumn 1979): 562.

178. John Keates, "Balancing Act," *Spectator* 243 (December 22, 1979): 29.

179. Helen Ruth Vaughn, review of *The Habit of Being*, by Flannery O'Connor, *New Catholic World* 222 (July–August 1979): 188.

180. Mary Gordon, "The Habit of Genius," *Saturday Review*, April 14, 1979, 43. Gordon's full quotation states her assumption about O'Connor: "Isolated as she was, O'Connor made and kept many friends through her correspondence."

181. Robert H. Brinkmeyer Jr., review of *The Habit of Being*, by Flannery O'Connor, *Southern Quarterly* 18, no. 2 (1980): 92.

182. Paul Granahan, review of *The Habit of Being*, by Flannery O'Connor, *Best Sellers* 40, no. 3 (June 1980): 109.

183. Jan Norby Gretlund, review of *The Habit of Being*, by Flannery O'Connor, *South Carolina Review* 12, no. 1 (Spring 1980): 61.

184. Sally Fitzgerald to Giroux, March 16, 1977.

185. Giroux to Sally Fitzgerald, April 7, 1977.

186. Robert B. Shaw, "Jane Austen in Milledgeville," *The Nation* 228, no. 16 (April 28, 1979): 474.

187. Friedman, "'The Human Comes Before Art,'" 114.

188. Eugene Current-Garcia, review of *The Habit of Being*, by Flannery O'Connor, *Southern Humanities Review* 14 (1979): 373.

189. Josephine Hendin, review of *The Habit of Being*, by Flannery O'Connor, *New Republic* 180, no. 10 (March 10, 1979): 35.

190. Janet Varner Gunn, review of *The Habit of Being*, by Flannery O'Connor, *American Literature* 53, no. 3 (November 1981): 522.

191. Brodhead, "A Life of Letters," 456.

192. Gray, review of *The Habit of Being*, 87.

193. See, for example, the *Atlantic Monthly*, where the reviewer states, "One stream of letters (most notably directed to a young woman known only as 'A') takes readers further into the forests of theology than most non-Catholics will want to travel, but they show the singular force and flexibility of her mind." Unsigned review of *The Habit of Being*, by Flannery O'Connor, *Atlantic Monthly* 243, no. 6 (June 1979): 96.

194. Robert Fitzgerald to Giroux, February 16, 1979.

195. Desmond, review of *The Habit of Being*, 289.

196. Tate, "The Village Theist," 364.

197. T. C. Holyoke, review of *The Habit of Being*, by Flannery O'Connor, *Antioch Review* 37, no. 3 (Summer 1979): 373.

198. "*The Habit of Being*," *Kirkus*, 109.

199. May, "Seekers and Finders," 498.

200. Ibid.

201. Orvell, "Blessed in Deprivation," 562.

202. David Livingstone, review of *The Habit of Being*, by Flannery O'Connor, *Maclean's*, April 23, 1979, 64.

203. Bette Howland, "An Unsuspecting Autobiographer," *Ms.* 8, no. 1 (July 1979): 39.

204. Giroux to John Loudon, June 17, 1985.

205. Giroux to Elmer O'Brien, March 19, 1990.

206. Giroux to Deborah Baker, September 21, 1992. Fitzgerald's papers are now housed at Emory University. Bruce Gentry, editor of the *Flannery O'Connor Review*, has described what Giroux called a "first draft" as more of a series of essays "written toward the greater work of putting it all together as a biography." Bruce Gentry, email message to author, October 3, 2013.

207. Herbert Mitgang, "Flanagan and Taylor Win Book Prizes," *New York Times*, January 8, 1980, c9.

208. Sally Fitzgerald, speech to the National Book Critics Circle, January 17, 1980. Farrar, Straus and Giroux Archives, NYPL.

209. Ibid. Emphasis in original.

Chapter 5. Adaptation and Reputation

1. Robert Giroux to Robert Fitzgerald, March 29, 1968. Farrar, Straus and Giroux Archives, New York Public Library. Unless otherwise stated, all letters are from this collection.

2. Boyum, *Double Exposure*, 175.

3. Giroux to Elizabeth McKee, June 30, 1966.

4. Giroux to Regina O'Connor, September 16, 1966.

5. Michael Fitzgerald, "Interview," *Wise Blood* DVD, directed by John Huston (Criterion Collection, 2009).

6. Ibid.

7. Madsen, *John Huston*, 212–13.

8. Vincent Canby, "Many Try, But 'Wise Blood' Succeeds," *New York Times*, March 2, 1980, D19.

9. David Thomson, "John Huston," 425. Huston's desire to adapt more literary works continued after *Wise Blood:* his next film was *Under the Volcano* and his last was *The Dead*.

10. Jim Harrison, *Off to the Side* (New York: Grove, 2002), 261. Quoted in Meyers, *John Huston*, 66. Huston's *The Maltese Falcon* was the third attempt to film Hammett's novel; Huston's success in adapting it came from his painstakingly replicating so much of the novel's exact dialogue and structure.

11. Geoffrey Nowell-Smith, "Loners and Sin," *New Statesman*, January 18, 1980, 102.

12. Benedict Fitzgerald, "Interview," *Wise Blood* DVD.

13. John Simon, "Christ Without Christ; Nijinsky Without Nijinsky," *National Review*, May 2, 1980, 543.

14. Joy Gould Boyum, "Two Artists: John Huston and Flannery O'Connor," *Wall Street Journal*, February 22, 1980, 21.

15. Huston was paid $125,000 instead of his usual $400,000. See Meyers, *John Huston*, 372.

16. Archer Winsten, "'Blood' Repels and Attracts," *New York Post*, February 18, 1980, 26.

17. Andrew Sarris, "Of Blood and Thunder and Despair," *Village Voice*, February 25, 1979, 39.

18. Andrew Sarris, "Blood Tells," *Village Voice*, October 8, 1979, 40.

19. Huston, *An Open Book*, 369.

20. "Nepotism Runs in the Blood," *Premiere*, December 1979, 9.

21. Grobel, *The Hustons*, 714.

22. Frank Rich, "The Sound and the Fury," *Time*, February 25, 1980, 50.

23. Gene Moskowitz, review of *Wise Blood*, directed by John Huston, *Variety*, June 6, 1979.

24. David Ansen, "Huston at His Best," *Newsweek*, March 17, 1980, 101.

25. Jim Robbins, review of *Wise Blood*, directed by John Huston, *Box Office*, April 14, 1980.

26. Rex Reed, "Huston Triumphs with 'Wise Blood,'" *New York Daily News*, February 27, 1980, 29.

27. O'Connor to Elizabeth McKee, February 17, 1949, in *The Habit of Being*, 9.

28. O'Connor to McKee, July 21, 1948, in *The Habit of Being*, 6.

29. O'Connor to McKee, February 3, 1949, in *The Habit of Being*, 9.

30. Press kit for *Wise Blood*, New Line Cinema, Archives of the New York Public

Library for the Performing Arts. All subsequent quotations from the press kit are from this source.

31. O'Connor to Elizabeth Bishop, April 23, 1960, in *The Habit of Being*, 391.

32. O'Connor to Betty Hester, September 24, 1955, in *The Habit of Being*, 105.

33. O'Connor to John Hawkes, September 13, 1959, in *The Habit of Being*, 350.

34. Michael Fitzgerald, "Interview," *Wise Blood* DVD.

35. O'Connor to John Hawkes, September 13, 1959, in *The Habit of Being*, 349.

36. Vincent Canby, "'Wise Blood,' Huston's 33d Feature," *New York Times*, September 29, 1979, 12.

37. Michael Fitzgerald, "Interview," *Wise Blood* DVD.

38. Grobel, *The Hustons*, 715.

39. Rich, "The Sound and the Fury," 50.

40. Jack Kroll, review of *Wise Blood*, directed by John Huston, *Newsweek*, October 22, 1979, 101.

41. Tim Pulleine, review of *Wise Blood*, directed by John Huston, *Sight and Sound*, Winter 1979–80, 57.

42. Ansen, "Huston at His Best," 101.

43. Rob Edelman, review of *Wise Blood*, directed by John Huston, *Films in Review*, January 1980, 115.

44. Ibid, 116.

45. Kathleen Carroll, "'Wise Blood' Is a Low-Budget Miracle," *New York Daily News*, February 18, 1980, 23.

46. Roger Angell, review of *Wise Blood*, directed by John Huston, *New Yorker*, February 25, 1980, 113.

47. Joe Lee Davis, "Outraged or Embarrassed," *Kenyon Review* 15 (Spring 1953), in Scott and Streight, *The Contemporary Reviews*, 23.

48. "Damnation of Man," *Savannah Morning News*, May 25, 1952, 40, in Scott and Streight, *The Contemporary Reviews*, 11.

49. "*Wise Blood* Guarantees to Frighten and Intrigue," *Wichita Eagle*, August 2, 1962, in Scott and Streight, *The Contemporary Reviews*, 187.

50. Winsten, "'Blood' Repels and Attracts," 26.

51. Melwyn Breen, "Satanic Satire," *Saturday Night*, July 19, 1952, 2–3, in Scott and Streight, *The Contemporary Reviews*, 18.

52. Stanley Kauffmann, "Unwise Bloods," *New Republic*, March 15, 1980, 24.

53. Philip French, "In the Bible Belt," London *Observer*, January 13, 1980, 14.

54. Robert Hatch, review of *Wise Blood*, directed by John Huston, *The Nation*, March 8, 1980, 283.

55. Boyum, "Two Artists," 21.

56. Ansen, "Huston at His Best," 101.

57. David Denby, review of *Wise Blood*, directed by John Huston, *New York*, March 10, 1980, 85.

58. Simon, "Christ Without Christ," 543.

59. Winsten, "'Blood' Repels and Attracts," 26.

60. Rich, "The Sound and the Fury," 50.

61. Stephen Farber, review of *Wise Blood*, directed by John Huston, *New West*, May 5, 1980.

62. Connie Koenenn, "Turn-ons and Turn-offs in Current Home Entertainment Releases," *Los Angeles Times*, April 15, 1986.

63. French, "In the Bible Belt," 14.

64. Robert Asahina, review of *Wise Blood*, directed by John Huston, *New Leader*, November 5, 1979, 24.

65. Gene Moskowitz, review of *Wise Blood*, *Variety*, June 6, 1979.

66. Howard Kissel, "Wise Blood," *Women's Wear Daily*, February 14, 1980, 20.

67. Carroll, "'Wise Blood' Is a Low-Budget Miracle," 23.

68. O'Connor, "The Grotesque in Southern Fiction" in *Mystery and Manners*, 40.

69. Hatch, review of *Wise Blood*, 283.

70. "Nepotism Runs in the Blood," 9.

71. Angell, review of *Wise Blood*, *New Yorker*, 114.

72. Ansen, "Huston at His Best," 101.

73. Farber, review of *Wise Blood*, *New West*, May 5, 1980.

74. Sarris, "Blood Tells," 40.

75. Carroll, "'Wise Blood' Is a Low-Budget Miracle," 23.

76. Rob Baker, "American Gothics," *Soho Weekly News*, October 11, 1979, 38.

77. Francine Prose, "*Wise Blood:* A Matter of Life and Death," *The Criterion Collection*, May 11, 2009, www.criterion.com/current/posts/1132-wise-blood-a-matter-of-life-and -death (accessed June 12, 2013); also included in supplemental material for the Criterion DVD edition of *Wise Blood*.

78. Canby, "Many Try, But *Wise Blood* Succeeds," D19.

79. Michael Ciment, "Two Encounters with John Huston," 138.

80. Ibid.

81. Angell, review of *Wise Blood*, *New Yorker*, 113.

82. Canby, "Many Try, But *Wise Blood* Succeeds," D19.

83. James McCourt, "Reports from the New York Film Festival," *Film Comment*, November/December 1979, 64.

84. David Sterrit, "Missing the Flannery O'Connor Mood," *Christian Science Monitor*, March 7, 1980, 19.

85. Nowell-Smith, "Loners and Sin," 102.

86. Asahina, review of *Wise Blood*, *New Leader*, November 5, 1979, 24.

87. Pulleine, review of *Wise Blood*, *Sight and Sound*, 57.

88. Michael Tarantino, review of *Wise Blood*, directed by John Huston, *Film Quarterly* 33, no. 4 (Summer 1980): 17.

89. Kauffmann, "Unwise Bloods," 24.

90. Angell, review of *Wise Blood*, *New Yorker*, 114.

91. Meyers, *John Huston*, 372.

92. Alan Yuhas, "As *The Great Gatsby* Opens, What Makes for a Good Adaptation Anyway?" *The Guardian*, May 7, 2013, www.guardian.co.uk (accessed May 22, 2013).

93. Harold Clurman, "New York Film Festival," *The Nation*, October 27, 1979, 409.

94. Sarris, "Of Blood," 39.

95. Boyum, *Double Exposure*, 71.

96. O'Connor, *Wise Blood*, 222.

97. Ibid, 224. Ellipses in original.

98. O'Connor to John Hawkes, September 13, 1959, in *The Habit of Being*, 349–50.

99. Ibid.

100. Boyum, "Two Artists," 21.

101. Denby, review of *Wise Blood*, *New York*, 85.

102. Kroll, review of *Wise Blood*, *Newsweek*, 101.

103. Ansen, "Huston at His Best," 101.

104. Ibid.

105. Pulleine, review of *Wise Blood*, *Sight and Sound*, 57.

106. Nowell-Smith, "Loners and Sin," 102.

107. French, "In the Bible Belt," 14.

108. Boyum, "Two Artists," 21.

109. Boyum, *Double Exposure*, 176.

110. Brett Taylor, "From Cuckoo Patient to Deadwood Doc: An Interview with Brad Dourif," *Shock Cinema*, Fall 2004, 33.

111. Isaac Rosenfeld, "To Win by Default," in Scott and Streight, *The Contemporary Reviews*, 17.

112. Angell, review of *Wise Blood*, *New Yorker*, 114.

113. "Dan Shor Interview," TV Store Online, http://blog.tvstoreonline.com/2013/05/actor-dan-shor-talks-with-tv-store.html, May 29, 2013 (accessed June 10, 2013).

114. Taylor, "From Cuckoo Patient to Deadwood Doc," 33.

115. Quoted in Grobel, *The Hustons*, 712.

116. Brad Dourif, "Interview," 2008, *Wise Blood* DVD.

117. Benedict Fitzgerald, "Interview," 2008, *Wise Blood* DVD.

118. Ibid.

119. Dourif, "Interview," *Wise Blood* DVD.

120. Grobel, *The Hustons*, 710.

121. O'Connor to Louise Abbot, [undated] Saturday, 1959, in *The Habit of Being*, 353.

122. Haddox, *Hard Sayings*, 39.

123. William Walsh, "Flannery O'Connor, John Huston, and *Wise Blood*: In Search of Taulkingham," *Flannery O'Connor Review* 9 (2011): 95.

124. Meyers, *John Huston*, 371.

125. Trailer for *Wise Blood*, 1980, *Wise Blood* DVD.

126. *Wise Blood*, directed by John Huston (1980; Macon, Georgia: The Criterion Collection, 2009), DVD.

127. See "Shining (romantic comedy)," *The Trailer Mash*, www.thetrailermash.com /shining-romantic-comedy (accessed May 22, 2013).

128. Canby, "Many Try, But 'Wise Blood' Succeeds," D19.

129. George Knight, "A Merited O'Connor Revival," *Tampa Tribune*, September 30, 1962, in Scott and Streight, *The Contemporary Reviews*, 192.

130. Harkins, *Hillbilly*, 206.

131. Denis Lim, "Huston's 'Wise Blood' Takes on the New Faith of a Nonbeliever," *Los Angeles Times*, May 10, 2009.

132. Meyers, *John Huston*, 372.

133. Huston, *An Open Book*, 370.

134. O'Connor to Cecil Dawkins, November 5, 1963, in *The Habit of Being*, 546.

135. O'Connor to Cecil Dawkins, November 8, 1963, in *The Habit of Being*, 547.

136. Ibid.

137. Press release for *The Displaced Person*, Archives of the New York Public Library for the Performing Arts.

138. Cecil Dawkins, "Thinking About Evil's Consequences," *New York World Journal Tribune*, December 25, 1966, 26.

139. Ibid.

140. Ibid.

141. Michael Smith, "Theatre: The Displaced Person," *Village Voice*, January 5, 1967, 17.

142. Richard Gilman, "Dark Amalgam," *Newsweek*, January 9, 1967, 71.

143. George Oppenheimer, "American Place Theatre Offers 'Displaced Person," *Newsday*, December 30, 1966, page unknown.

144. Ibid.

145. Robert Giroux to Robert Fitzgerald, December 29, 1966, Farrar, Straus and Giroux Archives, NYPL.

146. "Director Karin Coonrod Brings Flannery O'Connor Triptych to the Stage," *Columbia News*, November 16, 2001.

147. Karin Coonrod, "Director's Note," program for *Everything That Rises Must Converge*. New York Public Library for the Performing Arts.

148. Ibid.

149. Susan Srigley, "Flannery O'Connor in the Public Square: Karin Coonrod's *Everything That Rises Must Converge*," *Flannery O'Connor Review* 11 (2013): 99.

150. Bruce Weber, "Southern Stories, on the Stage and on Their Own," *New York Times*, November 3, 2001, A13.

151. David Cote, review of *Everything That Rises Must Converge*, directed by Karin Coonrod, *Time Out New York*, November 18, 2001, 149.

152. Jessica Winter, "A Doom of One's Own," *Village Voice*, November 6, 2001.

153. "Galley Proof: *A Good Man Is Hard to Find*," in Magee, *Conversations with Flannery O'Connor*, 5.

154. Ibid, 8.

155. Harvey Briet, "In and Out of Books: Visitor," *New York Times*, June 12, 1955, in Magee, *Conversations*, 11.

156. "Galley Proof," *Conversations*, 8.

157. O'Connor, "Writing Short Stories," in *Mystery and Manners*, 96.

158. O'Connor to Catharine Carver, May 24, 1955, in *The Habit of Being*, 83.

159. O'Connor to Robie Macaulay, May 18, 1955, in *The Habit of Being*, 82. O'Connor added the article to the television show's title.

160. O'Connor to Ben Griffith, June 8, 1955, in *The Habit of Being*, 84.

161. O'Connor to Elizabeth Fenwick Way, September 13, 1956, in *The Habit of Being*, 175.

162. O'Connor to Betty Hester, September 8, 1956, in *The Habit of Being*, 174.

163. O'Connor to Sally and Robert Fitzgerald, December 10, 1956, in *The Habit of Being*, 186.

164. O'Connor to Betty Hester, December 28, 1956, in *The Habit of Being*, 191.

165. O'Connor to Betty Hester, March 9, 1957, in *The Habit of Being*, 207.

166. O'Connor to Denver Lindley, March 6, 1957, in *The Habit of Being*, 206.

167. O'Connor to Betty Hester, March 9, 1957, in *The Habit of Being*, 208; O'Connor to Mrs. Rumsey Haynes, March 3, 1957, in *The Habit of Being*, 205.

168. O'Connor to Brainard and Frances Cheney, January 3, 1957, in Stevens, *Correspondence*, 47.

169. R. F. S., "Gene Kelly in Debut on 'Schlitz Playhouse," *New York Times*, March 2, 1957.

170. O'Connor, "Writing Short Stories," 94–95.

171. F. J. Fontinell to Elizabeth McKee, January 22, 1965, Farrar, Straus and Giroux Archives, NYPL.

172. Richard Gilman, "Flannery O'Connor," *Directions '65* television program, National Council of Catholic Men, April 25, 1965.

173. Gilman, "On Flannery O'Connor," *New York Review of Books* 13 (August 21, 1969): 24.

174. Gilman, "Flannery O'Connor."

175. Ibid.

176. Foote, *Genesis of an American Playwright*, 199.

177. Robert Donahoo, "A Tribute to Horton Foote, 1916–2009," *Flannery O'Connor Review* 7 (2009): 55.

178. Foote, *Genesis*, 183.

179. O'Connor to Betty Hester, August 24, 1956, in *The Habit of Being*, 171. Punctuation appears as in original.

Chapter 6. O'Connor and the Common (Online) Reader

1. *Goodreads*, www.goodreads.com/about/us (accessed July 18, 2015).

2. "Vulgar, adj.," *OED Online*, Oxford University Press, December 2014, www.oed .com (accessed January 29, 2015).

3. *Goodreads*, www.goodreads.com/about/us (accessed July 18, 2015). Besides its obvious volume of users, *Goodreads* is also the most valuable of the leading social reading sites because it accommodates longer reviews.

4. Lisa Nakamura, "'Words with Friends': Socially Networked Reading on *Goodreads*," *PMLA* 128, no. 1 (January 2013): 241.

5. Scott Turow, novelist and president of the Authors Guild, was a vocal critic of the takeover and stated that the acquisition stands as "a textbook example of how modern Internet monopolies can be built." Scott Turow, "Turow on Amazon/Goodreads: This is how modern monopolies can be built," *The Authors Guild*, March 29, 2013, www.authors guild.org (accessed September 2, 2013).

6. Jordan Weissmann, "The Simple Reason Why *Goodreads* Is So Valuable to Amazon," *Atlantic*, April 1, 2013, www.theatlantic.com (accessed August 24, 2013).

7. Julian Pinder, "Online Literary Communities: A Case Study of LibraryThing," in *From Codex to Hypertext: Reading at the Turn of the Twenty-First Century*, ed. Anouk Lang (Amherst: University of Massachusetts Press, 2012), 74–75.

8. Joel, review of *Wise Blood*, September 20, 2008, www.goodreads.com (accessed August 1, 2013).

9. Danielle Wilkie, review of *The Complete Stories*, July 8, 2008, www.goodreads.com (accessed August 10, 2013).

10. Propertius, review of *The Complete Stories*, June 11, 2013, Amazon.com (accessed August 9, 2013).

11. Richard, review of *The Complete Stories*, July 22, 2012, www.goodreads.com (accessed August 2, 2013).

12. Rebecca Saxon, review of *Three by Flannery O'Connor*, June 29, 2011, www.good reads.com (accessed August 9, 2013).

13. Lisa Norris, review of *Wise Blood*, May 29, 2012, www.goodreads.com (accessed August 1, 2013).

14. Heath Lowrance, review of *Wise Blood*, May 9, 2012, www.goodreads.com (accessed August 4, 2013).

15. Judi, review of *Wise Blood*, May 18, 1911, www.goodreads.com (accessed August 4, 2013).

16. Dylan H., review of *Wise Blood*, October 7, 2011, www.goodreads.com (accessed July 21, 2013).

17. Larry, review of *Wise Blood*, November 2, 2009, www.goodreads.com (accessed July 29, 2013).

18. Josh, review of *Wise Blood*, April 5, 2007, www.goodreads.com (accessed July 29, 2013).

19. A. M., review of *Wise Blood*, October 27, 2011, www.goodreads.com (accessed July 29, 2013).

20. Emily, review of *Wise Blood*, February 15, 2011, www.goodreads.com (accessed July 21, 2013).

21. Ricky German, review of *A Good Man Is Hard to Find*, October 15, 2012, www .goodreads.com (accessed July 29, 2013).

22. Richard, review of *The Complete Stories*, July 22, 2012, www.goodreads.com (accessed August 10, 2013).

23. Fussfehler, review of *A Good Man Is Hard to Find*, November 15, 2012, www.good reads.com (accessed August 4, 2013).

24. Matt, review of *The Complete Stories*, June 2, 2010, www.goodreads.com (accessed August 4, 2013).

25. Newengland, review of *Wise Blood*, November 2, 2012, www.goodreads.com (accessed August 10, 2013).

26. Becky Talbot, review of *The Violent Bear It Away*, February 23, 2013, www.good reads.com (accessed August 4, 2013).

27. James Stanley, review of *The Violent Bear It Away*, July 29, 2008, www.goodreads .com (accessed August 10, 2013).

28. Courtney, review of *Everything That Rises Must Converge*, March 5, 2012, www .goodreads.com (accessed August 1, 2013).

29. Paquita Maria Sanchez, review of *Everything That Rises Must Converge*, July 26, 2011, www.goodreads.com (accessed August 4, 2013).

30. Darwin8u, review of *Everything That Rises Must Converge*, October 29, 2012, www .goodreads.com (accessed August 4, 2013).

31. Peyton Von Amburgh, review of *The Complete Stories*, January 24, 2015, www .goodreads.com (accessed March 1, 2015).

32. Shelia, review of *Mystery and Manners*, April 15, 2011, www.goodreads.com (accessed August 10, 2013).

33. Trisha, review of *Everything That Rises Must Converge*, January 12, 2010, www .goodreads.com (accessed August 4, 2013).

34. Golden, review of *The Complete Stories*, September 30, 2010, www.goodreads.com (accessed August 4, 2013).

35. Jillian, review of *The Violent Bear It Away*, December 7, 2012, www.goodreads.com (accessed August 2, 2013).

36. Elliot, review of *Wise Blood*, June 1, 2012, www.goodreads.com (accessed August 6, 2013).

37. Kat, review of *Wise Blood*, October 12, 2010, www.goodreads.com (accessed August 9, 2013).

38. Jeffrey Taylor, review of *Wise Blood*, June 23, 2012, www.goodreads.com (accessed August 9, 2013).

39. Charles Weinstein, review of *Wise Blood*, Amazon.com, December 16, 2006 (accessed August 9, 2013).

40. Fiona Robson, review of *Wise Blood*, January 5, 2012, www.goodreads.com (accessed August 1, 2013).

41. Sera, review of *Wise Blood*, October 12, 2012, www.goodreads.com (accessed August 1, 2013).

42. Lena, review of *A Good Man Is Hard to Find*, December 29, 2011, www.goodreads.com (accessed August 17, 2013).

43. Christine Stafford, review of *Wise Blood*, March 1, 2012, www.goodreads.com (accessed August 22, 2013).

44. Stephanie, review of *A Good Man Is Hard to Find*, October 31, 2009, www.goodreads.com (accessed July 29, 2013).

45. Kathryn, review of *The Violent Bear It Away*, October 21, 2002, www.goodreads.com (accessed August 22, 2013).

46. Jo, review of *The Violent Bear It Away*, August 1, 2103, www.goodreads.com (accessed August 22, 2013).

47. Reese Clark, review of *Wise Blood*, September 11, 2011, www.goodreads.com (accessed August 24, 2013).

48. Amy, review of *Wise Blood*, June 6, 2011, www.goodreads.com (accessed August 21, 2013).

49. Anniebranson, review of *Wise Blood*, May 2, 2008, www.goodreads.com (accessed August 22, 2013).

50. Rebecca, review of *The Complete Stories*, May 8, 2010, www.goodreads.com (accessed August 12, 2013).

51. Tan August, review of *Wise Blood*, July 19, 2013, www.goodreads.com (accessed August 24, 2013).

52. Kevin, review of *Wise Blood*, August 3, 2011, www.goodreads.com (accessed August 24, 2013).

53. Jennifer, review of *Wise Blood*, April 28, 2013, www.goodreads.com (accessed August 9, 2013).

54. Adrian Stumpp, review of *Wise Blood*, October 28, 2009, www.goodreads.com (accessed August 17, 2013).

55. Tracy Kendall, review of *Wise Blood*, July 18, 2012, www.goodreads.com (accessed August 17, 2013).

56. Sean, review of *Wise Blood*, October 3, 2012, www.goodreads.com (accessed August 17, 2013).

57. Tim Ferreira, review of *Wise Blood*, June 10, 2013, www.goodreads.com (accessed August 24, 2013).

58. Matt Bianco, review of *Wise Blood*, December 26, 2012, www.goodreads.com (accessed August 24, 2013).

59. Buzz Borders, review of *A Good Man Is Hard to Find*, August 11, 2011, www.goodreads.com (accessed August 11, 2013).

60. Jeff, review of *The Complete Stories*, July 28, 2013, www.goodreads.com (accessed August 9, 2013).

61. Mike, review of *The Violent Bear It Away*, April 4, 2008, www.goodreads.com (accessed August 1, 2013).

62. Dominic, review of Carson McCullers, *The Ballad of the Sad Café and Other Stories*, January 30, 2011, www.goodreads.com (accessed August 9, 2013).

63. Roby, review of *A Good Man Is Hard to Find*, August 23, 2011, www.goodreads.com (accessed July 22, 2013).

64. C. J. Lipsky, review of *The Complete Stories*, July 24, 2011, www.goodreads.com (accessed August 31, 2013).

65. Alan Bajandas, review of *Wise Blood*, July 19, 2009, www.goodreads.com (accessed July 22, 2013).

66. Donovan Foote, review of *Wise Blood*, July 6, 2012, www.goodreads.com (accessed August 17, 2013).

67. Rebecca Stout, review of *Wise Blood*, January 22, 2013, www.goodreads.com (accessed August 17, 2013).

68. Caroline, review of *Wise Blood*, November 12, 2008, www.goodreads.com (accessed August 17, 2013).

69. Dan Karuna, review of *Wise Blood*, March 11, 2008, www.goodreads.com (accessed August 17, 2013).

70. Steven Taylor, review of *Wise Blood*, September 25, 2009, www.goodreads.com (accessed August 17, 2013).

71. Arti, review of *A Good Man Is Hard to Find*, September 29, 2011, www.goodreads.com (accessed August 17, 2013).

72. Jasonlylescampbell, review of *Everything That Rises Must Converge*, May 31, 2012, www.goodreads.com (accessed August 17, 2013).

73. Betsy, review of *Wise Blood*, January 12, 2012, www.goodreads.com (accessed August 18, 2013).

74. Kevin, review of *Wise Blood*, August 3, 2007, www.goodreads.com (accessed August 18, 2013).

75. Stefani, review of *Wise Blood*, July 15, 2009, www.goodreads.com (accessed August 18, 2013).

76. Vanessa, review of *Everything That Rises Must Converge*, July 26, 2011, www.goodreads.com (accessed August 18, 2013).

77. Ibtisam Helen, review of *A Good Man Is Hard to Find*, September 6, 2007, www.goodreads.com (accessed August 18, 2013).

78. Brett, review of *Wise Blood*, October 23, 2011, www.goodreads.com (accessed August 31, 2013).

79. Tim, review of *The Complete Stories*, January 8, 2008, www.goodreads.com (accessed August 18, 2013).

80. Stefani, review of *Wise Blood*, July 9, 2009, www.goodreads.com (accessed August 18, 2013).

81. Jenn(ifer), review of *Wise Blood*, July 2, 2012, www.goodreads.com (accessed August 18, 2013).

82. J. S. Balley, review of *A Good Man Is Hard to Find*, June 29, 2011, www.goodreads.com (accessed August 18, 2013).

83. Rochelle Torke, review of *A Good Man Is Hard to Find*, October 2, 2007, www.goodreads.com (accessed August 18, 2013).

84. Anna, review of *A Good Man Is Hard to Find*, July 29, 2007, www.goodreads.com (accessed August 18, 2013).

85. Danny, review of *A Good Man Is Hard to Find*, February 27, 2013, www.goodreads.com (accessed August 19, 2013).

86. Carmen, review of *A Good Man Is Hard to Find*, October 25, 2002, www.goodreads.com (accessed August 18, 2013).

87. Grace Jensen, review of *A Good Man Is Hard to Find*, July 22, 2013, www.goodreads.com (accessed August 18, 2013).

88. Joab Jackson, review of *A Good Man Is Hard to Find*, November 10, 2012, www.goodreads.com (accessed August 18, 2013).

89. Jana, review of *A Good Man Is Hard to Find*, June 25, 2010, www.goodreads.com (accessed August 9, 2013).

90. Paul, review of *Wise Blood*, October 19, 2007, www.goodreads.com (accessed August 18, 2013).

91. Goldfield, *Still Fighting the Civil War*, 7.

92. "New Creative Writers," *Library Journal*, February 15, 1952, 354, in Scott and Streight, *The Contemporary Reviews*, 3.

93. Walter Elder, "That Region," *Kenyon Review* 17 (Autumn 1955): 661–70, in Scott and Streight, *The Contemporary Reviews*, 58.

94. Tim, review of *A Good Man Is Hard to Find*, September 15, 2012, www.goodreads.com (accessed August 18, 2013).

95. Julie, review of *Everything That Rises Must Converge*, May 7, 2013, www.goodreads.com (accessed August 18, 2013).

96. Steve Abercrombie, review of *Everything That Rises Must Converge*, May 27, 2011, www.goodreads.com (accessed August 18, 2013).

97. Lori, review of *Everything That Rises Must Converge*, December 18, 2012, www.goodreads.com (accessed August 18, 2013). Emphasis in original.

98. Dave Hikegrin, review of *Everything That Rises Must Converge*, December 1, 2012, www.goodreads.com (accessed August 18, 2013).

99. Margot, review of *Everything That Rises Must Converge*, August 5, 2012, www.goodreads.com (accessed August 18, 2013).

100. Steven H, review of *A Good Man Is Hard to Find*, June 16, 2007, www.goodreads.com (accessed August 31, 2013).

101. Annie Schoening, review of *The Complete Stories*, February 4, 2008, www.goodreads.com (accessed August 18, 2013).

102. Sara Shepherd, review of *A Good Man Is Hard to Find*, June 11, 2013, www.goodreads.com (accessed August 18, 2013).

103. Mike, review of *A Good Man Is Hard to Find*, November 25, 2011, www.goodreads.com (accessed August 18, 2013).

104. Gena, review of *Wise Blood*, July 24, 2010, www.goodreads.com (accessed August 9, 2013).

105. Jeff Golick, review of *Wise Blood*, June 29, 2013, www.goodreads.com (accessed August 9, 2013).

106. Cobb, *Away Down South*, 1.

107. O'Connor to Robert Giroux, November 12, 1960, in *The Habit of Being*, 417.

108. O'Connor, "Some Aspects of the Grotesque in Southern Fiction," in *Mystery and Manners*, 38.

109. "I have found that anything that comes out of the South is going to be called grotesque by the Northern reader, unless it is grotesque, in which case it is going to be called realistic." Ibid, 40.

110. Harvey Breit, "Galley Proof: *A Good Man Is Hard to Find*," in Magee, *Conversations with Flannery O'Connor*, 8.

111. Ellmann, *James Joyce*, 557.

112. MillCityPress, review of *A Good Man Is Hard to Find*, June 20, 2007, www.goodreads.com (accessed August 31, 2013).

113. Rhonda, review of *A Good Man Is Hard to Find*, January 20, 2009, www.goodreads.com (accessed August 31, 2013).

114. Matthew Jankiewicz, review of *A Good Man Is Hard to Find*, April 15, 2012, www.goodreads.com (accessed August 31, 2013).

115. Regan Sharp, review of *The Complete Stories*, www.goodreads.com, April 1, 2011 (accessed August 5, 2013).

116. O'Connor, "The Life You Save May Be Your Own," in *A Good Man Is Hard to Find*, 53.

117. C. Ross Mullins, "Flannery O'Connor: An Interview," *Jubilee* 11 (June, 1963): 32–35, in Magee, *Conversations with Flannery O'Connor*, 103.

118. Elisabeth Jansen, review of *Everything That Rises Must Converge*, June 2, 2011, www.goodreads.com (accessed August 24, 2013).

119. Emily, review of *A Good Man Is Hard to Find*, June 14, 2010, www.goodreads.com (accessed August 24, 2013).

120. Gary Ganong, review of *A Good Man Is Hard to Find*, June 6, 2011, www.goodreads.com (accessed August 24, 2013).

121. Megan, review of *A Good Man Is Hard to Find*, August 17, 2009, www.goodreads.com (accessed August 24, 2013).

122. Bruce Marr, review of *The Violent Bear It Away*, November 25, 2010, www.goodreads.com (accessed August 24, 2013).

123. Nathan, review of *A Good Man Is Hard to Find*, September 28, 2012, www.goodreads.com (accessed August 22, 2013).

124. Jeremy Purves, review of *Mystery and Manners*, April 9, 2009, www.goodreads .com (accessed August 24, 2103).

125. Lane, review of *Mystery and Manners*, April 9, 2009, www.goodreads.com (accessed August 23, 2103).

126. Sabina Chen, review of *The Complete Stories*, May 23, 2007, www.goodreads.com (accessed August 24, 2013).

127. Corrine Wasilewski, review of *The Complete Stories*, February 10, 2013, www.good reads.com (accessed August 24, 2013).

128. Pam Newman, review of *A Good Man Is Hard to Find*, September 1, 2012, www .goodreads.com (accessed August 24, 2013).

129. Elaine, review of *A Good Man Is Hard to Find*, September 13, 2012, www.good reads.com (accessed August 23, 2013).

130. Beverly, review of *A Good Man Is Hard to Find*, January 29, 2012, www.goodreads .com (accessed August 23, 2013).

131. Skylar Burris, review of *The Violent Bear It Away*, August 15, 2010, www.goodreads .com (accessed August 31, 2013).

132. Catherine, review of *The Complete Stories*, July 30, 2008, www.goodreads.com (accessed August 24, 2013).

133. Gaby, review of *The Complete Stories*, June 18, 2007, www.goodreads.com (accessed August 24, 2013).

134. Ezra Furman, review of *The Complete Stories*, May 14, 2007, www.goodreads.com (accessed August 24, 2013).

135. David Hammond, review of *The Complete Stories*, June 23, 2011, www.goodreads .com (accessed August 24, 2013).

136. Sara Pauff, review of *The Complete Stories*, August 8, 2010, www.goodreads.com (accessed August 24, 2013).

137. Kristi, review of *The Complete Stories*, November 26, 2008, www.goodreads.com (accessed August 24, 2013).

138. Erik Rollwage, review of *The Complete Stories*, February 6, 2012, www.goodreads .com (accessed August 24, 2013).

139. Alicia, review of *The Complete Stories*, March 25, 2011, www.goodreads.com (accessed August 24, 2013).

140. Lindsay, review of *Everything That Rises Must Converge*, March 19, 2010, www .goodreads.com (accessed August 24, 2013).

141. Shane, review of *The Complete Stories*, June 10, 2012, www.goodreads.com (accessed August 13, 2013).

142. Cheeseblab, review of *The Complete Stories*, December 27, 2010, www.goodreads .com (accessed August 11, 2013).

143. Jacob, review of *The Complete Stories*, July 2, 2009, www.goodreads.com (accessed August 17, 2013).

144. Eliza Griffith, review of *The Complete Stories*, October 12, 2011, www.goodreads .com (accessed August 24, 2013).

145. Allen Smith, review of *The Complete Stories*, June 1, 2008, www.goodreads.com (accessed August 24, 2013).

146. Clark, review of *The Complete Stories*, June 13, 2010, www.goodreads.com (accessed August 24, 2013).

147. Angie Harmon, review of *The Complete Stories*, May 5, 2013, www.goodreads.com (accessed August 11, 2013).

148. Mei, review of *The Violent Bear It Away*, May 9, 2013, www.goodreads.com (accessed August 24, 2013).

149. O'Connor, *The Violent Bear It Away*, 16.

150. Joe, review of *The Violent Bear It Away*, February 5, 2011, www.goodreads.com (accessed August 24, 2013).

151. O'Connor, *The Violent Bear It Away*, 34.

152. Ibid, 16.

153. Diane, review of *The Violent Bear It Away*, March 2, 2010, www.goodreads.com (accessed August 24, 2013).

154. Rowland Bismark, review of *The Violent Bear It Away*, September 19, 2010, www .goodreads.com (accessed August 24, 2013).

155. Judy Krueger, review of *The Violent Bear It Away*, September 28, 2012, www .goodreads.com (accessed August 20, 2013).

156. Marissa, review of *The Violent Bear It Away*, July 10, 2008, www.goodreads.com (accessed August 20, 2013).

157. Paul Bryant, review of *The Violent Bear It Away*, August 21, 2013, www.goodreads .com (accessed August 20, 2013).

158. Ricky Orr, review of *The Violent Bear It Away*, September 19, 2009, www .goodreads.com (accessed August 20, 2013).

159. Ryan, review of *The Violent Bear It Away*, October 10, 2010, www.goodreads.com (accessed August 24, 2013).

160. O'Connor to John Hawkes, September 13, 1959, in *The Habit of Being*, 350. On the subject of how readers react to Rayber and Mason, a student of mine once remarked, "It's funny how readers will automatically question Mason but never Rayber. Perhaps O'Connor should have drawn even larger and more startling figures."

161. Bunting, "An Afternoon with Walker Percy," 47.

162. Wood, *Flannery O'Connor*, 30.

163. Andrew Warsinske, review of *The Violent Bear It Away*, February 7, 2010, www .goodreads.com (accessed August 24, 2013).

164. Charlaralotte, review of *The Violent Bear It Away*, March 13, 2009, www.goodreads .com (accessed August 24, 2013).

165. Paul Hinman, review of *The Violent Bear It Away*, March 14, 2011, www.goodreads.com (accessed August 24, 2013).

166. Erick Nordenson, review of *The Violent Bear It Away*, June 18, 2010, www.goodreads.com (accessed August 24, 2013).

167. Diane, review of *The Violent Bear It Away*, March 2, 2010, www.goodreads.com (accessed August 17, 2013).

168. Melissa, review of *The Violent Bear It Away*, December 12, 2012, www.goodreads.com (accessed August 24, 2013).

169. O'Connor, "The Fiction Writer and His Country," in *Mystery and Manners*, 34.

170. Michael Tucker, review of *A Good Man Is Hard to Find*, June 11, 2012, www.goodreads.com (accessed August 11, 2013).

171. C. J. Lipsky, review of *The Complete Stories*, July 24, 2011, www.goodreads.com (accessed August 11, 2013).

172. Kaylee, review of *The Complete Stories*, August 15, 2011, www.goodreads.com (accessed August 11, 2013).

173. Matt Middlebrook, review of *The Complete Stories*, May 26, 2012, www.goodreads.com (accessed August 2, 2013).

174. Jenny, review of *The Complete Stories*, December 31, 2014, www.goodgreads.com accessed March 1, 2015).

175. N W James, review of *The Complete Stories*, November 24, 2014, www.goodreads.com (accessed March 1, 2015).

176. Larry Bassett, review of *The Complete Stories*, November 19, 2011, www.goodreads.com (accessed August 2, 2013).

177. Stephen Hyter, review of *A Good Man Is Hard to Find*, August 5, 2011, www.goodreads.com (accessed August 11, 2013).

178. Joy Lesknick, review of *Everything That Rises Must Converge*, August 6, 2012, www.goodreads.com (accessed August 11, 2013).

179. Ed, review of *Everything That Rises Must Converge*, August 21, 2011, www.goodreads.com (accessed August 11, 2013).

180. O'Connor to Betty Hester, September 1, 1963, in *The Habit of Being*, 537.

181. As mentioned in my introduction, in *The Cambridge Introduction to Mark Twain*, Peter Messent notes that the novel's reception has changed over time and explains that, upon its release in 1885, American readers were upset not because of Twain's treatment of race but because he supposedly glorified juvenile delinquency. See Messent, *The Cambridge Introduction to Mark Twain*, 12–14.

182. Ellen, review of *Everything That Rises Must Converge*, June 25, 2010, www.goodreads.com (accessed August 4, 2013).

183. Ryan Wolf, review of *Everything That Rises Must Converge*, November 8, 2010, www.goodreads.com (accessed August 4, 2013).

184. Cullen, review of *A Good Man Is Hard to Find*, April 17, 2013, www.goodreads.com (accessed August 2, 2013).

185. Melissa, review of *A Good Man Is Hard to Find*, August 21, 2007, www.goodreads.com (accessed August 11, 2013).

186. Lisa N, review of *Everything That Rises Must Converge*, December 31, 2010, www.goodreads.com (accessed August 11, 2013).

187. David, review of *Everything That Rises Must Converge*, July 1, 2012, www.goodreads.com (accessed August 2, 2013).

188. Karolyn Sherwood, review of *A Good Man Is Hard to Find*, April 1, 2012, www.goodreads.com (accessed August 11, 2013).

189. Tracy Nicolaysen, review of *Everything That Rises Must Converge*, February 10, 2009, www.goodreads.com (accessed August 3, 2013).

190. Smith Nickerson, review of *A Good Man Is Hard to Find*, April 12, 2012, www.goodreads.com (accessed August 4, 2013).

191. O'Connor, "The Life You Save May Be Your Own," in *A Good Man Is Hard to Find*, 57.

192. Karen, review of *Everything That Rises Must Converge*, July 14, 2009, www.goodreads.com (accessed August 7, 2013).

193. Becky, review of *A Good Man Is Hard to Find*, April 8, 2012, www.goodreads.com (accessed August 24, 2013).

194. C, review of *Everything That Rises Must Converge*, December 17, 2012, www.goodreads.com (accessed August 6, 2013).

195. Lily Brent, review of *Everything That Rises Must Converge*, October 3, 2008, www.goodreads.com (accessed August 6, 2013).

196. Amber, review of *A Good Man Is Hard to Find*, December 31, 2008, www.goodreads.com (accessed August 4, 2013).

197. Alexis Quinian, review of *The Complete Stories*, January 23, 2009, www.goodreads.com (accessed August 7, 2013).

198. Valerie, review of *The Complete Stories*, May 21, 2013, www.goodreads.com (accessed August 24, 2013).

199. Jamie, review of *Everything That Rises Must Converge*, August 13, 2011, www.goodreads.com (accessed August 3, 2013).

200. Sarah Walker, review of *A Good Man Is Hard to Find*, August 7, 2007, www.goodreads.com (accessed August 24, 2013).

201. O'Connor, "A Good Man Is Hard to Find," in *A Good Man Is Hard to Find*, 22.

202. Chrissy, review of *A Good Man Is Hard to Find*, April 4, 2013, www.goodreads.com (accessed August 24, 2013).

203. Martha, review of *A Good Man Is Hard to Find*, August 27, 2009, www.goodreads.com (accessed August 24, 2013).

204. Northpapers, review of *A Good Man Is Hard to Find*, July 25, 2013, www.goodreads.com (accessed August 24, 2013).

205. See J. Bottum, "Flannery O'Connor Banned," *Crisis* 18, no. 9 (October 2000): 48–49.

206. "Flannery O'Connor," www.goodreads.com (accessed September 19, 2015).

207. Steven Salaita, review of *A Good Man Is Hard to Find*, July 2, 2009, www.good reads.com (accessed August 31, 2013).

208. Rhonda, review of *A Good Man Is Hard to Find*, January 20, 2009, www.good reads.com (accessed August 11, 2013).

209. Marc Goldstein, review of *The Violent Bear It Away*, March 20, 2013, www .goodreads.com (accessed August 24, 2013).

210. Paquita Maria Sanchez, review of *A Good Man Is Hard to Find*, January 13, 2001, www.goodreads.com (accessed August 31, 2013).

211. Dara, review of *Wise Blood*, June 24, 2013, www.goodreads.com (accessed August 24, 2013).

212. Matt Hanson, review of *A Good Man Is Hard to Find*, February 12, 2008, www .goodreads.com (accessed August 17, 2013).

213. Consuelo, review of *The Violent Bear It Away*, April 1, 2014, www.goodreads.com (accessed March 1, 2015).

Conclusion

1. O'Connor to Elizabeth and Robert Lowell, March 17, 1953, in *The Habit of Being*, 57.

2. O'Connor to Betty Hester, June 28, 1956, in *The Habit of Being*, 163.

3. "A Good Man Is Hard to Find."

4. O'Connor to John Lynch, November 6, 1955, in *The Habit of Being*, 114.

5. O'Connor to Betty Hester, December 16, 1955, in *The Habit of Being*, 126.

6. Transcript of the *Galley Proof* television program filmed in May 1955, in Magee, *Conversations with Flannery O'Connor*, 8.

7. O'Connor to Cecil Dawkins, in *The Habit of Being*, 307.

8. O'Connor to Elizabeth and Robert Lowell, in *The Habit of Being*, 20.

9. W. A. Sessions, introduction to *A Prayer Journal*, viii.

10. Mary Loftus, "'Straightforward as a Gunshot': Exploring Flannery O'Connor's Tough-Minded Faith," *Emory News Center*, http://news.emory.edu/stories/2013/09 /spirited_flannery_oconnor_lecture/campus.html (accessed January 21, 2015).

11. Lindsay Gellman, "Newly Discovered Journal Reveals Glimpse of Young Flannery O'Connor," *Wall Street Journal*, November 19, 2013, http://blogs.wsj.com/speakeasy /2013/11/19/newly-discovered-personal-journal-reveals-glimpse-of-young-flannery -oconnor (accessed February 2, 2015).

12. Marian Ryan, "The Prayers of Flannery O'Connor," *Slate*, November 6, 2013, www .slate.com/articles/arts/books/2013/11/flannery_o_connor_and_catholicism_a_prayer _journal_reviewed.html (accessed January 30, 2015).

13. Hilton Als, "Genius Breaking Through," *New York Review of Books* 61, no. 13 (August 14, 2014), www.nybooks.com/articles/archives/2014/aug/14/flannery-oconnor -genius-breaking-through (accessed September 19, 2015).

14. Patrick Samway, review of *A Prayer Journal*, *Flannery O'Connor Review* 12 (January 1, 2014): 117.

15. Max Radwin, "Lost 'Journal' Reveals a Candid, Meditative Side to Flannery O'Connor," *Michigan Daily*, November 22, 2013, www.michigandaily.com/arts/11book -review-flannery-oconnor22 (accessed September 19, 2015).

16. James Parker, "The Passion of Flannery O'Connor," *Atlantic*, October 23, 2013, www.theatlantic.com/magazine/archive/2013/11/the-passion-of-flannery-oconnor /309532 (accessed September 19, 2015).

17. Sarah Gordon, review of *A Prayer Journal*, *Georgia Review* 67, no. 4 (January 1, 2013): 756.

18. Patrick Reardon, review of *A Prayer Journal*, *Chicago Tribune*, December 20, 2013.

19. Carlene Bauer, "God's Grandeur: The Prayer Journal of Flannery O'Connor," *Virginia Quarterly Review* 90, no. 1 (January 6, 2014), www.vqronline.org/gods-grandeur -prayer-journal-flannery-oconnor (accessed September 19, 2015).

20. Casey N. Cep, "Inheritance and Invention: Flannery O'Connor's Prayer Journal," *New Yorker*, November 12, 2013, www.newyorker.com/books/page-turner/inheritance -and-invention-flannery-oconnors-prayer-journal (accessed September 19, 2015).

21. "*A Prayer Journal*," Goodreads.com, accessed January 21, 2015.

22. O'Connor, *The Violent Bear It Away*, 4.

23. O'Connor, "Some Aspects of the Grotesque in Southern Fiction," in *Mystery and Manners*, 37.

24. O'Connor to Betty Hester, February 13, 1960, in *The Habit of Being*, 374.

25. O'Connor to John Hawkes, March 3, 1961, in *The Habit of Being*, 434.

26. O'Connor to Cecil Dawkins, January 26, 1962, in *The Habit of Being*, 463.

27. Richard Gilman, "On Flannery O'Connor," *New York Review of Books* 13 (August 21, 1969): 24–26, in Scott and Streight, *The Contemporary Reviews*, 395.

28. O'Connor to Cecil Dawkins, October 26, 1958, in *The Habit of Being*, 301.

29. Cep, "Inheritance and Invention," *New Yorker*.

30. Andrea DenHoed, "Flannery O'Connor's Manhattan Memorial," *New Yorker*, November 8, 2014, www.newyorker.com/books/page-turner/flannery-oconnors-manhattan -memorial (accessed September 19, 2015).

31. Ellen Douglas, "Inside Flannery O'Connor's Universe," *New Republic*, July 5, 1975, www.newrepublic.com/article/117146/inside-flannery-oconnors-universe (accessed September 19, 2015).

32. Ibid.

33. Cobb, *Away Down South*, 3.

34. Goldfield, *Still Fighting the Civil War*, 6.

35. Cox, *Dreaming of Dixie*, 82.

36. Johnson, "Preface to the Plays of William Shakespeare," 423.

37. Zinn, *The Southern Mystique*, 218.

Bibliography

Archive and Manuscript Sources

Everything That Rises Must Converge, directed by Karin Coonrod. Press kit and production materials. New York Public Library for the Performing Arts.

Farrar, Straus and Giroux, Inc. records. Manuscripts and Archives Division. New York Public Library. Astor, Lenox, and Tilden Foundations.

Wise Blood, directed by John Huston. Press kit and production materials. New York Public Library for the Performing Arts.

Primary and Secondary Sources

Barasch, Frances K. "Theories of the Grotesque." In *Encyclopedia of Contemporary Literary Theory: Approaches, Scholars, Terms*. Ed. Irene Rima Makaryk. Toronto: University of Toronto Press, 1993. 84–89.

Berg, A. Scott. *Maxwell Perkins: Editor of Genius*. New York: Berkley, 2008.

Bloom, Harold, ed. *Flannery O'Connor: Bloom's Modern Critical Views*. New York: Chelsea House Publishers, 1986.

Borges, Jorge Luis. *Labyrinths*. Ed. Donald A. Yates and James E. Irby. New York: New Directions, 1988.

Bornstein, George, and Theresa Tinkle. *The Iconic Page in Manuscript, Print, and Digital Culture*. Ann Arbor: University of Michigan Press, 1998.

Boswell, James. *The Life of Samuel Johnson*. New York: Penguin, 2008.

Boyum, Joy Gould. *Double Exposure: Fiction into Film*. New York: Universe Books, 1985.

Bunting, Charles T. "An Afternoon with Walker Percy." In *Conversations with Walker Percy*. Ed. Lewis A. Lawson and Victor A. Kramer. Jackson: University Press of Mississippi, 1985. 40–55.

Cash, Jean W. *Flannery O'Connor: A Life*. Knoxville: University of Tennessee Press, 2002.

Chesterton, G. K. *Chesterton on Dickens*. Vol. 15 of *The Collected Works of G. K. Chesterton*. San Francisco: Ignatius Press, 1989.

———. *Orthodoxy*. Hollywood, Fla.: Simon & Brown, 2012.

Ciment, Michael. "Two Encounters with John Huston." In *John Huston: Interviews*. Ed. Robert Emmet Long. Jackson: University Press of Mississippi, 2001. 135–49.

Cobb, James C. *Away Down South: A History of Southern Identity*. New York: Oxford University Press, 2005.

Cox, Karen L. *Dreaming of Dixie: How the South Was Created in American Popular Culture*. Chapel Hill: University of North Carolina Press, 2011.

Donaldson, Scott. ed. *The Cambridge Companion to Hemingway*. Cambridge: Cambridge University Press, 1996.

Edel, Leon. *The Prefaces of Henry James*. Folcroft, Pa.: The Folcroft Press, 1970.

Elie, Paul. *The Life You Save May Be Your Own: An American Pilgrimage*. New York: Farrar, Straus and Giroux, 2003.

Ellmann, Richard. *James Joyce*. New York: Oxford University Press, 1983.

Foote, Horton. *Genesis of an American Playwright*. Waco, Tex.: Baylor University Press, 2004.

Friedman, Melvin J., and Lewis A. Lawson. *The Added Dimension: The Art and Mind of Flannery O'Connor*. New York: Fordham University Press, 1966.

Genette, Gérard. *Paratexts: Thresholds and Interpretations*. Trans. Jane E. Lewin. Cambridge: Cambridge University Press, 1997.

Gentry, Bruce, and Craig Amason, eds. *At Home with Flannery O'Connor: An Oral History*. Milledgeville, Ga.: The Flannery O'Connor–Andalusia Foundation, 2012.

Goldfield, David. *Still Fighting the Civil War*. Baton Rouge: Louisiana State University Press, 2002.

Goldstein, Philip, and James L. Machor, eds. *New Directions in American Reception Study*. Oxford: Oxford University Press, 2008.

Gooch, Brad. *Flannery: A Life of Flannery O'Connor*. New York: Little, Brown, 2009.

Grobel, Lawrence. *The Hustons*. New York: Charles Scribner's Sons, 1989.

Haddox, Thomas H. *Hard Sayings: The Rhetoric of Christian Orthodoxy in Late Modern Fiction*. Columbus: Ohio State University Press, 2013.

Harkins, Anthony. *Hillbilly: A Cultural History of an American Icon*. New York: Oxford University Press, 2004.

Hazlitt, William. *Lectures on the Dramatic Literature of the Age of Elizabeth*. London: John Warren, 1821.

Huston, John. *An Open Book*. New York: Alfred A. Knopf, 1980.

Johnson, Samuel. "Preface to the Plays of William Shakespeare." In *Samuel Johnson: The Major Works*. Ed. Donald Greene. New York: Oxford University Press, 2008. 419–56.

Machor, James L. "The American Reception of Melville's Short Fiction in the 1850s." In *New Directions in American Reception Study*. Ed. Philip Goldstein and James L. Machor. Oxford: Oxford University Press, 2008. 87–98.

Madsen, Axel. *John Huston: A Biography*. New York: Doubleday, 1978.

Magee, Rosemary M., ed. *Conversations with Flannery O'Connor.* Jackson: University Press of Mississippi, 1987.

Martin, Carter H. *The True Country: Themes in the Fiction of Flannery O'Connor.* Nashville: Vanderbilt University Press, 1968.

Mencken, H. L. *The Impossible H. L. Mencken.* Ed. Marion Elizabeth Rodgers. New York: Doubleday, 1991.

Messent, Peter. *The Cambridge Introduction to Mark Twain.* Cambridge: Cambridge University Press, 2007.

Meyers, Jeffrey. *John Huston: Courage and Art.* New York: Crown Archetype, 2011.

Morson, Gary Saul. *The Boundaries of Genre: Dostoevsky's Diary of a Writer and the Traditions of Literary Utopia.* Austin: University of Texas Press, 1981.

O'Connor, Flannery. *The Complete Stories.* New York: Farrar, Straus and Giroux, 1971.

——. *Flannery O'Connor: The Cartoons.* Ed. Kelly Gerald. Seattle: Fantagraphics Books, 2012.

——. *A Good Man Is Hard to Find.* New York: Harcourt Brace Jovanovich, 1977.

——. *The Habit of Being.* Ed. Sally Fitzgerald. New York: Vintage Books, 1979.

——. Introduction to *A Memoir of Mary Ann.* The Dominican Nuns of Our Lady of Perpetual Help Home. Savannah: Frederic C. Beil, 1991.

——. *Mystery and Manners: Occasional Prose.* Ed. Sally and Robert Fitzgerald. New York: Macmillan, 1969.

——. *A Prayer Journal.* New York: Farrar, Straus and Giroux, 2013.

——. *The Violent Bear It Away.* New York: Farrar, Straus and Giroux, 2007.

——. *Wise Blood.* 2nd ed. New York: Farrar, Straus and Giroux, 1962.

Ohmann, Richard. *Politics of Letters.* Middletown, Conn.: Wesleyan University Press, 1987.

Orwell, George. "Inside the Whale." In *Essays.* New York: Everyman's Library, 2002. 211–49.

Quinn, John J., ed. *Esprit: A Journal of Thought and Opinion* 8, no. 1 (Winter 1964).

Rabinowitz, Peter L. *Before Reading: Narrative Conventions and the Politics of Interpretation.* Ithaca: Cornell University Press, 1987.

Rodden, John. *The Politics of Literary Reputation: The Making and Claiming of "St. George" Orwell.* New York: Oxford University Press, 1989.

Rogers, Jonathan. *The Terrible Speed of Mercy: A Spiritual Biography of Flannery O'Connor.* Nashville: Thomas Nelson, 2012.

Schwartz, Lawrence H. *Creating Faulkner's Reputation: The Politics of Modern Literary Criticism.* Knoxville: University of Tennessee Press, 1988.

Scott, R. Neil. *Flannery O'Connor: An Annotated Reference Guide to Criticism.* Milledgeville, Ga.: Timberlane Books, 2002.

Scott, R. Neil, and Irwin H. Streight, eds. *Flannery O'Connor: The Contemporary Reviews.* Cambridge: Cambridge University Press, 2009.

Stevens, C. Ralph, ed. *The Correspondence of Flannery O'Connor and the Brainard Cheneys.* Jackson: University Press of Mississippi, 1986.

Templin, Charlotte. *Feminism and the Politics of Literary Reputation: The Example of Erica Jong.* Lawrence: University Press of Kansas, 1995.

Thomson, David. "John Huston." In *The New Biographical Dictionary of Film.* New York: Alfred A. Knopf, 2002. 424–25.

Trimmer, Joseph F. *The National Book Awards for Fiction: An Index to the First Twenty-Five Years.* Boston: G. K. Hall, 1978.

West, James L. W. *The American Literary Marketplace Since 1900.* Philadelphia: University of Pennsylvania Press, 1988.

———. "The Iconic Dust Jacket: Fitzgerald and Styron." In *The Iconic Page in Manuscript, Print, and Digital Culture.* Ed. George Bornstein and Theresa Tinkle. Ann Arbor: University of Michigan Press, 1998. 269–84.

Whitt, Margaret Earley. *Understanding Flannery O'Connor.* Columbia, S.C.: University of South Carolina Press, 1995.

Wise Blood. DVD. Directed by John Huston. The Criterion Collection, 2009.

Wood, Ralph C. *Flannery O'Connor and the Christ-Haunted South.* Grand Rapids, Mich.: William B. Eerdmans, 2004.

Zinn, Howard. *The Southern Mystique.* New York: Simon & Schuster, 1964.

Index

Merton, Thomas, 69, 77, 92, 100
Meyers, Jeffrey, 144, 150
Montaigne, Michel de, 17
Mystery and Manners (O'Connor), 88–90, 162, 169, 177

National Book Award, 105–8
Nelson, Marilyn, 189, 192–93
New Line Cinema, 135, 151

Oates, Joyce Carol, 1, 85, 105
O'Connor, Flannery: 9, 100, 159, 189; on adaptations, 155–56, 161; biographies of, 9, 111; bravery of, 71, 127; compared with other artists, 172–73; death of, 65, 79; illness of, 70–71, 85–87, 129, 190; literature, assumptions about, 88, 131, 160; as outsider, 102, 162; and peacocks, 72–75; prizes received, 64, 105–6, 131; and race, 7, 184, 186, 187–88; and reviewers, 12, 16, 44–45, 52, 53, 77; as Roman Catholic, 107, 178, 195–96; as satirist, 21–22, 54; scholarly works on, 4, 8; as southern author, 12–14, 45, 52, 67, 69, 76, 109, 110, 159, 197; and southern religion, 137
O'Connor, Flannery, works: 69, 91–92, 166–67; character types in, 102–3; difficulty of understanding, 54, 89, 170–71; grotesque elements of, 16–19, 54, 69, 79; humor in, 54–55, 137; limited range of, 77, 83–84, 103–4, 178–79; racism of characters in, 183–88; as "realistic," 174–75; Roman Catholic themes of, 20–21, 23–25, 34–36, 40, 43–44, 49–53, 57, 63, 68, 149, 176–77; southern reception of, 14–15; theoretical audiences of, defined, 42–44; universal themes of, 45, 53, 76, 92, 102, 106, 176, 190. *See also individual works*
O'Connor, Regina, 82, 108, 111; and Flannery's letters, 113, 115–25; on Flannery's work, 124–25
Ohman, Richard, 5, 8
Orwell, George, 50, 51

paratexts, 26
"Parker's Back" (O'Connor), 81, 181

Parker's Back: An Opera in Two Acts (Hayes), 159
peacocks, 72, 90, 105
Percy, Walker, 105, 181
Poe, Edgar Allan, 9, 17, 172
Poirier, Richard, 78
Porter, Katherine Anne, 68, 71
Powers, J. F., 69, 106, 114
Prayer Journal, A (O'Connor), 193–94
Prescott, Orville, 48, 60
Price, Richard, 5
Pritchett, V. S., 86

Quinn, John J., 67, 84, 88

Rabinowitz, Peter J., 4, 10, 40–41
racism, O'Connor's depictions of, 183–88
Reed, Rex, 136
reputation, literary: and author's letters, 120; and awards, 107, 109; and character types, 102; defined, 6, 8–9, 26; evolution of, 54, 58; fluidity of, 104; and O'Connor's critics, 69, 79, 80–81; and O'Connor's inner circle, 82, 96, 125, 133; and online reviews, 164–66, 172; and readers' religious beliefs, 176–78; and watchwords, 195
"Revelation" (O'Connor), 47, 78, 81, 146
Rich, Frank, 136, 138
"River, The" (O'Connor), 42, 43, 50, 87, 147; and film adaptation, 133, 163
Rodden, John, 3, 8
Rosenfeld, Isaac, 21–22, 85
Roth, Philip, 20

Sarris, Andrew, 135, 144
Schlitz Playhouse, 7
Schwartz, Lawrence H., 81
Selby, John, 36, 99, 136, 143
Sessions, William A., 193
Simon, John, 135, 140
Sophocles, 77, 163, 172
South, American: clichés about, 174, 176, 196–97; in Coonrod's *Everything That Rises Must Converge*, 159; Dawkins on,

Made in the USA
Lexington, KY
31 March 2018